D1593716

Patterns of
Metropolitan
Policing

Patterns of Metropolitan Policing

Elinor Ostrom
Roger B. Parks
Department of Political Science
University of Indiana, Bloomington

Gordon P. Whitaker
Department of Political Science
University of North Carolina at Chapel Hill

Ballinger Publishing Company • Cambridge, Massachusetts
A Subsidiary of J.B. Lippincott Company

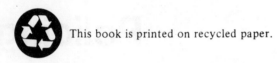

The research was funded by the National Science Foundation (Research Applied to National Needs Division) under Grant NSF GI-43949. The authors gratefully acknowledge this support. Any findings, inferences, views, or opinions expressed herein are, however, those of the authors and do not necessarily reflect those of the National Science Foundation.

International Standard Book Number: 0-88410-783-3

Library of Congress Catalog Card Number: 77-25466

Printed in the United States of America

Library of Congress Cataloging in Publication Data

Ostrom, Elinor.
   Patterns of metropolitan policing.

   1. Police—United States. I. Parks, Roger B., joint author.
II. Whitaker, Gordon P., joint author. III. Title.
HV8138.O758   363.2'0973   77-25466
ISBN 0-88410-783-3

Contents

List of Figures

List of Maps

List of Tables

Preface: The Nature of This Volume

If we could first know where we are and whither we are tending, we could better judge what to do and how to do it.

—Abraham Lincoln

This volume presents a broad overview of the current organization of police services in metropolitan America—in Lincoln's words "where we are." We examine police service delivery arrangements as they existed in 1974 and 1975 in and among police agencies serving small- to medium-sized metropolitan areas across the country. These areas constitute much of metropolitan America; yet they are often ignored in discussions of metropolitan policing.

No field of local public service has been studied by more national commissions or subjected to more recommendations for change than has local policing. The Wickersham Commission Report, written in 1931, was only the first in a long series recommending major changes in local police organization. More recently both the President's Commission on Law Enforcement and Administration of Justice in 1967 and the National Advisory Commission on Criminal Justice Standards and Goals in 1973 have recommended sweeping changes in the organization of police agencies—particularly those serving metropolitan areas. Similarly, the Advisory Commission on Intergovernmental Relations and the Committee for Economic Development have also recommended major changes.

In the course of our research we have had opportunities to discuss these reports and recommendations with police officials across the country. These officials frequently commented that while the commission studies and proposals were often all right in abstract terms, many suggestions were not relevant to the specific situations confronting local police. The flaw police officials identified in many different ways was that quite often commission members and staff personnel proposing changes "didn't know the territory." Most commissions and agencies making recommendations are staffed by individuals familiar with, at best, a limited number of areas. Reforms that might be appropriate for those areas are not always relevant when applied in a sweeping fashion to all metropolitan areas.

The most significant finding of our report is that there are patterns within the diversity of policing arrangements in metropolitan America. The areas we studied vary widely in the number of agencies conducting police services, in the size and types of those agencies, in the internal organization of the agencies, and in the interorganizational arrangements linking the agencies together and to the citizen-consumers they serve. Yet with few exceptions local police understood and made use of the divisions of policing that were practiced in their own metropolitan area.

We hope our description of the patterns presented in this report will help scholars and practitioners to better "know the territory." With this wider knowledge their recommendations for changing the police industry may be more considered and relevant. To be relevant their recommendations will surely have to be less sweeping than those of the past. It is unlikely that a uniform set of recommendations can be applicable to all the many different metropolitan areas.

Across the country efforts are being made to initiate changes in police organization. But what is known about the way police agencies are presently organized and interrelated in metropolitan areas or about the effects of organization on performance? None of the major national recommendations for change cite empirical evidence to support their contentions. The data presented in those reports are largely compilations of the numbers of agencies providing general municipal or county-level police services in metropolitan areas. Although the number of agencies is indeed large, simple sums and lists of agencies do not provide information about the types of arrangements among agencies that may or may not exist in metropolitan areas. Nor do such lists provide any evidence about the relative performance of the individual police agencies.

The assumption is often made that most police agencies must provide training, crime lab, and other expensive specialized services for themselves. Is this correct? The assumption is often made that most municipal police agencies cannot pursue a fleeing suspect beyond their boundaries. Is this true? The assumption is often made that little coordination and cooperation exist among police agencies. How much cooperation is there? The assumption is often made that extensive duplication of police services exists due to the fragmentation and the degree of overlap in the American federal system. How much duplication is there?

For future public policies to be based on information rather than on assumptions, an accurate picture of the broad spectrum of organizational arrangements existing across the country is needed. Such a description is necessary for successful adoption of new public policies. How can we know what we should change unless we know what is there? This volume is an attempt to begin to answer that need.

The next phase of our research will examine what differences in the outcomes for police agencies and the citizens they serve result from differences in internal and interorganizational arrangements. We believe that organizational forms, both internal to police agencies and among agencies and their citizenry, exert important influences upon the effectiveness, equity, efficiency, and responsiveness of the police industry.

In our continuing research we plan to examine the direction and strength of these influences. In the interim, however, we hope you find this volume useful. The many different patterns of organization are alternatives that citizens and police have adopted. Our description of these options may be helpful to those considering changes in their own areas.

Elinor Ostrom
Roger B. Parks
Gordon P. Whitaker

Aknowledgments

The authors owe an enormous debt of gratitude to many people. All over the country busy public officials took time from their schedules to meet with us, to provide us with data, and to read our preliminary reports. We hope that this report provides them with a composite overview of police services delivery that adds to the knowledge that each so generously contributed to this study. We wish to thank all of these individuals for their help and kindness.

We were also helped by the work of a very active, enthusiastic, incisive, and articulate National Board of Consultants:

Dr. John Angell
Criminal Justice Center
University of Alaska
Anchorage, Alaska

Dennis L. Bliss
Deputy Attorney General
State of New Jersey
Trenton, New Jersey

Col. James P. Damos
Chief of Police
University City, Missouri

Paul F. Dunn, Director
Law Enforcement Council
National Council on Crime
  and Delinquency
Hackensack, New Jersey

Dr. John A. Gardiner
Department of Political Science
University of Illinois—
   Chicago Circle
Chicago, Illinois

Lt. Col. Adolphe C. Jacobsmeyer
Assistant Chief of Police
St. Louis Metropolitan Police Dept.
St. Louis, Missouri

Joseph H. Lewis
Director of Evaluation
Police Foundation
Washington, D.C.

Edgar Likins, Associate Director
Center for Criminal Justice
  Training
Indiana University
Indianapolis, Indiana

J.P. Morgan, President
Public Safety Consultants
St. Petersburg, Florida

Robert P. Owens
Chief of Police
Oxnard, California

Dr. Dennis C. Smith
Graduate School of Public
  Administration
New York University
New York, New York

The Board met six times during this phase of the project. At each meeting the members actively reviewed our plans and made many important contributions to the project.

Our project managers at the National Science Foundation, Vaughn Blankenship, Trudi Miller, and Frank Scioli, have all contributed valuable advice and support. We also received very helpful suggestions from two separate NSF Site Review teams who reviewed this volume and other products of the project.

The three principal investigators are deeply appreciative of the contributions of staff members at the Workshop in Political Theory and Policy Analysis, Indiana University, and at the Center for Urban and Regional Studies, University of North Carolina at Chapel Hill. The research staff has contributed actively to all stages of the research design, development of research instruments and field procedures, and to actual fieldwork itself. Many of the innovative aspects of this study result from the valuable contributions of this very capable group:

Frank Anechiarico	Thomas Kramer	Marlene Rodenbeck
Paula Baker	Stephen Mastrofski	Eric Scott
Thomas Banes	John McIver	Elaine Sharp
Mike Binford	Gary Miller	William Tabor
Frances Bish	Marc Mishkin	Ronald Tedrow
Ken Cahill	Darwin Morgan	Fred Towe
Donald Coles	Nancy M. Neubert	Larry Wagner
Gary Gray	Stephen Percy	Dan Wilson
Vicki Greene	Barry Price	Carl Young
Phillip Gregg		

Martha Vandivort, Systems Analyst, assisted by John Chadwick and Max Rayfield, did the complex job of building a large data base and handled the data management problems associated with integrating data from a number of diverse sources.

We had the good fortune of working with an extremely responsible and careful coding staff under the able guidance of Data Processing

Supervisors Susan Gillie, Lenell Nussbaum, and Diane Eubanks, and Assistant Data Processing Supervisors Adrienne Kaplan and Barbara Metz:

Lisa Carrol	Rebecca Korenich	Dale Ogden
Mark Giaquinta	Robert Korenich	Deborah Puchrik
Richard Henderson	Phyllis Lee	Mona Sawyer
Kim Hubbard	Janet Lerner	Earl Singleton
Paula Killelea	Brenda Lott	Anita Swansiger
John Kolena	Nancy Mattingly	Dan Wiltshire

Andrea Lapeyre, Administrative Assistant at Indiana, and Sally Bernard, Administrative Secretary at North Carolina, were responsible for all the administrative activities that held this project together.

Mary Zielinski and Gillian Nevin supervised a skilled secretarial and support staff:

Mary Abramson	Pam Hill	Mary Munchel
Trisha Bracken	Patty Hodson	Philip Nevin
Donna Brawner	Owie Ikponmwosa	Carol Parks
Edna Bryan-Cummins	Claude Lapeyre	Lorna Schofield
Bea Carrol	Bethsaida Lee	Diane Singleton
Judy Clark	Sue Lytle	Lisa Slezak
Melanie Cloghessy	Ralph Miller	Eileen Walters
Delores Cowden	Jane Moon	Patty Zielinski
Debbie Gray		

Sally Bernard, Marsha Brown, Phyllis McNamara, Mary Turk, Mary Wagner, and Mary Zielinski typed and retyped the several drafts of this volume with skill, good will, and concern. Mary Zielinski typed and proofed for consistency the entire final draft. Mary Rosenson edited this volume, helping to translate our reports into more readable form. Spencer Ballard ran and reran the tables. We also wish to thank Vincent Ostrom for the many hours he devoted to reading and commenting on this volume and other reports from the project.

Readers interested in a less detailed summary report of this project should refer to *Policing Metropolitan America* by Elinor Ostrom, Roger B. Parks, and Gordon P. Whitaker, published in 1977 by the National Science Foundation and available from the U.S. Government Printing Office (Stock Number 038−000−00317−8).

This volume was prepared with the support of National Science Foundation Grant GI 43949. Any opinions, findings, conclusions, or recommendations expressed in it are those of the authors and do not necessarily reflect the views of NSF.

The research project was one of four funded by the Research Applied to National Needs (RANN) Division of the National Science Foundation under Program Solicitation 73—28 to study the organization of service delivery in metropolitan areas for these services: police, fire, public health, and solid waste. Publications from the other studies funded under this solicitation may be obtained from:

Fire:

Dr. Lois MacGillivray
Center for Population Research
  and Service
Research Triangle Institute
Box 12194
Research Triangle Park,
  North Carolina 27709

Public Health:

Dr. Patrick O'Donoghue, President
Spectrum Research, Inc.
789 Sherman, Suite 500
Denver, Colorado 80203

Solid Waste:

Dr. E.S. Savas
Graduate School of Business
Columbia University
New York, New York 10027

The long hours, the attempt to present error-free data, and the sheer volume of work almost overwhelmed all of us at times. However, the skill, good spirit, spontaneity, and willingness to persevere on everyone's part kept us going. We hope our joint product will contribute to an understanding of the patterns of organization in the complex field of metropolitan policing.

Elinor Ostrom
Roger B. Parks
Gordon P. Whitaker

Summary

This report describes the ways in which police are organized to patrol, control traffic, and conduct criminal investigations in small- to medium-sized metropolitan areas. It also describes the supply of radio communications, pretrial detention services, entry-level training, and crime laboratory analysis to police departments serving metropolitan areas.

We detail the different kinds of agencies supplying these police services and the patterns of fragmentation, dominance, independence, duplication, coordination, and alternation that characterize the delivery of these services. We explore regional differences, metropolitan area size differences, and differences in state law that affect the organization of police services delivery. Our findings suggest that no one way of organizing police services delivery is necessarily better than all other ways. Proposals for change must take into account existing organizational structure and local service requirements. Many already existing arrangements should be considered as possible options.

This report is descriptive. It explains how police agencies divide among them the work of policing metropolitan areas. Comparable data on the quality of police services are not available. To evaluate the effectiveness, efficiency, equity, and responsiveness of alternatives in police organization it is necessary to observe the ways in which organization influences service delivery activities and the consequences different ways of performing police activities have for the particular community being served.

WHAT IS IN THIS BOOK

Chapter 1: Introduction

Despite the many reform proposals that have been made in recent years, little is known about police organization in metropolitan areas. There has even been uncertainty about the number of police agencies serving these areas. Our industry approach, which uses concepts of producers and consumers of police services, contrasts with traditional research based upon an organizational approach. The industry approach permits us to explore "interorganizational" arrangements for service delivery. We ask not only how many agencies supply each service, but who receives the service and whether agencies serving the same recipients alternate, coordinate, or duplicate service delivery.

Chapter 2: The Metropolitan Areas

The areas studied are Standard Metropolitan Statistical Areas (SMSAs) under 1.5 million in population and lying within only one state. We chose a random sample of 80 of the 200 such SMSAs. The sample was stratified by Federal Administrative Region. Data were collected from state sources and from individual police agencies during the last half of 1974 and 1975. As much as three-person weeks of fieldwork were required in those SMSAs with great organizational complexity. Telephone and mail contacts supplemented our in-person data collection.

Chapter 3: Studying the Organization of Police Services Delivery

This chapter explains our research methodology and contains definitions of the measures we used to examine the organization of police services delivery: measures of fragmentation, multiplicity, independence, autonomy, and dominance. We also define different production relationships following our industry model: regular production, irregular production, alternation, coordination, and duplication. We explain our data display form—the service matrix—which allows us to characterize service exchanges between producers and consumers.

Chapter 4: An Introduction to Direct Services

Direct police services are those supplied directly to citizens by police agencies. Some producers of these services conduct only one or two of the three direct services we studied: patrol, traffic control, and criminal investigation. Others conduct all of them. However, all parts of any given metropolitan area receive each service from at least one producer. In this chapter we present data on municipal producers, county producers, state producers, college and university campus producers, federal producers, and special district and private producers. We discuss the services produced by each type of agency.

Chapter 5: General Area Patrol

Most patrol is conducted by municipal and county police agencies, although campus police, military police, and other special district agencies are important in some SMSAs. General area patrol duties occupy the largest number of personnel in most local police agencies. We present data on the agencies conducting patrol services, the operational organization of patrol agencies, patrol deployment and citizen-to-patrol officer ratios, variations in patrol practices, and the relationship between agency size and operational structure.

We find that more consolidated patrol arrangements are not necessarily better. Larger departments do *not* translate their relative personnel advantage into as high an on-street presence as do small- to medium-sized agencies. The larger departments characteristically have fewer officers on the street for every 10,000 citizens served. Arrangements that divide responsibility for metropolitan area patrol may, therefore, increase the number of officers assigned to general area police patrol.

Chapter 6: Traffic Control Services

Although much traffic control is conducted by local police agencies, state police and highway patrols make an important contribution to this service. Alternation of traffic control is common with a state agency controlling traffic on major thoroughfares, while municipal or county law enforcement agencies patrol traffic and investigate accidents on other streets and roads. These arrangements are quite diverse, however, and in some areas there is little or no alternation of this type.

Traffic control specialists are generally used by state agencies and by the largest local departments. Most local police agencies assign traffic duties to general patrol officers. Neither alternate production nor the use of police generalists is seen by police officials as creating confusion about traffic control responsibilities. Examination of the operation of a specific metropolitan area traffic control system is required to determine whether more or less organizational diversity would be beneficial in that particular area.

Chapter 7: Criminal Investigation

Many more local police agencies investigate residential burglary than investigate homicide. Small municipal, campus, and special district police agencies are least likely to investigate homicides. Homicide investigation in their service areas is conducted by the county or a larger city agency with overlapping jurisdiction. Many of the smaller agencies that do investigate homicide coordinate their efforts with those of detectives from another agency. Larger agencies are more likely to assign detectives rather than police generalists to investigations.

Chapter 8: An Overview of Direct Service Delivery Patterns

We find definite patterns of working relationships among the varied producers of metropolitan police services. Strict duplication of services is almost nonexistent in the production of direct police services in most SMSAs. Alternate arrangements between producers exist for traffic control in many metropolitan areas. Coordination of criminal investigations is especially widespread for homicide investigation. Much more intensive examination of the practices and impacts of police services delivery is needed to assess the value of current organizational arrangements.

Chapter 9: An Introduction to Auxiliary Services

This chapter introduces four auxiliary services used by police agencies in the production of direct services: radio communications, adult pretrial detention, entry-level training, and crime laboratory analysis. Because these auxiliary activities are designed to serve police agencies, they are organized quite differently from police services supplied directly to citizens. Except for radio communications, the proportion of direct service producers who also produce their own auxiliary services is quite low. Large direct service agencies are more likely to produce their own auxiliary services; however, only 1 of the 1,454 local producers in the 80 SMSAs supplies all the services we studied.

Chapter 10: Radio Communications

About 70 percent of all direct service producers supply their own radio communications. Other direct service agencies obtain radio communications services from specialized communications agencies or from neighboring direct service agencies. About 80 percent of county police and sheriffs' departments dispatch for other departments. We find little duplication in the production of this service, although there is some alternation of production. Arrangements for sharing radio frequencies and monitoring radios of other police agencies are common in our metropolitan areas.

Three fourths of all local direct service producers that also produce radio communications assign four or fewer full-time employees to dispatch duties. The employment of civilians for dispatch duties is widespread. Smaller agencies that produce their own radio communications tend to use a substantially larger proportion of their personnel to produce this service than do larger agencies. Some economies of scale appear in the production of this auxiliary service.

Chapter 11: Adult Pretrial Detention

Most metropolitan areas are served by only one nonmilitary producer of pretrial detention. In the Northeast there is little involvement of direct service agencies in the production of pretrial detention. In other regions sheriffs typically supply detention and direct services; there is little duplication in the production and consumption of this service. SMSAs with two or more nonmilitary detention facilities are usually multicounty metropolitan areas with producers serving each county using only the jail in that county.

Facilities differ for jails of different types. Half the municipal police departments with their own jails have room for fewer than 20 inmates. Two thirds of the municipal departments with their own jails assign no employees to full-time detention duties. Eighty percent of the county sheriffs' departments have a capacity of over 50 inmates and over five employees assigned full time to detention. Most jails operated by detention specialists (agencies conducting no direct police services) have capacity for over 100 inmates and employ at least 20 full-time jail personnel.

Chapter 12: Entry-Level Training

More than 90 percent of all local direct service producers require some entry-level training of all recruits. In all but two states, entry-level training for at least some officers is required by state legislation. These state requirements are exceeded by about half of the agencies. Over half the departments requiring entry-level training require more than 240 hours. Larger local direct service producers are more likely to require entry-level training, to require longer number of hours of training, and to require that training be completed during the first six months of service.

While municipal police departments make up over half the agencies producing entry-level training, regional, state, and federal training academies play an important role in the production of entry-level training. Most small police departments send their recruits to regional and state academies or to an academy operated by a large local department.

Chapter 13: Crime Laboratory Analysis

We focus on one type of commonly requested laboratory service requiring expert competence: chemical analysis. This service is available to virtually all metropolitan police agencies. Patterns of organization for chemical analysis generally share more common features than differences. Few direct police agencies conduct their own laboratory analysis. Chemical analysis in most areas is dominated by state laboratories. However, there is greater dependency upon local agencies in the West than in other regions. Also, agencies in larger metropolitan areas tend to use local labs for chemical analysis of evidence.

Chapter 14: An Overview of Auxiliary Service Delivery Patterns

Our findings differ markedly from those we would expect from reading some of the major reports on police organization that have appeared during the last decade. We find a much richer network of interrelationships among agencies, and a much higher use of auxiliary services in general, than we would have expected. Where there are economies of scale in production of auxiliary services, these can (and in practice may already) be realized through production of these services by larger agencies or by specialists that supply them to smaller direct service agencies.

Chapter 15: Police Agency Cooperation: Patterns of Mutual Aid and Cross-Deputization

Informal interagency assistance is common in the 80 metropolitan areas. Almost 90 percent of the agencies that patrol assist other police agencies, while over 90 percent report receiving assistance. Both formal and informal mutual assistance are more frequent in smaller departments. Most states also authorize police to pursue suspects across jurisdiction boundaries, although the extent of this authorization varies from state to state. Interagency assistance and the existence of fresh pursuit legislation seem to be common responses to the jurisdictional fragmentation of metropolitan areas.

Chapter 16: Dividing the Work of Metropolitan Policing

The work of policing metropolitan areas in the United States is divided up in many ways. One division is geographic. Different officers are assigned responsibility for serving different parts of the SMSA. Another way to divide the work of metropolitan policing is to assign officers to particular services and have them restrict their activities to those services. Specialized assignments may be made with personnel employed by a single agency or with personnel employed by separate, service-specific agencies. Similarly, geographic division of policing can be made within a single department or by dividing the SMSA among numerous departments.

Whether it is preferable to have all service production facilities contained in a single department or to have departments organized along either geographic or service-specific lines is an issue that requires further study. Some think that having all services within the same department facilitates communication and coordination of the separate services. In studying SMSAs with extensive division of services among agencies, we have, however, found considerable interdepartmental communication and coordination of service. Alternative ways of organizing the delivery of police services in metropolitan areas need to be evaluated on the basis of how well they meet local service needs. Such evaluation must take into account the consequences of organization for police activities and the impact of those activities on the citizens served.

 *Chapter 1*

Introduction

Police services in metropolitan America are delivered by a wide variety of agencies through various kinds of arrangements with each other and with the citizens in the communities being served. Local, county, state, and federal agencies are all involved in the day to day conduct of such basic police services as patrol, traffic control, and the investigation of residential burglaries and homicides.

Some political jurisdictions receive all these services from a single police department. Quite commonly, however, several agencies serve residents of the same political community. One may patrol at night, another during the day. One may control traffic on major thoroughfares, while another controls traffic on secondary streets and roads. Some police departments produce their own radio communications, entry-level training, pretrial detention, or crime lab analysis. Most obtain these auxiliary services from other agencies.

DIVERSITY IN SERVICE DELIVERY

Is this diversity harmful? Does it lead to confusion among police agencies over the division of responsibility for delivery of police services? Does it leave some areas without service while duplicating services to other areas? Our findings show that the answers to these questions are most often *no*. In general, police in metropolitan areas are not confused about who is to conduct which police services and where they are to be conducted. Patrol, traffic control, and criminal investigation are supplied to all parts of the 80 metropolitan areas we studied. There is little duplication of service. In most areas where two or more police departments conduct the same service they divide the work so that each complements the other. Cooperation and interagency assistance are commonplace.

While most police agencies do not produce their own entry-level training, pretrial detention, or chemical analysis of evidence, almost without exception they use these services. In a few instances confusion does exist over poorly defined jurisdictional boundaries. And there are cases of rivalry among the agencies serving a metropolitan area. But blanket criticism of current organizational arrangements for metropolitan policing is unwarranted.

In this volume we identify the patterns of police service delivery that bring order to the activities of the various producers of direct and auxiliary police services in small- to medium-sized metropolitan areas of the United States. Much has been written about the internal operations and problems of very large central city police departments. The New York City Police Department, the Chicago Police Department, the Los Angeles Police Department, and similar large city police agencies have been studied extensively. They are the models used explicitly or implicitly in judging other police departments across the country.

But little has been written about the ways in which smaller police agencies work in relation to each other in small- and medium-sized urban areas of the country. Some studies have counted the number of police agencies serving metropolitan areas and concluded that too many departments exist in most metropolitan areas. Many observers have expressed concern about the existence of small departments. In their opinion these agencies cannot possibly provide the wide range of services offered by large central city police departments. Major changes in the law enforcement systems of metropolitan areas have been proposed. These changes are being considered without much information (other than the number and size distribution of agencies) about how services are delivered.

THE DESCRIPTIVE FUNCTION
OF THIS VOLUME

This volume is an attempt to fill part of that gap. It is an interim report from an ongoing study of the organizational arrangements for the production of police services in the nation's small- and medium-sized metropolitan areas. Later reports will evaluate different organizational arrangements in terms of effectiveness, efficiency, equity, and responsiveness. This report—a comprehensive overview of the descriptive stage of the project—does not attempt to evaluate which ways of producing police services are the most effective, efficient, equitable, or responsive. What it does do, however, is present the first broad overview of the ways in which police agencies work independently or with one another to produce basic police services required by residents of metropolitan areas.

THE INDUSTRY APPROACH

In this study we take an "industry approach" rather than an "organizational approach" [1]. That is, we systematically examine some specific police services within what is more generally called police service, and we look at the organizational arrangements for producing these different services.

Let us illustrate the difference. Observers using an organizational approach to study police find that most departments having fewer than 150 full-time sworn officers do not have their own crime laboratories. These observers typically conclude that citizens served by these departments lack the advantages crime labs can offer to investigators. But in using an industry approach we are interested in determining whether the residents served by smaller police departments are, in fact, covered by crime lab services. We ask whether agencies with overlapping jurisdictions, such as county or state police agencies, provide crime lab facilities to smaller police agencies, or whether smaller agencies contract for such services from another local police department or a nonpolice agency, such as a local hospital or private laboratory.

Observers using an organizational approach may argue that if economies of scale exist in the production of certain police services, all police agencies should be made large enough (through consolidation or merger, for instance) to gain these economies. But observers using an industry approach will ask whether these economies can be achieved by organizing large, specialized agencies to produce a particular service rather than including all police service production within one agency.

In the private goods and services market we are familiar with the difference between retailers and wholesalers. We are also familiar with the differences between neighborhood, quick-service, limited selection establishments and broad-spectrum supermarkets or full-scale department stores. These differences can be instructive in examining organizational arrangements for supplying public goods and services. We do not find each political jurisdiction isolated. For services to be available to citizens each agency need not produce the full range of services itself.

USING THE INDUSTRY APPROACH
TO EXAMINE SERVICE DELIVERY

Using an industry approach we examine three important police services delivered directly to citizens: general area patrol, traffic control, and criminal investigation. We also examine patterns of service delivery for four auxiliary services consumed in the production of direct services by a direct service agency. These services are radio communications, adult pretrial detention, entry-level training, and criminal laboratory analysis. For each metropolitan area and for each service we have determined which agencies produce the service and who are the service recipients.

Several forms of service delivery are possible. The service recipient may decide to establish its own agency to produce the service. This is the case, for instance, when a municipality (which may be considered the service recipient for citizen consumers) organizes its own police agency to produce general area patrol services. This is also the case when an individual police agency (which may be considered the service recipient for police officers receiving support services) organizes its own radio communications unit. However, not all service recipients produce their own services; some contract for services from other agencies. A municipality may pay the county sheriff an annual fee to produce pretrial detention, for example, or the county or state may pay the municipality for certain services.

Some forms of service delivery are established by state law. In Virginia, for instance, state legislation authorized the formation of a state criminal laboratory facility that may be used by any police agency in the state. No fees or separately written agreements are necessary. Service recipients may also receive the same service from more than one producer. All police departments in the United States may draw upon the laboratory facilities of the FBI, even though these agencies may have access to county, state, or their own crime labs.

Questions Answered Using This Approach

By examining production and consumption patterns in metropolitan areas a number of questions will be answered in this volume. Some are:

- *How many* agencies produce the direct services in each metropolitan area?
- What are the *characteristics* of the agencies producing these services?

- How many political jurisdictions make decisions about policing in each metropolitan area?
- How much *duplication* of direct service production is there?
- How do *agency characteristics* and *patterns* of service delivery relate to the density of on-street patrol in metropolitan areas?
- What *types* of agencies produce auxiliary services for direct service producers?
- Is there greater *specialization* among auxiliary service producers than among direct service producers?
- What *types* of agencies produce their own auxiliary services?
- What types of *duplication* occur in auxiliary services?

The second and third sections of this report answer these and related questions for the metropolitan areas we studied. The fourth section examines several specific patterns of interagency relationships. We answer such questions as:

- What are the *legal grounds* for *inter* and *intra*state fresh pursuit?
- What *patterns* of crossdeputization occur in different types of metropolitan areas?
- What types of agencies participate most actively in different forms of *mutual assistance*?

Before turning directly to our findings, however, we discuss the concepts and methods used in this study. In the next chapter we describe the 80 metropolitan areas included in this study and our methods of data collection, and in Chapter 3 we discuss in detail our concepts and methodology. Then we turn to discussion of each of the individual services included in the study.

 *Chapter 2*

The Metropolitan Areas Studied
and Methods of Data Collection

This chapter describes how we conducted this study: how
we drew our sample of metropolitan areas and how we
collected data about police service producers in those
metropolitan areas selected. These data have been placed on file
with the Inter-University Consortium for Political and Social Research at the University of Michigan in Ann Arbor. Readers of this
volume interested in doing further data analysis may obtain the
data by corresponding directly with the Consortium. Documentation
on the data file itself will be supplied with the data.

In this chapter we present information about our sampling
methods to allow readers to evaluate the degree to which our findings can be generalized. We also present information about our data
collection methods to allow an evaluation of the validity of the information collected.

THE METROPOLITAN AREAS STUDIED

Two hundred Standard Metropolitan Statistical Areas (SMSAs) met
the National Science Foundation's criteria for initial inclusion in
this study [1]. These criteria were a 1970 SMSA population of less
than 1.5 million and an SMSA boundary (defined by the U.S. Bureau of the Census) that did not cross state lines. The first criterion
reflected a desire to focus on the less studied areas of the country.
Police departments in the very large metropolitan areas have been
frequently studied by national commissions, state and federal agencies, and social scientists. The second criterion resulted from a desire

to determine the impact of state laws and policies on metropolitan policing. Restriction to single-state SMSAs was expected to sharpen analysis on this question.

In 1970 more than 67 million Americans—approximately one third of the U.S. population—lived in these 200 metropolitan areas. This population, moreover, was nearly half the nation's people living outside the 16 largest metropolitan areas. The 200 SMSAs ranged from 55,959 population (Meriden/Connecticut) to 1,421,869 (Seattle-Everett/Washington). Population density ranged from 19 persons per square mile (Reno/Nevada) to 12,963 persons per square mile (Jersey City/New Jersey).

The 200 SMSAs cover a broad spectrum of places where Americans live and receive police services. Saginaw/Michigan, with a 1970 population of 219,743 is the median-sized SMSA in the 200. Fifty-five percent of the 200 metropolitan areas had a 1970 population of less than 250,000; 20 percent had more than 500,000 residents. Metropolitan areas in the Midwest were generally smaller, while those in the West tended to be larger. Metropolitan areas in the Northeast were most densely populated, and those in the West generally had much lower population densities [2].

The 80 SMSA Sample

To keep our research manageable within 18 months we drew a 40 percent stratified sample of metropolitan areas from each of the 10 regions used for administrative purposes by the U.S. Department of Justice and other federal agencies. This produced a list of 80 SMSAs for study. Stratification by region ensured a wide distribution across the country so that significant state and regional variations might be observed. Map 2–1 shows the boundaries used for stratification and shows the 80 SMSAs.

The 80 SMSAs include metropolitan areas of many sizes, population densities, and types. They are located in 31 states. Three of the 80 SMSAs had more than one million residents in 1970. Ten had fewer than 100,000. Population densities in the 80 SMSAs ranged from 31 persons per square mile in the Great Falls/Montana SMSA to more than 3,000 persons per square mile in the Paterson-Clifton-Passaic/New Jersey SMSA. The distribution of population size and density across the 80 SMSAs closely reflects the full 200 (Table 2–1). The distribution of population size is slightly lower in the 80 than in the 200, and population density is very slightly higher. But neither deviation is large.

Restricting SMSAs to those with populations of less than 1.5 million excluded metropolitan areas containing the largest American

Map 2–1. The 80 Metropolitan Areas and the 10 Federal Regions

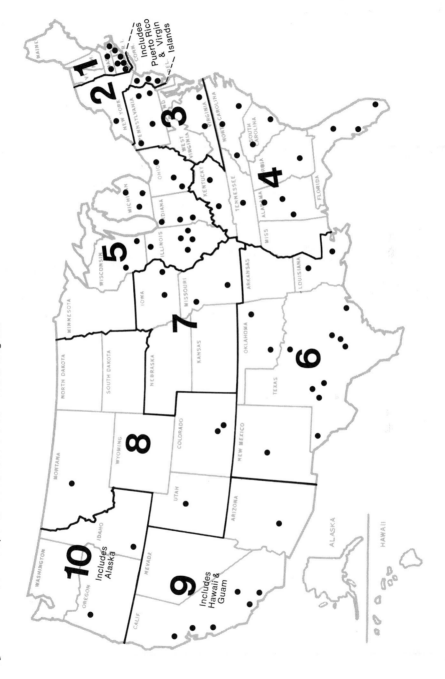

Table 2–1.   Distribution of Metropolitan Area Size and Population Density: 200 SMSAs and 80 SMSA Sample

	200 Metropolitan Areas	80 SMSA Sample	Percent of SMSAs in Region in Size and Density Classes[a]							
			Northeast		Midwest		South		West	
			200 SMSAs	80 SMSA Sample	200 SMSAs	80 SMSA Sample	200 SMSAs	80 SMSA Sample	200 SMSAs	80 SMSA Sample
	200	80	47	18	51	20	68	29	34	13
SMSA population (1970)										
50,000 to 124,999	45	21	23	22	18	30	28	28	18	23
125,000 to 249,999	64	27	32	39	43	45	28	24	24	31
250,000 to 499,999	52	20	26	28	24	10	26	31	29	31
500,000 and Larger	39	12	19	11	16	15	18	17	29	15
SMSA population density (persons per square mile)										
0 to 150	52	21	6	0	12	10	34	31	59	77
151 to 300	62	25	21	11	39	50	37	38	21	15
301 to 600	50	18	26	33	39	30	21	21	12	0
Over 600	36	16	47	56	10	10	9	10	9	8

Note: Columns may not total 100 percent due to rounding errors.

[a] Regions 1, 2, and 3 are in the Northeast region; Regions 5 and 7 constitute the Midwest; Regions 4 and 6, the South; and Regions 8, 9, and 10, the West.

cities. But major cities are included in our sample of 80 SMSAs. Two (Phoenix and San Antonio) have more than 500,000 residents within the city boundaries. Another nine cities in the 80 areas studied have between 250,000 and 500,000 residents within the city [3]. Twenty-three cities have populations between 100,000 and 250,000. These medium- to large-sized cities ensure that we include examples of "big city" and "central city" problems in our analyses.

But our study also includes the full range of additional types of areas police serve, including smaller central and suburban cities and towns (90 percent of the municipal police agencies in the 80 metropolitan areas serve cities having fewer than 50,000 residents—about 50 percent of these are municipalities with 5,000 or fewer inhabitants), unincorporated county areas contiguous to more built-up cities, and rural areas. The heavy focus of previous research and literature on the problems of very large cities has led some to overlook problems of policing in these other areas. A full list of the 80 metropolitan areas studied, their estimated populations in 1973, and their population densities is shown in Table 2-2 [4].

DATA COLLECTION METHODS

This report is based on three types of information. Our central concern was to collect data on all producers of the police services selected for study in each of the 80 SMSAs. We also needed information on the service areas receiving each direct service and on the state laws that pertain to the organization of policing in each state. Each type of data required different collection techniques. This section discusses our data on police service producers, service areas, and state laws and summarizes the ways in which they were assembled.

Police Service Producer Data

Both the organization of individual police service producers and the relationships among producers are of concern to us in this volume. We examined three police services supplied directly to citizens: patrol, traffic control, and criminal investigation. We also examined four auxiliary services used by police in the production of direct services: entry-level training, radio communications, crime laboratory analysis, and adult pretrial detention.

Six broad questions guided our producer data collection. For each producer we sought to determine:

- Which direct and auxiliary services does it produce?
- Who receives these services?

Table 2–2.   The 80 Metropolitan Area Sample: Region, SMSA Population, and Density

	SMSA Population (1970)	SMSA Population Density (Persons per Square Mile in 1970)	Estimated SMSA Population (1973)
Region 1			
Brockton/Massachusetts	189,820	1,157	202,985
Meriden/Connecticut	55,959	2,332	56,686
New Bedford/Massachusetts	152,642	1,075	153,602
New Britain/Connecticut	145,269	1,729	145,037
Norwalk/Connecticut	120,099	1,668	120,135
Pittsfield/Massachusetts	79,727	569	79,059
Waterbury/Connecticut	208,956	954	216,476
Worcester/Massachusetts	344,320	728	347,778
Region 2			
Paterson-Clifton-Passaic/ New Jersey	1,357,930	3,188	1,355,437
Rochester/New York	882,667	381	888,037
Trenton/New Jersey	303,968	1,333	315,489
Vineland-Millville-Bridgeton/ New Jersey	121,374	243	129,609
Region 3			
Altoona/Pennsylvania	135,356	255	136,285
Erie/Pennsylvania	263,654	324	272,504
Newport News-Hampton/Virginia	292,159	1,155	302,206

Reading/Pennsylvania	296,382	344	305,064
Roanoke/Virginia	181,436	599	190,324
Scranton/Pennsylvania	234,107	516	235,037
Region 4			
Albany/Georgia	89,639	277	95,017
Asheville/North Carolina	145,056	221	148,800
Birmingham/Alabama	739,274	272	755,827
Charleston/South Carolina	303,849	148	312,447
Fayetteville/North Carolina	212,042	324	216,230
Greensboro–Winston-Salem–High Point/North Carolina	605,713	274	630,708
Greenville/South Carolina	299,730	233	324,237
Huntsville/Alabama	228,239	169	229,753
Lexington/Kentucky	174,323	623	184,604
Nashville/Tennessee	541,160	336	555,539
Orlando/Florida	428,003	352	515,160
Owensboro/Kentucky	79,486	172	81,157
Tampa–St. Petersburg/Florida	1,012,504	777	1,164,301
Tuscaloosa/Alabama	116,029	87	121,826
West Palm Beach/Florida	348,753	172	412,075

(Table 2–2. continued overleaf)

Table 2-2. continued

	SMSA Population (1970)	SMSA Population Density (Persons per Square Mile in 1970)	Estimated SMSA Population (1973)
Region 5			
Akron/Ohio	679,239	752	677,130
Bay City/Michigan	117,339	262	119,037
Bloomington–Normal/Illinois	104,389	89	114,842
Champaign–Urbana/Illinois	163,281	163	163,806
Decatur/Illinois	125,010	216	124,742
Gary–Hammond–East Chicago/Indiana	633,367	675	640,777
Grand Rapids/Michigan	539,225	380	552,917
Hamilton/Ohio	226,207	480	237,348
Jackson/Michigan	143,274	205	144,922
Kenosha/Wisconsin	117,917	434	120,841
La Crosse/Wisconsin	80,468	178	82,725
Lafayette–West Lafayette/Indiana	109,378	219	111,768
Rockford/Illinois	272,063	339	271,150
Springfield/Illinois	161,355	184	167,737
Springfield/Ohio	157,115	391	157,520
Terre Haute/Indiana	175,143	117	175,372

Region 6			
Albuquerque/New Mexico	315,774	270	353,957
Austin/Texas	295,516	292	341,776
Baton Rouge/Louisiana	285,167	621	305,064
El Paso/Texas	359,291	340	390,046
Galveston-Texas City/Texas	169,812	426	176,025
Lawton/Oklahoma	108,144	100	102,165
Midland/Texas	65,433	70	65,937
Monroe/Louisiana	115,387	181	121,818
Odessa/Texas	91,805	101	93,072
San Angelo/Texas	71,047	47	73,150
San Antonio/Texas	864,014	441	932,069
Tulsa/Oklahoma	475,264	126	489,382
Waco/Texas	147,553	148	152,899
Wichita Falls/Texas	126,322	83	125,810
Region 7			
Cedar Rapids/Iowa	163,213	228	164,275
Des Moines/Iowa	268,130	464	294,448
St. Joseph/Missouri	86,915	215	86,896
Springfield/Missouri	152,929	226	165,598

(Table 2-2. *continued overleaf*)

Table 2-2. continued

	SMSA Population (1970)	SMSA Population Density (Persons per Square Mile in 1970)	Estimated SMSA Population (1973)
Region 8			
Colorado Springs/Colorado	235,972	109	283,688
Great Falls/Montana	81,804	31	84,519
Provo–Orem/Utah	137,776	68	158,119
Pueblo/Colorado	118,238	49	124,193
Region 9			
Bakersfield/California	329,271	40	335,570
Oxnard–Simi Valley–Ventura/California	378,497	203	419,903
Phoenix/Arizona	968,487	103	1,126,607
Salinas–Seaside–Monterey/California	247,450	74	255,479
San Jose/California	1,066,421	820	1,156,738
Santa Barbara–Santa Maria–Lompoc/California	264,324	97	276,761
Vallejo-Fairfield-Napa/California	250,955	156	262,827
Region 10			
Boise/Idaho	112,230	108	127,874
Salem/Oregon	186,658	98	199,531
Total: 80 SMSAs	23,034,194		24,308,261

- Do any other producers serve the same areas or agencies?
- How is the producer formally organized?
- How are personnel allocated and deployed?
- What formal interagency agreements is the producer involved in?

Answers to these questions were coded on two detailed, standardized research instruments: (1) a matrix coding form used to generate our service delivery matrices and measures and (2) an individual producer coding form for information about the personnel and internal operations of each direct service producer. The first form was completed for all 1,827 producers included in the study. The second form was completed for the 1,454 direct service producers only. Chapter 3 describes our service delivery matrices and measures.

We used a mixed strategy in collecting the data about each producer. This strategy involved obtaining information from state records, from the county sheriffs' and larger police agencies in each metropolitan area, and from individual producers themselves. We relied heavily on in-person interviews, supplemented by mail and telephone interviews and by compilations of previously collected data where available. Data collection was conducted from June 1974 to September 1975.

Before going to a particular SMSA we visited its state capital. In the state capital we usually visited the state criminal justice planning agency, the agency empowered by state legislation to supervise entry-level training in the state, the state police headquarters, and all other agencies that might have data relevant to the six broad questions outlined above. We started our data collection efforts at the state capital for several reasons. First, we wished to inform state public officials about our study, its purpose, and what sorts of data would come from it. Second, we were aware that many state agencies were actively engaged in regular data collection from local police agencies. It would waste our time and that of local police officials to collect data from them that had just been collected by a state agency. Further, such duplication of research efforts can create considerable aggravation among police officials. This aggravation can be avoided if careful initial steps are taken.

In total, we spent more than 60 person-days in state capitals and talked to some 300 individuals located in over 250 state agencies. We received much cooperation wherever we visited. For state agencies producing direct services in the study SMSAs, we were usually able to obtain the number of sworn and civilian personnel assigned to each SMSA in the state and other types of agency information. We supplemented these data in interviews with the division commander serving each SMSA to determine relationships between his state agency and other producers serving the metropolitan area.

Most state agencies were interested in the type of data we were collecting and helped us gain valid data at least cost to the local producers. In several instances, recently administered questionnaires that contained items similar to those on our forms were copied for us. Preliminary drafts of reports soon to be issued were also made available. The data contained in regular state reports were reviewed and brought to our attention.

From our state capital visits we were able to obtain a good overview of how police responsibilities are divided among different types of agencies in each state. Local variations are, of course, important; however, knowing whether the state highway patrol generally does or does not conduct criminal investigation or general area patrol inside incorporated cities helped us ask pertinent questions when talking with local producers. In some states the state highway patrol is severely restricted in the number of police services it produces. In others it has wide responsibilities. The division of responsibility for patrol in the rural portions of metropolitan areas between state and county agencies varies considerably from one state to another.

In many cases we were able to precode some data before we did our initial fieldwork in a particular SMSA. By posting relevant data before visiting a particular producer we could use the in-person interview to verify information obtained from the state data source. Such verification accomplished two purposes. First, it helped us to evaluate the accuracy of the data we had already obtained. Second, it enabled us to inform the local agency that we had made a considerable investment in time and effort to try to get as much information as possible about that agency from state files. If the agency wished (or, if we learned from our first verification questions that the posted data were inaccurate—due mostly to the passage of time) we then obtained all data directly from the local producer.

One problem we faced early was obtaining an accurate list of producers supplying police services in each metropolitan area. We began with the best lists currently available—one of police agencies published by the FBI (the NCIC Agency Identifiers list) [5] and a second of incorporated places in each SMSA obtained from U.S. Census Bureau tapes.

Within a particular SMSA we usually visited each sheriff or county police chief before visiting other police producers in the SMSA. We often spent three hours or more with the sheriff and his staff. We reviewed our lists of producers with them and usually obtained a complete list of producers serving each county in the SMSA. In addition to these lists, we also reviewed a map of the county. We asked specific questions about all potential sites for special police forces. These questions included:

- Who patrols in this airport, in this park, or on this campus?
- Is there any special investigative force not normally producing investigation services that responds to particular types of incidents, such as homicides or traffic fatalities?
- Are there any special arrangements for patrolling on freeways, tollways, bridges, state highways, or county roads?

Wherever the sheriff's department dispatched other agencies in the area we also obtained information about these. We learned how many sworn officers were employed, when each agency was on duty, and what types of services each dispatched agency produced. We also obtained information about the services produced by the sheriff's department itself, personnel allocation and deployment, services obtained from others, personnel practices, and other information.

Our next visits within a metropolitan area were usually to larger municipal police departments. There we again obtained specific information about the department. We also obtained information about other producers with which the department had regular working relationships. We visited as many of the smaller direct service producers as we could in each SMSA, including campus police and other special district agencies. Where it was impossible to visit all direct service producers, we mailed a questionnaire to agencies not included in our in-person visits. To follow up these mailings we interviewed direct service producers by telephone.

More than 250 person-days were spent in the 80 SMSAs. In-person interviews were conducted with members of more than 600 police agencies. Often more than a single member of a police department was interviewed to obtain all the information needed. An additional 300 agencies were contacted by telephone. Over 200 agencies responded to mail questionnaires, and many of these agencies were also telephoned to check information. Data for the other 300 direct service producers were coded using information about them from state agencies, from county sheriffs, and from other agencies located in the metropolitan areas.

We asked each direct service producer where it sent entry-level recruits for training. We learned about training academies from their answers. Agencies using crime laboratory services were our major sources of information about crime laboratory producers. We learned about specialized detention and communications producers from the police departments using their services.

One perplexing problem in collecting data about relationships *among* agencies is what to do with conflicting information. In most instances we received consistent information about the relationships among state, county, municipal, and other producers. Some conflicts of interpretation were encountered, however. For example, a county sheriff indicated that his department conducted regular traffic patrol throughout the county—both in the incorporated and unincorporated areas of the county. Municipal police departments in that county indicated that the county sheriff's department did *not* regularly conduct traffic patrol within their boundaries.

How did we resolve such conflicts? Obviously, considerable judgment goes into any coding decision made when information conflicts. Consistency with other information was our main criterion for making such coding decisions. Where, for example, the personnel and number of patrol cars available to the sheriff were quite limited (given the size of the county), and where *all* municipal police departments within the county indicated that the sheriff did *not* patrol within their boundaries, we assumed that the municipalities were correct. We assumed that the sheriff felt bound to indicate his "legal" jurisdiction rather than his current service delivery patterns.

In other situations of conflicting information we called back several of the departments involved to determine in more detail the relationships among them. By persistent questioning we were usually able to code these relationships with a high degree of confidence in our accuracy and validity. However, we are aware—and the reader and future user of our data should also be aware—that our judgment was involved in coding these data. We made such decisions with considerable investment in time, going back over our notes, talking by phone with participants, and trying to gain a consistent view before we made a final coding decision.

Service Area Data

Because our concern is to describe police service delivery, we are interested not only in the police agencies, but in the types of areas they serve. We needed to be able to describe those characteristics of service areas that might be expected to affect the delivery of services. We obtained data relating to three broad questions about service areas:

- How large is the territory of the service area?
- How many people live in the service area?
- What are the age, income, race, mobility, and housing attributes of the service area population?

Data on service area size were obtained from the 1970 U.S. decennial census and from maps obtained in the metropolitan areas. Because census data are generally aggregated to the boundaries of local *governmental* units, it was frequently necessary for us to calculate the service area size by subtracting from a unit, such as a city, the various service enclaves within the city limits.

For example, the City of Fayetteville, North Carolina, included 24 square miles in 1970. The Fayetteville State University campus (within the City of Fayetteville) encompassed one square mile, representing the size of the FSU patrol service area. The size of the City of Fayetteville patrol service area is, thus, 24 minus 1, or 23 square miles. A similar "remaindering" process was required for most counties in the study—subtracting the areas of incorporated municipalities having their own police forces and areas served by other noncounty producers.

The data on population and housing in the service areas of the 80 SMSAs were obtained from the 1970 Census and from 1973 estimates. As with service area territorial size, it was necessary to obtain data on enclaves and subtract these from the totals for the governmental units commonly used for census aggregation. We used both Fourth and Fifth Count tabulations. In some cases we used individual block statistics from the Metropolitan Area Reports. We obtained 1973 population estimates for all areas possible.

Data on State Laws

Five broad areas of state law were researched by law students using the library of the Indiana University School of Law. Legal experts in each state were then asked to check the accuracy and currency of the coding. The areas of research were:

- State laws relating to "fresh pursuit" of suspected felons and misdemeanants beyond the boundaries of an officer's jurisdiction.
- State laws relating to the recruitment of peace officers.
- State laws relating to the training of police recruits.
- State laws relating to the authority to produce direct and auxiliary police services, including powers of arrest.
- State laws authorizing or regulating intergovernmental agreements.

The data were collected using detailed standardized formats. Data were collected on each of the 50 states. The required information was obtained from state statutes. Legislation in effect on June 30, 1974, inclusive, was the primary data collected. However, changes in state law effective July 1, 1974, and thereafter were noted.

Although the state statutory codes of the 50 states were the primary source of data collection, alternative sources were utilized in the areas of recruitment and training. In these areas, rules and regulations made by state commissions charged with rule-making authority by state statute were specifically noted and included in the data on state laws. Additionally, case law was reviewed in annotated state codes to aid in the interpretation of the legislation.

※ *Chapter 3*

Studying the Organization
of Police Services Delivery

In this chapter we explain our research methodology. First we define the specific police services included in our study. Then we list the types of agencies producing these services, and we discuss the various service recipients. Next we explain the production relationships between the agencies and the service recipients. Based on this information we develop our structural measures; that is, we devise ways to look at and analyze the different patterns of organization of police services delivery in the various metropolitan areas [1].

Readers who are interested in a particular aspect of police service delivery may wish to skip over this chapter initially, but the major terms used throughout the rest of the report are defined here, and a careful reading of this chapter is recommended at some point [2]. For the reader's further convenience, a glossary of terms explained in this chapter is included as Appendix A.

POLICE SERVICES

Police perform a variety of tasks, some of which are direct services to citizens. We examine the delivery of three direct services: (1) patrol, (2) traffic control, and (3) criminal investigation.

These three services represent a variety of police activities and include many of the most time consuming and/or high priority police services provided to citizens. For our purposes, delivery of these services involves activity by officers who have "extraordinary powers of arrest" in the conduct of the service. We refer to them as "sworn officers." Private watchmen, guards, and private investigators are, thus, excluded from the study.

We define the three direct services as follows:

Patrol is the organized surveillance of public places within a specified territory and response to reports of suspected criminal acts for the purpose of preventing crime, apprehending offenders, or maintaining public order. Officers on patrol also frequently respond to calls that are not crime related.

Traffic control includes monitoring vehicular traffic and investigation of traffic accidents. Because traffic patrol assignments may differ from traffic accident investigation assignments, we examine the delivery of each.

Criminal investigation is activity undertaken to identify alleged criminals, to gather evidence for criminal proceedings, or to recover stolen goods. Because both the investigative techniques and the agencies that do the investigations sometimes differ depending on the type of crime, we focus our attention on two types of investigations: homicide investigation and residential burglary investigation. The more serious offense, homicide, occurs less often than residential burglary, an often encountered felony.

Auxiliary services are used by police agencies in the production of direct services. We include four: (1) radio communications, (2) adult pretrial detention, (3) entry-level training, and (4) crime laboratory analysis.

Some of the agencies that produce direct services also produce their own auxiliary services. Some do not produce auxiliary services for themselves, but obtain them from other direct service police agencies. Still other police departments receive auxiliary services from specialized agencies that do not produce direct services. These specialized agencies include community colleges and technical institutes that provide entry-level training; hospital laboratories that provide chemical analysis for criminal investigation; and answering services and fire departments that dispatch police department radio patrol cars.

Our study includes any agency that regularly supplies any of the four auxiliary services to a direct service police agency. The four auxiliary services studied are defined as follows:

Radio communications is the relaying of requests for police assistance to officers in the field and the receipt of radioed requests for information or assistance from officers in the field.

Adult pretrial detention is the holding of an adult after arraignment, but before final court disposition of a case. Only agencies empowered to hold individuals in their facilities for more than 24 hours are included. We do not include agencies with only temporary "lockups" as producers of adult pretrial detention services.

Entry-level training is the department-required training of recruits for an agency producing direct police services. By department-required we do not ignore or disregard state requirements; instead, we consider the number of training hours that a department specifies for its recruits. For many this requirement is the state minimum. For some the departmental requirement greatly exceeds the state minimum.

Crime laboratory analysis is the processing of evidence by persons whose testimony is accepted as "expert" for presentation in court. Various kinds of laboratory analyses are required in criminal and accident investigation. We limit our attention to the identification of narcotics and the chemical analysis of other substances, such as blood and hair.

AGENCIES

We include in this study any agency whose officers have extraordinary powers of arrest and that produces patrol and/or criminal investigation and/or traffic control. Further, we include any agency that supplies radio communications, adult pretrial detention, entry-level training, or crime laboratory analysis to a direct service producer. This involves the study of many different types of agencies, most of which are located in the 80 SMSAs, although many are not.

Auxiliary service producing agencies need not be located in the metropolitan area they serve. Many police departments, for instance, send recruits to training academies located outside their metropolitan area. Such training academies are included in our study as producers of entry-level training for the metropolitan areas they serve. In fact, any of the four auxiliary services we examine may be produced by an agency located outside 1 of the 80 SMSAs.

Direct services may also be produced by agencies headquartered outside the SMSA, although personnel from such agencies must work inside the metropolitan area. In many states traffic patrol and accident investigation on major thoroughfares within SMSAs are conducted by a state agency. Some metropolitan areas receive patrol services or criminal investigation from state agencies; in such cases we include the state agency as a metropolitan police producer.

Federal agencies have many roles in metropolitan policing. However, much of the work of federal law enforcement agencies concerns administration of federal programs rather than the delivery of the three types of direct police services discussed in this report. So, although the Federal Bureau of Investigation is present in all SMSAs, we did not include the FBI as a producer of criminal investigation in SMSAs where it does not regularly investigate residential burglary or homicide.

There are portions of some SMSAs where the federal government has either exclusive or concurrent jurisdiction. Military bases, national parks and forests, and Indian reservations are three types of areas where the federal government may have exclusive jurisdiction. Federal agencies with exclusive jurisdiction are solely responsible for providing patrol, traffic control, and burglary and homicide investigation. Federal agencies producing any of those direct services in 1 of the 80 SMSAs are included in the study.

Where federal jurisdiction is concurrent, federal, state, county, and/or local agencies may produce direct police services. We include all agencies that actually produce such services on a federal site. We also find that local, county, and state agency use of the FBI crime lab varies significantly across SMSAs. The FBI is reported here as a producer of crime lab analysis wherever local, county, state, or federal agencies investigating burglary or homicide use the FBI lab on a regular basis.

Because our interest is in the producers of police services for a metropolitan area, we count each federal, state, or other agency as a *producer* in each metropolitan area it serves. This count of SMSA producers is, of course, greater than the sum of the separate *agencies* involved in police service production in the 80 SMSAs. For most of the analyses we present, the number of producers in each of the SMSAs is the appropriate measure. We clearly distinguish those instances in which we refer only to agencies. For example, the FBI, a single *agency*, regularly produces one or more of the services we are studying in 41 of the 80 metropolitan areas. The total number of FBI SMSA producers is, therefore, 41. As another example, the North Carolina Highway Patrol serves each of the three North Carolina metropolitan areas studied and is counted as an SMSA producer in each area.

Table 3–1 shows the frequencies of the various types of agencies and SMSA producers studied.

SERVICE RECIPIENTS

For each of the police services studied, identifying the agencies producing the service was the first step in our research. The second step was to identify the service recipient for the service. "Service areas" were identified for each *direct service*. By definition, each service area had a 1973 resident population of at least 100, some way of making collective decisions about police services in the area, and a distinct legal arrangement with a producer of a direct police service. Thus, for each direct service the population of the metropolitan area is divided into mutually exclusive service areas, each served by one or more producers.

The service areas for one direct service may differ from the service areas for another direct service, since a community of people may have one arrangement for general area patrol and another for traffic control or criminal investigations. Many service areas are cities, towns, or villages. A residential campus or military base is a service area if it has a distinct arrangement for providing patrol, traffic control, or burglary or homicide investigation services to dormitory residents or base personnel.

For example, if a college within a city does not have its own police force and its campus is patrolled by the city police department, then the campus is not a separate service area: its population is considered part of the city service area. However, if a college within a city has its own arrangements for policing, it is considered a service area, and the rest of the city is considered a separate service area. The unincorporated parts of counties in most states are separate service areas. Residents living in these county "remainders" receive their direct services regularly from the county sheriff or county police department, while the residents of other service areas within the county receive services from other agencies (and occasionally from the county as well).

Direct services are delivered directly to residents of a community, while auxiliary services are used in the production of direct services. *Auxiliary service recipients* are the producers of direct police services. While most direct service producers use all auxiliary services, a few do not send their recruits for entry-level training, and some do not use any radio communications.

AGENCIES AND SERVICE RECIPIENTS: PRODUCTION RELATIONSHIPS

Police services are produced regularly most of the time. By "regular" production of a direct service we mean that the producer makes the

Table 3–1. Direct and Auxiliary Service Police Agencies and Producers in the 80 SMSAs

	Agencies	SMSA Producers
Local Government Agencies		
Municipal police	958	965
Cities, towns, and villages	791	795
New England town police	51	51
Township police	116	119
Other Municipal Agencies	47	50
Airport police	11	11
Dispatch centers	14	15
Others (e.g., parks, fire departments, detention centers, hospitals, housing authorities)	22	24
Special District Agencies	32	32
Campus police	18	18
Others (e.g., airports and Indian reservations)	14	14
Unincorporated Areas	3	3
Private Agencies	47	48
Campus police	31	31
Others (e.g., answering services, chemical laboratories)	16	17
County Government Agencies	167	181
Sheriffs' departments and county police	110	113
Detention centers	20	22
Prosecutors	10	16
Park police	10	10
Others (e.g., dispatch centers, coroners, training academies)	17	20

State Government Agencies	173	287
State police and highway patrols	31	80
State criminal investigation bureaus	9	21
Park police	11	18
Campus police	74	78
Training academies	24	42
Others (e.g., chemical laboratories, capitol police, detention centers, hospitals)	24	48
Federal Government Agencies	89	207
Military base police	69[a]	94
Military investigative agencies	4	44
Federal Bureau of Investigation	1	41
Other nonmilitary agencies (e.g., Park Service, Veterans Administration, Bureau of Indian Affairs, Drug Enforcement Administration, Bureau of Alcohol, Tobacco, and Firearms)	15	28
Agencies Established by Intergovernmental Agreements	43	54
Training academies	31	42
Others (e.g., dispatch centers, crime laboratories)	12	12
TOTALS	1,559	1,827

[a]This is the number of separate military units directly responsible to local base commanders.

service available on a routine basis to individuals in the area it serves. Regular production of auxiliary service occurs when the service is routinely produced for the police agency being served.

By "irregular" production we mean that the service is produced only in unusual circumstances. If, for example, a municipal police department investigates all reported homicides in a city, but the state police occasionally assist in homicide investigation, the municipal police is considered a regular producer and the state police an irregular producer for that city. Although we have found some irregular production relationships for all services, most of our analyses examine the regular production of each service.

In observing the patterns of police production we found that several forms of production involve *simultaneous regular production by more than a single producer for any given service recipient.* Three forms of simultaneous regular production are so important that we developed special ways to code and measure them. These forms of simultaneous regular production are (1) coordination, (2) alternation, and (3) duplication.

Coordination occurs when two or more producers interact in planning regular service production for the same service recipient. In many service areas homicide investigations are simultaneously conducted by several agencies who coordinate their activities. Even though two or more agencies work on the case, they maintain a single case record and share information. This is a strict definition of coordination requiring interaction in the planning and the production of a specific service. Occasional cooperation and mutual assistance among agencies do not constitute coordination as defined here. (In Chapter 15 we discuss mutual assistance and occasional cooperation.)

Alternation occurs when two agencies produce a service for the same service area, but systematically divide their production activities over space, over time, or among clientele. *Alternation in space* often occurs with parks, airports, tollways, and bridges—places that rarely have a residential population. Often the producers who serve these places are different from those who serve the rest of the service area. Yet, these places with separate service delivery are usually only a small part of the entire service area. This pattern is coded in a distinct manner to avoid implying that two regular producers serve an entire service area.

A second variation is *alternation in time.* For example, a small municipal police department may dispatch for itself between 8 a.m. and 4 p.m. and be dispatched by the sheriff's department between

4 p.m. and 8 a.m. The municipal department and the sheriff's department alternate in time in supplying radio communications services for the municipal police department.

A third form of alternation also occurs—*alternation among clientele*. Two agencies produce a service for the same area during the same times, but for different groups of people. For example, military and civilian police departments may patrol streets together—but each pays primary attention to a different clientele. Or, two agencies produce adult pretrial detention for the same police department, but one detains male inmates and one detains female inmates. This is another instance of alternation in clientele.

Service alternation may be either exclusive or nonexclusive. When, for example, the alternating producer is the only producer of patrol services on a freeway (and the regular producer for the consuming unit never patrols the freeway), we consider this exclusive alternation in space. But when the alternating producer is not the only producer on the freeway and the regular department also patrols, the alternation is considered nonexclusive.

Duplication in service delivery occurs when two or more regular producers supply a service to the same consuming unit without coordination or alternation.

SERVICE DELIVERY MATRICES
AND MEASURES

For each direct and each auxiliary service a particular producer can have either no production relationship, an irregular production relationship, or a regular production relationship with each service recipient. If the production relationship is regular, it might be coordinated, alternated, duplicated, or independent. For each service we classify the relationship (or lack thereof) between each producer of that service and all service recipients and enter the specific relationships in the cells of a service delivery matrix.

In this matrix producers are arrayed as the rows (across), and service recipients are arrayed as the columns (down). From the coding of these individual service delivery matrices for each direct and auxiliary service for each of the 80 SMSAs we construct service delivery measures that enable us to compare service delivery across the 80 SMSAs.

Because an understanding of this process is crucial to an understanding of much of the data presented later in this volume, we describe the use of service delivery matrices and the derivation of service delivery measures from them in some detail, using the Fayetteville/

North Carolina SMSA as an example. Fayetteville is a convenient example for this purpose. About half the 80 metropolitan areas we studied have larger populations and about half have smaller populations. The patterns of police service delivery in Fayetteville are not "typical"—no single SMSA exemplifies the diversity we have found. Rather, the Fayetteville area illustrates our techniques for describing the service delivery patterns in a metropolitan area. Furthermore, since the Fayetteville area has only a few police agencies and so is less complex than many of the areas in our study, it is easy to use as an example.

The Fayetteville SMSA (defined by the U.S. Census Bureau as Cumberland County) covers 654 square miles of the North Carolina coastal plain. Like many of the 80 SMSAs we studied, much of the area is rural. The urbanized area of Cumberland County includes the city of Fayetteville, two smaller towns, and two military installations, as well as portions of the unincorporated county.

Map 3—1 shows that urban development is concentrated in the northwestern third of the county. The city of Fayetteville, with about 58,000 residents in 1973, is a center for tobacco and cotton marketing and textile and chemical manufacturing. But the area's major industry is the military. The combined population of Fort Bragg and Pope Air Force Base is 80 percent as great as the city of Fayetteville. The entire town of Spring Lake and parts of Fayetteville are residential and commercial service areas for military personnel. Hope Mills is a quiet, rural village that is being transformed into a middle income suburb for Fayetteville's civilian population. About half the SMSA population lives in unincorporated areas, and these residents are heavily concentrated in the northwestern part of the county near the military bases.

Since relationships between traffic patrol producers and service areas in the Fayetteville SMSA are quite simple and clear-cut, they are used as our first example of a service matrix. For traffic patrol the SMSA divides into seven service areas. Each military installation in Cumberland County is a traffic patrol service area, as are the municipalities of Spring Lake and Hope Mills. Because Fayetteville State University within the city of Fayetteville receives traffic patrol from its own Safety Division, it is also a traffic patrol service area. The remainder of the city of Fayetteville is a sixth traffic patrol area and the remainder of Cumberland County a seventh. Each service area is represented by a column on the matrix in Table 3—2. The exclusive population of each service area is reported across the bottom of the chart.

Map 3—1. Map of Fayetteville/North Carolina SMSA

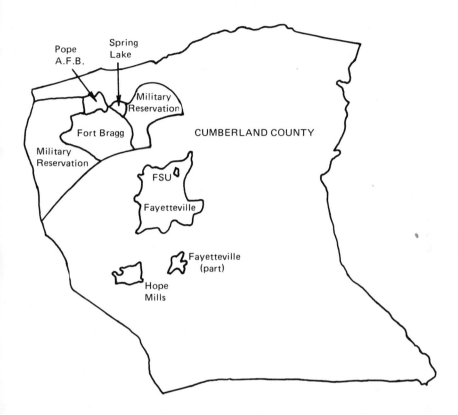

Each of these service areas receives regular production from one—and only one—producer of traffic patrol (coded as an "R" for regular production on the matrix). These producers are shown across the rows of the service matrix. The pattern made by the diagonal line of Rs in the traffic patrol service matrix reflects the 1 to 1 relationship between producers and service areas. Note that in this SMSA a state producer—the North Carolina Highway Patrol—regularly produces traffic patrol in the unincorporated portion of Cumberland County.

Working with the defined terms and the illustrative traffic patrol service matrix for Fayetteville, we can now explain some service delivery measures and show how they are computed for the Fayetteville SMSA. These are the measures that express the various characteristics of service delivery structure for all the service areas in the 80 SMSAs.

Table 3–2.   Traffic Patrol Service Matrix: Fayetteville/North Carolina SMSA

Agency Producing Service	Traffic Patrol Service Areas						
	Fort Bragg	Pope Air Force Base	Hope Mills	Spring Lake	Fayetteville State University	Remainder of the City of Fayetteville	Remainder of Cumberland County
U.S. Army Military Police	R–O						
U.S. Air Force Security Police		R–O					
Hope Mills Police Department			R–O				
Spring Lake Police Department				R–O			
Fayetteville State University Safety Division					R–O		
Fayetteville Police Department						R–O	
North Carolina Highway Patrol							R–N
Exclusive Population	46,995	400	2,506	4,124	1,643	56,456	104,103

R — denotes regular service.   O — denotes service by an area's "own" agency.
N — denotes service by an agency *not* directly responsible to the service area's governing authority.

DEFINITIONS OF OUR
STRUCTURAL MEASURES

"Fragmentation," "multiplicity," and "duplication" are terms often used to describe the relationships among local governmental units in metropolitan areas. Fragmentation, multiplicity, and duplication are repeatedly cited as causes for many of the ills of police service delivery in these areas [3]. But for all the use of these terms, they have rarely been defined. How many service areas must there be within a metropolitan area for fragmentation to be a problem? How many police agencies within a metropolitan area must there be for multiplicity to be a problem? For example, how can SMSAs that range in population from 50,000 to 1.5 million be compared in terms of multiplicity? Is the presence of 10 police departments in an SMSA of 50,000 population the same as the presence of 10 police departments in an SMSA of 1.5 million? How much duplication exists when we take account of regular arrangements for coordination and alternation of service?

Questions such as these must be answered as we deal with the policy issues for which this report is intended to provide information. We hope that the definitions that follow will help the reader by providing a useful framework for approaching these critical policy issues of police services delivery.

Fragmentation

When a metropolitan area is described as fragmented, it could have many producers and few service areas; it could have a few producers and many service areas; or it could have many producers and many service areas. Because of this ambiguity, we usually do not know which case is being discussed when the term fragmentation is used. Until the uses of the term are sorted out, empirical work to determine the relative effects of different forms of fragmentation cannot be undertaken.

For direct services we define fragmentation as the number of service areas receiving the particular direct service within the metropolitan area. For auxiliary services, fragmentation is defined as the number of police departments in the metropolitan area receiving the particular auxiliary service. In other words, fragmentation is a measure of the number of separate entities, either service areas or direct service producers, that are service recipients.

Metropolitan areas with larger populations tend to have more service areas, and we want to be able to compare SMSAs while holding population constant. Therefore, we also define a relative measure of fragmentation for direct services. "Relative fragmentation" is the number of service areas per 100,000 residents. This measures the extent to which the metropolitan area is divided for purposes of making collective decisions about police service delivery. Because each service area is subject to a separate governing authority, the more service areas, the less consolidated the decision making regarding provision of the police service.

To calculate traffic patrol fragmentation in the Fayetteville metropolitan area, the number of traffic patrol service areas in the SMSA is counted. As Table 3−2 shows, there are seven service areas, represented by the seven columns under the "Traffic Patrol Service Area" heading. Fragmentation for this service is, therefore, 7. Relative fragmentation of traffic patrol is 3.24, calculated by dividing the number of service areas by the SMSA population in 100,000s.

Multiplicity

We define multiplicity as the number of producers of a particular service in a metropolitan area. As with fragmentation, comparison among metropolitan areas is facilitated by controlling for population size. Multiplicity relative to population is defined as the number of producing units for a given police service per 100,000 SMSA residents. This measure is an inverse indicator of the degree to which an area has consolidated production of each police service. The lower the number of producers per 100,000 population, the greater the consolidation.

An alternative way of measuring consolidation is to relate the number of producers of a service to the number of organized service recipients (multiplicity relative to service recipients). The ratio of the number of direct service producers to the number of service areas in an SMSA is a second inverse indicator of the degree of consolidation in that SMSA. An SMSA with 7 patrol producers serving 10 service areas is *less* consolidated than an SMSA with 60 patrol producers serving 100 service areas, according to this measure.

To return to the Fayetteville SMSA, seven producers patrol traffic (listed in the "Agency Producing Service" column in Table 3−2). Multiplicity of traffic patrol in the Fayetteville SMSA is, therefore, 7. Multiplicity relative to population is 3.24 (seven producers divided by 2.16 hundred-thousand residents). Multiplicity relative to service recipients is 1, because there is one producing unit for each traffic patrol service area in the Fayetteville SMSA.

Independence

Another aspect of service delivery structure concerns the types of distinct legal arrangements between a producing unit and each of its service areas. Many police agencies are bureaus of their local governing authority. The extent of service "independence" in an SMSA is the fraction of all service recipients receiving regular service from their "own" producer.

All but one of the traffic patrol service areas shown in Table 3-2 receive service from their own service producer. (For our purposes a military base commander and a college campus administration are both "local governing authorities.") The North Carolina State Highway Patrol produces traffic patrol in the unincorporated, off-base area of Cumberland County and is not a bureau of the local governing authority for the county. The other six service areas have their own producers. Independence of traffic patrol in the Fayetteville SMSA is, therefore, 0.86 (6/7).

"Relative independence" is the fraction of the SMSA population served by own production units. In the Fayetteville metropolitan area 48 percent of the population is located in the unincorporated, off-base area of Cumberland County and is served by the State Highway Patrol. The other 52 percent of the population is served by own producers. Relative independence of traffic patrol in the Fayetteville SMSA is, therefore, 0.52.

Autonomy

Another aspect of service delivery structure is the extent to which service areas rely exclusively on their own producers for any particular service. We refer to this exclusive reliance as "autonomy." Autonomy of traffic patrol is the proportion of the service areas receiving traffic patrol exclusively from their own police producer. In the Fayetteville SMSA traffic patrol autonomy is the same as independence since six out of seven of the service areas receive traffic patrol exclusively from their own producer. In other SMSAs traffic patrol independence and autonomy are often different. "Relative autonomy" is the proportion of the population of the metropolitan area living in service areas that regularly receive traffic patrol exclusively from their own police agency. Relative autonomy for traffic patrol in the Fayetteville SMSA is the same as relative independence.

Dominance

Some police producers serve many service areas, while others serve only a single area. Some serve large populations; others serve much smaller groups of residents. Each of these differences between police service producers is a way in which an agency is more or less dominant in producing service in a metropolitan area. We define the "dominant" producer of a service in an SMSA as the one serving the largest resident population on a regular basis. For traffic patrol in the Fayetteville SMSA this is the North Carolina State Highway Patrol. "Dominance" is the proportion of the service areas in the SMSA served by the dominant producer. In this case the Highway Patrol serves one of the seven service areas; therefore, service area dominance is 0.14.

"Relative dominance" is the proportion of the SMSA population regularly served by the dominant producer. The North Carolina State Highway Patrol regularly patrols traffic only in the unincorporated and off-base part of Cumberland County; the population of that area is 104,103, or 48 percent of the SMSA population. Therefore, relative dominance for traffic patrol in Fayetteville is 0.48. Table 3−3 summarizes the service delivery measures presented thus far. The Fayetteville SMSA scores are shown.

Measures of Alternation, Coordination, and Duplication

Homicide investigation in the Fayetteville SMSA provides examples of alternation and coordination of service delivery. No duplication of regular service was found in Fayetteville for any of the services we studied. However, we discuss the measures of all three forms of service delivery in this section.

First, examining the measures presented in the preceding sections, we find that homicide investigation in the Fayetteville SMSA has a different delivery structure than does traffic patrol (see Table 3−4). Fayetteville State University's Security Division does not investigate homicides. Homicides on campus are investigated by the Fayetteville City Police just like homicides occurring elsewhere in the city. So fragmentation for homicide investigation is 6. Seven producers regularly investigate homicides in the metropolitan area. An eighth— the State Bureau of Investigation—is only irregularly involved in homicide investigations. Multiplicity for this service is, therefore, 7. Independence is 0.67 since four of six service areas have their own homicide investigation producers.

Autonomy of homicide investigation is 0.33 since two of the four service areas with their own producers for homicide investigation also regularly receive homicide investigation services from another producer. Residents of the two areas relying exclusively on their own producer for homicide investigation comprise three quarters of the SMSA population, yielding a relative autonomy for homicide investigation of 0.75. Service area dominance for homicide investigation is 0.50. Three of the six service areas are served by the Cumberland County Sheriff, the dominant producer. Relative dominance is 0.51,

Table 3-3. Some Service Delivery Measures for Traffic Patrol: Fayetteville/North Carolina SMSA

Fragmentation = Number of service areas for traffic patrol
= Number of columns on the traffic patrol service chart
= 7

Relative Fragmentation = Number of service areas for traffic patrol per 100,000 residents
= Fragmentation divided by SMSA population in 100,000s
= 7/2.16227
= 3.24

Multiplicity = Number of regular producers of traffic patrol
= Number of rows on the traffic patrol service chart
= 7

Multiplicity Relative to Population = Number of regular producers of traffic patrol per 100,000 residents
= Multiplicity divided by SMSA population in 100,000s
= 7/2.16227
= 3.24

Multiplicity Relative to Service Recipients = Number of regular producers of traffic patrol per service area
= Multiplicity divided by fragmentation
= 7/7
= 1.00

(Table 3-3. continued overleaf)

Table 3–3. continued

Independence	= Proportion of service areas receiving regular traffic patrol from their own producers
	= Number of columns having an "O" entry divided by fragmentation
	= 6/7
	= 0.86
Relative Independence	= Proportion of SMSA population receiving regular traffic patrol from their own producers
	= Sum of the exclusive populations of the service area columns having an "O" entry divided by total SMSA population
	= (46,995 + 400 + 2,506 + 4,124 + 1,643 + 56,456)/216,227
	= 0.52
Autonomy	= Proportion of service areas receiving regular traffic patrol *exclusively* from their *own* producers
	= Number of columns with one "RO" entry and no other "A," "C," or "R" entry divided by the number of service areas
	= 6/7
	= 0.86
Relative Autonomy	= Proportion of SMSA population receiving traffic patrol *exclusively* from their *own* producer
	= Sum of the exclusive population of the service area columns having one "RO" entry and no other "A," "C," or "R" entry divided by total population
	= (46,995 + 400 + 2,506 + 4,124 + 1,643 + 56,456)/216,227
	= 0.52

Dominance

= Proportion of service areas receiving regular, alternate, or coordinated service from the producer with the largest serviced population

= Number of columns with an "R," "A," or "C" in the row of the producer with the largest serviced population divided by the number of service areas

= 1/7

= 0.14

Relative Dominance

= Proportion of SMSA population receiving regular, alternate, or coordinated service from the producer with the largest serviced population

= Sum of the exclusive populations of the columns having an "R," "A," or "C" in the row of the producer with the largest serviced population divided by the total population

= 104, 103/216, 227

= 0.48

Table 3–4.   Homicide Investigation Service Matrix: Fayetteville/North Carolina SMSA

Agency Producing Service	Homicide Investigation Service Areas					
	Fort Bragg	Pope Air Force Base	Hope Mills	Spring Lake	Fayetteville	Remainder of Cumberland County
U.S. Army Criminal Investigations Division	Ac-N					
Federal Bureau of Investigation	Ac-N	Ac-N				
U.S. Air Force Office of Special Investigations		Ac-N				
Hope Mills Police Department			C-O			
Spring Lake Police Department				C-O		
Fayetteville Police Department					R-O	
Cumberland County Sheriff's Department			C-N	C-N		R-O

North Carolina State Bureau of Investigation			I-N	I-N	I-N	I-N
Exclusive Population	46,995	400	2,506	4,124	58,099	104,103

Ac — denotes alternation in clientele in production of the service.
R — denotes regular production of the service.
C — denotes coordinated production of the service.
I — denotes irregular production of the service.
O — denotes service by an area's "own" agency.
N — denotes service by an agency *not* directly responsible to the service area's governing authority.

reflecting the sheriff's investigation of homicides in areas with just over half the population of the entire metropolitan area.

Alternation of homicide investigations occurs in two of the six service areas. On both of the military bases in the SMSA the FBI is responsible for homicides involving civilians, while the respective military investigation agencies handle homicides in which only military personnel are involved. Alternation is defined as the fraction of all service areas receiving alternate service. For homicide investigation in the Fayetteville SMSA this is 0.33.

"Relative alternation" is the fraction of the SMSA population served by alternate producers. Fort Bragg's population is 46,995, and Pope Air Force Base has 400 residents. So, a total of 47,395 residents live in areas subject to alternate homicide investigation. This is 22 percent of the SMSA population, and relative alternation is, therefore, 0.22.

Coordination of homicide investigation regularly occurs in two of the six service areas in the Fayetteville SMSA. Both the Spring Lake and Hope Mills Police Departments coordinate investigations of homicides within their jurisdictions with the Cumberland County Sheriff's detectives. The extent of coordination is the fraction of all service areas with regular service from two or more producers that coordinate their investigations. In the Fayetteville SMSA this proportion is 0.33.

"Relative coordination" is the proportion of the SMSA population living in service areas where homicide investigation is coordinated. Hope Mills has 2,506 residents and Spring Lake has 4,124. This is 0.03 of the population of the metropolitan area. Note that while the proportion of service areas with alternate service is the same as the proportion of service areas with coordinated service (0.33 in both cases), relative alternation of homicide investigation is over seven times as great as relative coordination of homicide investigation.

Duplication of homicide investigation does not occur in any of the six service areas of the Fayetteville metropolitan area. That is, in all service areas where more than one producer is regularly involved in homicide investigation, these producers either alternate in the cases they investigate (the military bases) or they coordinate their investigations (the small towns). Duplication is the proportion of service areas receiving regular service from more than one producer where these producers do not alternate or coordinate in production of the service. For homicide investigation in the Fayetteville SMSA this proportion is 0.0.

"Relative duplication" is the proportion of the metropolitan area's population served by duplicate producers. In the Fayetteville SMSA none of the population is served by duplicate producers, so the relative duplication is 0.0. Table 3—5 presents a summary of the service delivery measures for homicide investigation in the Fayetteville SMSA.

Auxiliary Service Patterns

The measures examined so far are for direct services. The measures appropriate for describing auxiliary service delivery patterns are quite similar, but there are some important differences. Table 3—6 is the service matrix for entry-level training in the Fayetteville SMSA. The rows represent the service producers, just as in the direct service matrices discussed previously. The columns on the entry-level training matrix are producers of direct police services who use training services. As with the direct service matrices, the columns represent service recipients, but for auxiliary services these are direct police service producers rather than service areas.

There are eight producers of entry-level training for direct service police agencies in the Fayetteville metropolitan area: multiplicity is 8 for this service. Eleven direct service producers use entry-level training services: fragmentation is 11. For auxiliary services the population served by the direct service producers is not pertinent since the service recipients are producers and not service areas. Therefore, measures relative to population are not calculated for auxiliary services. But measures relative to numbers of sworn officers can be useful. In addition to computing the number of producers of an auxiliary service per direct service producer, we can also compute the number of producers of an auxiliary service per 1,000 sworn officers employed by direct service producers using that auxiliary service when this is a useful measure of service delivery (Table 3—7).

A second change in computation is for measures of dominance. For auxiliary services, dominance is defined as the proportion of producers of direct police services using an auxiliary service who receive that service from the auxiliary service producer serving the largest number of such direct service producers. (For direct services the dominant producer is identified as the producer serving the largest population rather than the greatest number of service areas.)

Table 3–5.   Service Delivery Measures for Homicide Investigation: Fayetteville/North Carolina SMSA

Fragmentation	=	Number of service areas for homicide investigation
	=	Number of columns on the homicide investigation service chart
	=	6
Relative Fragmentation	=	Number of service areas for homicide investigation per 100,000 residents
	=	Fragmentation divided by SMSA population in 100,000s
	=	6/2.16277
	=	2.77
Multiplicity	=	Number of regular producers of homicide investigation
	=	Number of rows on the homicide investigation service chart
	=	7
Multiplicity Relative to Population	=	Number of regular producers of homicide investigation per 100,000
	=	Multiplicity divided by SMSA population in 100,000s
	=	7/2.16277
	=	3.24
Multiplicity Relative to Service Recipients	=	Number of regular producers of homicide investigation per service area
	=	Multiplicity divided by fragmentation
	=	7/6
	=	1.17
Independence	=	Proportion of service areas receiving regular homicide investigation from their own producer
	=	Number of columns having an "O" entry divided by fragmentation
	=	4/6
	=	0.67

Relative Independence	=	Proportion of SMSA population receiving regular homicide investigation from their own producers
	=	Sum of the exclusive populations of the service area columns having an "O" entry divided by total SMSA population
	=	$(2,506 + 4,124 + 58,099 + 104,103)/216,227$
	=	0.78

Autonomy	=	Proportion of service areas receiving regular homicide investigation *only* from their *own* producer
	=	Number of columns with one "RO" entry and no other "A," "C," or "R" entry divided by the number of service areas
	=	2/6
	=	0.33

Relative Autonomy	=	Proportion of SMSA population receiving homicide investigation *only* from their *own* producer
	=	Sum of the exclusive populations of the service area columns having one "RO" entry and no other "A," "C," or "R" entry divided by total population
	=	$(58,099 + 104,103)/216,227$
	=	0.75

Dominance	=	Proportion of service areas receiving regular, alternate, or coordinated service from the producer with the largest serviced population
	=	Number of columns with an "R," "A," or "C" in the row belonging to the producer with the largest serviced population divided by the number of service areas
	=	3/6
	=	0.50

(Table 3-5. continued overleaf)

Table 3–5. continued

Relative Dominance = Proportion of SMSA population receiving regular, alternate, or coordinated service from the producer with the largest serviced population

= Sum of the exclusive populations of the columns having an "R," "A," or "C" in the row of the producer with the largest serviced population divided by the total population

= (2,506 + 4,214 + 104,103)/216,227

= 0.51

Alternation = Proportion of service areas receiving regular homicide investigation from alternate producers

= Number of columns on the homicide investigation chart having at least one "A" divided by fragmentation

= 2/6

= 0.33

Relative Alternation = Proportion of SMSA population receiving alternate homicide investigation services

= Sum of exclusive populations of columns having at least one "A" divided by total SMSA population

= (46,995 + 400)/216,227

= 0.22

Coordination = Proportion of service areas receiving regular homicide investigation from coordinating producers

= Number of columns on the homicide investigation chart having at least one "C" divided by fragmentation

= 2/6

= 0.33

Relative Coordination	=	Proportion of SMSA population receiving coordinated homicide investigation services
	=	Sum of exclusive populations of columns having at least one "C" divided by total SMSA population
	=	(2,506 + 4,124)/216,227
	=	0.03
Duplication	=	Proportion of service areas receiving regular, nonalternating, noncoordinated service from two or more producers
	=	Number of columns on the homicide investigation chart having more than one "R" divided by fragmentation
	=	0
Relative Duplication	=	Proportion of SMSA population receiving regular, nonalternating, noncoordinated service from two or more producers
	=	Sum of exclusive populations of columns having more than one "R" divided by total SMSA population
	=	0

Table 3–6. Entry-Level Training Service Matrix for Fayetteville/North Carolina SMSA

Agencies Producing Service	Agencies Being Served										
	U.S. Army Military Police	U.S. Air Force Security Police	U.S. Air Force Office of Special Investigations	Federal Bureau of Investigation	Hope Mills Police Department	Spring Lake Police Department	Fayetteville Police Department	Fayetteville State University Safety	Cumberland County Sheriff's Department	North Carolina Highway Patrol	North Carolina State Bureau of Investigation
U.S. Army Military Police	R–N										
U.S. Air Force Security Police		R–N									
U.S. Air Force Office of Special Investigations			R–O								
Federal Bureau of Investigation				R–O							
Fayetteville Technical Institute					R–N	R–N	R–N	R–N	R–N		
North Carolina Highway Patrol										R–O	
North Carolina State Bureau of Investigation											R–O
Johnston Technical Institute						R–N					
Number of Sworn Officers	491	92	3	—	5	5	125	10	153	32	5

R — denotes regular provision of basic training.   O — denotes "own" production.   N — denotes service supplied by other agency.

Table 3–7. Service Delivery Measures for Entry-Level Training: Fayetteville/North Carolina SMSA

Fragmentation	=	Number of agencies receiving entry-level training
	=	Number of columns on the entry-level training service chart
	=	11
Multiplicity	=	Number of regular producers of entry-level training
	=	Number of rows on the entry-level training service chart
	=	8
Multiplicity Relative to Service Recipients	=	Number of regular producers of entry-level training per agency using entry-level training
	=	Multiplicity divided by fragmentation
	=	8/11
	=	0.73
Multiplicity Relative to Sworn Officers	=	Number of regular producers of entry-level training per 1,000 sworn officers employed by producers using entry-level training
	=	Multiplicity divided by the sum of sworn officers (in 1,000s) employed by agencies using entry-level training in the SMSA
	=	8/0.921
	=	8.69
Independence	=	Proportion of serviced agencies producing entry-level training for themselves
	=	Number of columns having an "O" entry divided by fragmentation
	=	4/11
	=	0.36

(Table 3–7 continued overleaf)

Table 3–7. continued

Autonomy	=	Proportion of serviced agencies receiving entry-level training *only* from themselves
	=	Number of columns with one "RO" entry and no other "A," "C," or "R" entry divided by fragmentation
	=	4/11
	=	0.36
Dominance	=	Proportion of serviced agencies receiving entry-level training from the producer who produces for the largest number of serviced agencies
	=	Number of columns having an "R," "A," or "C" in the row of the producer with the largest number of "R," "A," and "C"s divided by fragmentation
	=	5/11
	=	0.45
Alternation	=	Proportion of serviced agencies receiving entry-level training from alternate producers
	=	Number of columns having at least one "A" divided by fragmentation
	=	0
Coordination	=	Proportion of serviced agencies receiving entry-level training from agencies that regularly coordinate training
	=	Number of columns having at least one "C" divided by fragmentation
	=	0
Duplication	=	Proportion of serviced agencies receiving entry-level training from two or more producers without coordination or alternation
	=	Number of columns having more than one "R" divided by fragmentation
	=	1/11
	=	0.09

UPCOMING CHAPTERS

The measures of police services delivery described in this chapter will be used extensively in Chapters 5 through 13. These chapters focus on each of the specific direct and auxiliary services studied. In each chapter the measures are used to describe patterns of service delivery characteristic of that service in the 80 SMSAs studied. The measures are also being used in analyses for a series of technical articles written by members of the study team. A list of these publications appears in Appendix C.

✳ *Chapter 4*

An Introduction
to Direct Services

Patrol, traffic control, and the investigation of residential burglary and homicide are conducted by many different types of agencies in the metropolitan areas of the United States. Some agencies conduct only one or two of these basic police services; others conduct all of them. Nevertheless, all parts of a metropolitan area receive each service from at least one producer.

Many of these agencies are local, serving only jurisdictions within a single SMSA. A few are state or federal agencies, however, with personnel conducting police services in more than one metropolitan area. Each state and federal agency is coded and is counted as a producer in each of the metropolitan areas it serves. Local agencies are typically producers in only a single SMSA. There are 1,454 producers of the direct services we studied in the 80 SMSAs. When our interest is in the delivery of police services within each metropolitan area, this count of producers is more appropriate than a count of separate agencies involved in service production. We first discuss the agencies supplying police services and then consider the service producers within each SMSA.

AGENCIES PRODUCING DIRECT SERVICES

Different types of agencies conduct different services. For example, there are almost 1,300 agencies supplying patrol, but fewer than 900 conducting homicide investigations. Municipal police departments account for more than 70 percent of the agencies that conduct each of the direct services we studied (Figure 4-1). The proportion of

Figure 4−1.   Types of Agencies Producing Direct Services in 80 SMSAs

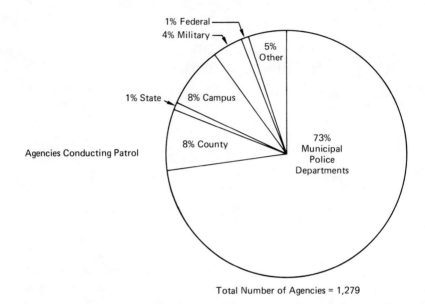

1% Federal
4% Military
5% Other
1% State
8% Campus
8% County
73% Municipal Police Departments

Agencies Conducting Patrol

Total Number of Agencies = 1,279

1% Federal
3% Military
3% Other
3% State
7% Campus
5% County
78% Municipal Police Departments

Agencies Conducting Traffic Accident Investigation

Total Number of Agencies = 1,153

Figure 4–1. (continued) Types of Agencies Producing Direct Services
in 80 SMSAs

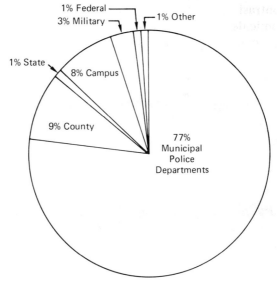

Agencies Conducting
Residential Burglary
Investigation

Total Number of Agencies = 1,040

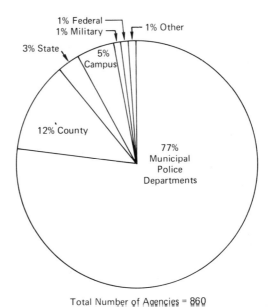

Agencies Conducting
Homicide Investigation

Total Number of Agencies = 860

other types of agencies varies according to the service. County police and sheriffs are about 10 percent of the patrol and burglary and homicide investigation agencies, but only 5 percent of the traffic accident investigation agencies. State law enforcement agencies, in contrast, are about 3 percent of the traffic accident investigation and homicide investigation agencies, and only 1 percent of the agencies that conduct the other services.

Campus police agencies represent 5 or more percent of the total for each of these services. Military law enforcement agencies account for less than 5 percent of the agencies conducting each of these services. Nonmilitary federal agencies account for only about 1 percent for each service. Other agencies are about 5 percent of the patrol agencies, but are only 1 percent of the criminal investigation agencies.

DIRECT SERVICE PRODUCERS
IN EACH SMSA

Most metropolitan areas have state or federal, as well as local, producers of direct services. State and federal agencies usually supply direct services to several SMSAs. Thus, the total number of producers for the 80 metropolitan areas is greater than the number of agencies supplying those services.

The kind of governing authority responsible for an agency producing police services is an important consideration. Legal authority to conduct police services and financial support for those services differs according to the kind of governing authority involved. Different sorts of agencies also commonly produce different combinations of police services. Most municipal, New England town, and township police departments conduct all the services studied. We consider them as a single group: "municipal police departments." County sheriffs' departments and county police departments are also discussed as a group. State police, highway patrols, and bureaus of criminal investigation constitute a third group of producers in our discussions of direct service delivery patterns.

College and university police commonly produce patrol and traffic control, with fewer of them investigating crimes. We consider all campus police in a single category, regardless of the kind of governing authority responsible for the campus. Military law enforcement agencies are considered as a single group. Nonmilitary federal agencies constitute another group. The final category of direct police service delivery patterns is composed of "other" agencies, whether municipal, county, state, special district, or private. A few of these agencies investigate crimes, but most are patrol and/or traffic control producers.

Municipal Producers

Municipal police departments are the most numerous producers of direct services. More than 60 percent of the producers of patrol, traffic control, and criminal investigation in the 80 metropolitan areas are municipal police. Table 4–1 shows a regional breakdown of the proportion of producers of direct services that are municipal police departments.

Municipal producers are especially prevalent in New York and New Jersey (Region 2), in Virginia and Pennsylvania (Region 3), and in Illinois, Indiana, Michigan, Ohio, and Wisconsin (Region 5). Townships, as well as separately incorporated cities, towns, and villages, have organized independent police departments in many of these metropolitan areas. Municipal police departments constitute fewer than half the producers of direct police services in the Rocky Mountain states (Region 8)—Colorado, Utah, and Montana in our sample —and in California and Arizona (Region 9). Federal reservations are relatively most common in the western parts of the country. (One fourth of the producers of direct police services in these areas are military or civilian federal agencies.)

The police departments of cities, towns, and villages are by far the most numerous kind of municipal agencies producing police services. Most of these departments patrol, control traffic, and investigate both residential burglary and homicide, although one in seven does not investigate homicide. A similar proportion investigates neither burglary nor homicide (Table 4–2). New England town police are even more likely to conduct all the direct services we studied. In other parts of the country criminal investigations are conducted for some municipal departments by the county sheriff or police. Because there are no county police agencies in the New England SMSAs studied, almost all town police conduct this service for their own service areas.

Township police are found in the Mid-Atlantic states and the Great Lakes states (Regions 2, 3, and 5). About two thirds of the producers of this type conduct all of the direct services we studied. One in 10 investigates burglary but not homicide, and 2 in 10 do not investigate either burglary or homicide.

County Producers

County sheriffs' departments, county police departments, and county prosecutors' police account for about 7 percent of the producers of patrol, traffic control, and criminal investigation in the metropolitan areas studied. Except in the New England states, county sheriffs' departments or county police have responsibility for serving

Table 4–1.   Production of Direct Police Services in the 80 Metropolitan Areas: Region and Type of Producer

Location	Number of Direct Police Producers	Percent of Direct Police Producers That Are						
		Municipal Police Departments	County Police and Sheriffs	State Police Agencies	Campus Police	Military Police	Federal Police Producers	Other Police Producers
Total	1,454	64	7	7	7	6	3	6
Northeast								
Region 1	87	69	0	18	10	0	0	2
Region 2	162	82	6	3	3	0	0	7
Region 3	143	78	1	4	6	4	2	5
Midwest								
Region 5	275	74	9	6	6	1	1	3
Region 7	54	65	7	7	4	2	4	11
South								
Region 4	305	62	9	7	10	6	2	4
Region 6	182	49	10	9	10	11	5	6
West								
Region 8	48	44	8	10	6	19	6	6
Region 9	170	43	7	4	9	15	8	13
Region 10	28	68	21	7	0	0	0	4

Note: Rows may not total 100 percent due to rounding errors.

much of the territory within metropolitan areas, some of which is urban, but much of which is rural. New England town police conduct these services in rural parts of metropolitan areas in those states. County producers also often coordinate investigations with municipal and special district police departments and supply them with auxiliary services.

Sheriffs' departments are the most numerous of the county producers of direct police services (Table 4−3). Most of these agencies conduct all of the direct services studied, although a quarter of them do not conduct traffic patrol or accident investigation. A few of the metropolitan areas studied have sheriffs' departments that maintain pretrial detention facilities, but conduct no direct police service. In still other metropolitan areas there are sheriffs' departments whose duties are entirely court related and that supply none of the services we studied. Neither kind of sheriff's department is included in this discussion of direct service producers.

Only five county police departments operate in the 80 metropolitan areas. Two of these do no criminal investigation, while the other three conduct burglary and homicide investigations as well as patrol and traffic control. Ten of the counties in the 80 SMSAs have prosecutors' detectives engaged regularly in criminal investigation. Ten metropolitan areas also have county park police. None of the county park police conducts criminal investigations. All of them patrol, and three fifths also control traffic.

State Producers

State police, highway patrols, and state bureaus of investigation are another group of agencies producing direct services (Table 4−4). State agencies control traffic on at least some highways in each of the 80 SMSAs. In one third of the metropolitan areas the highway patrol or state police also conduct criminal investigations. Thirteen other metropolitan areas in the sample of 80 receive the investigative services of state bureaus of investigation. Overall, state agencies constitute about 7 percent of the producers of the direct police services we studied.

Campus Police

College and university police departments commonly supply patrol and traffic control, but many do not investigate crimes. We discuss all campus police in a single category, regardless of the kind of governing authority responsible for the campus. State, county, and municipal colleges and universities are not the only kinds of campuses with their own law enforcement agencies. Many private

Table 4–2.   Types of Municipal Producers and the Services They Conduct

	Number Reporting	Percent of Producers Conducting		
		Patrol Only	Patrol and Traffic Control	Patrol, Traffic, and Burglary Investigation
City, town, and village police departments	770	a	15	14
New England town police	51	—	—	4
Township police	116	5	14	12

ª Less than half of one percent.

Table 4–3.   Types of County Producers and the Services They Conduct

	Number Reporting	Percent of Producers Conducting		
		Patrol Only	Patrol and Traffic Control	Patrol, Traffic, and Burglary Investigation
Sheriffs' departments	93	—	—	—
County police departments	5	—	40	—
County prosecutors' detectives	10	—	—	—
County park police	10	40	60	—
Other county agencies	2	—	—	100

colleges and universities also have campus police conducting patrol, traffic control, and criminal investigation. Campus police account for another 7 percent of the producers of direct police services in the 80 SMSAs.

Campus police departments at state colleges and universities are somewhat more likely to investigate homicides than are the other kinds of campus police. Special district colleges and universities are most likely to have their police conducting only patrol or only patrol and traffic control. But a comparison of Table 4–2 with Table 4–5

Table 4—2. continued

		Percent of Producers Conducting		
Patrol, Traffic, Burglary and Homicide Investigation	*Traffic Control Only*	*Patrol and Criminal Investigation*	*Traffic Control and Criminal Investigation*	*Criminal Investigation Only*
70	—	a	a	—
94	2	—	—	—
65	1	3	—	—

Table 4—3. continued

		Percent of Producers Conducting		
Patrol, Traffic, Burglary and Homicide Investigation	*Traffic Control Only*	*Patrol and Investigation*	*Traffic and Investigation*	*Investigation Only*
71	—	28	—	1
60	—	—	—	—
—	—	—	—	100
—	—	—	—	—
—	—	—	—	—

shows that campus police departments are much less likely than municipal police to conduct all the direct services we studied.

Military Producers

Military law enforcement agencies also supply direct police services in metropolitan areas. Forty-eight base police units serve Army, Navy, Air Force, and Marine Corps installations in the 80 SMSAs (Table 4—6). Almost all these patrol and control traffic, and more than half also investigate burglary. Investigations of homicides and

Table 4—4.   Types of State Producers and the Services They Conduct

		Percent of Producers Conducting		
	Number Reporting	*Patrol Only*	*Patrol and Traffic Control*	*Patrol, Traffic, and Burglary Investigation*
State police and highway patrols	80	—	6	—
State criminal investigation agencies	13	—	—	—

[a]Includes eight irregular producers of burglary investigation.

Table 4—5.   Types of Campus Producers and the Services They Conduct

		Percent of Producers Conducting		
	Number Reporting	*Patrol Only*	*Patrol and Traffic Control*	*Patrol, Traffic, and Burglary Investigation*
Special district college and university campus police	14	36	43	—
State college and university campus police	64	2	16	30
Private college and university campus police	30	—	20	40

of more serious burglaries on federal military reservations are under-taken by military investigation agencies: the Army Criminal Investigations Division, the Naval Special Investigations Office, and the Air Force Office of Special Investigations. Several of the metropolitan areas have more than one installation of the same branch of the military and, therefore, have several base police producers, but only a single military investigation unit. Eighty of the 1,454 direct service producers (6 percent) are military units.

Table 4−4. continued

Percent of Producers Conducting				
Patrol, *Traffic,* *Burglary* *and Homicide* *Investigation*	*Traffic* *Control* *Only*	*Patrol and* *Investigation*	*Traffic* *and* *Investigation*	*Investigation* *Only*
32ª	49	—	13	—
—	—	—	—	100

Table 4−5. continued

Percent of Producers Conducting				
Patrol, *Traffic,* *Burglary* *and Homicide* *Investigation*	*Traffic* *Control* *Only*	*Patrol and* *Investigation*	*Traffic* *and* *Investigation*	*Investigation* *Only*
21	—	—	—	—
52	—	2	—	—
30	—	10	—	—

Nonmilitary Federal Producers

Nonmilitary federal agencies constitute another group of producers. The Federal Bureau of Investigation is regularly involved in burglary and homicide investigation on federal reservations in 26 of the 80 metropolitan areas. These are SMSAs with military or other federal reservations. The FBI and other federal investigative agencies, such as the Bureau of Alcohol, Tobacco, and Firearms and the Drug Enforcement Administration, conduct investigations in all metropoli

Table 4–6.   Types of Military and Civilian Federal Producers and the Services They Conduct

	Number Reporting	*Percent of Producers Conducting*		
		Patrol Only	*Patrol and Traffic Control*	*Patrol, Traffic, and Burglary Investigation*
Military base police	48	12	23	58
Military investigation agencies	32	—	—	—
Federal Bureau of Investigation	26	—	—	—
Other federal agencies (Veterans' Authority Hospital Police, Bureau of Indian Affairs, National Parks)	14	7	36	21

tan areas. The enforcement of federal laws is not within the scope of this study, however, except on federal reservations where federal law supplants state law as the general criminal code.

Federal agencies producing patrol, traffic control, or burglary and homicide investigation in these federal jurisdictions include the Veterans' Administration, the National Park Service, and the Bureau of Indian Affairs. These agencies produce direct police services in a variety of combinations, usually including patrol and traffic control. Forty of the 1,454 direct service producers (3 percent) are nonmilitary federal agencies.

Other Police Producers

Other municipal agencies—airport police, park police, housing authority police, for example—are not commonly involved in criminal investigation; however, most producers of this type patrol, and over half control traffic as well (Table 4–7).

Some independent local special districts, such as public school districts, airport districts, and park districts, have established their own police agencies. About one fourth of these local special district police patrol, but conduct none of the other services we studied. Half patrol and control traffic; few investigate burglaries or homicides.

Table 4—6. continued

Percent of Producers Conducting				
Patrol, Traffic, Burglary and Homicide Investigation	Traffic Control Only	Patrol and Investigation	Traffic and Investigation	Investigation Only
4	—	—	—	2
—	—	—	—	100
—	—	—	—	100
29	—	—	—	7

Intergovernmental agencies have been created for a variety of purposes in the United States. Few of these include the provision of direct police services, however. Only five intergovernmental agencies are involved in direct police service in the 80 metropolitan areas. Two of these are special interagency investigations organizations created explicitly for conducting criminal investigations. The others are agencies, such as the Port Authority of New York and New Jersey, that have broader public service responsibilities, but conduct police services as a part of that broad mandate.

Traffic control is the common service produced by these agencies. There are state park police in 18 of the 80 SMSAs. Most of these patrol and control traffic, and a few conduct investigations of burglaries and homicides as well. Other state agencies include capitol police, hospital police, and motor vehicle registries. These agencies produce direct police services in a wide range of combinations, as shown in Table 4—7.

Few private organizations (other than the private colleges and universities discussed above) are responsible for the provision of the direct police services we studied. We encountered only one in the 80 metropolitan areas.

Residents of a few unincorporated areas hire sworn officers to

Table 4—7. Types of Other Producers and the Services They Conduct

	Number Reporting	*Percent of Producers Conducting*		
		Patrol Only	*Patrol and Traffic Control*	*Patrol, Traffic, and Burglary Investigation*
Other municipal agencies (airport police, park police, housing authority police)	19	37	58	—
Local special district agencies	13	23	54	23
Intergovernmental agencies	5	—	40	—
State park police	18	17	61	6
Other state agencies (state capitol police, hospital police)	17	12	23	18
Other private agencies	1	—	100	—
Unincorporated areas	3	—	100	—

patrol and control traffic in their neighborhoods. We found three such producers in the 80 metropolitan areas. The practice of hiring private guards or watchmen is much more extensive than this listing would indicate. However, most private patrols are not empowered to exercise special powers of arrest and, thus, were not included in this study.

Table 4—7. continued

	Percent of Producers Conducting			
Patrol, Traffic, Burglary and Homicide Investigation	*Traffic Control Only*	*Patrol and Investigation*	*Traffic and Investigation*	*Investigation Only*
—	—	5	—	—
—	—	—	—	—
—	20	—	—	40
17	—	—	—	—
18	23	6	—	—
—	—	—	—	—
—	—	—	—	—

CATEGORIES OF SERVICE PRODUCERS

These categories—municipal, county, state, campus, military, federal, and other—will most frequently be used in this volume. However, when the number of producers from one of these groups is extremely small, the group will be collapsed into the "other police" category.

Chapter 5

General Area Patrol

Patrol is the most visible police service. In most police agencies the patrol force constitutes the largest section of the department and has the most contact with citizens. Recent trends in police organization—among them the introduction of team policing—suggest that in the future even more police officers in many departments will be assigned to patrol. This represents a shift from an earlier trend toward specialization of officer assignment [1].

Many types of police agencies conduct general area patrol. In addition to municipal and county police departments, numerous campus police, military base police, and police of other special districts patrol public places in the 80 metropolitan areas we studied. The work of patrolling metropolitan areas is usually divided among several producers. Patrol is supplied by a single producer in only 1 of the 80 SMSAs.

Most producers of patrol are small. Two thirds of the local agencies we studied have 20 or fewer sworn officers. But these small producers supply only 20 percent of the total patrol force. They do allocate disproportionately large numbers of sworn personnel to patrol, however. Because most small police agencies emphasize patrol over other types of direct service, they generally have about twice as many officers on patrol for every 1,000 residents of the areas they patrol when compared with larger local departments.

Almost all service areas have their own patrol producers. Contracting and other arrangements for patrol exclusively by outside agencies are rare, although they do occur. On the other hand, only about half the service areas receive patrol exclusively from their own agencies. Most of the service areas with two or more producers of patrol do not have duplication of this service, however. The patrolling agencies in most cases alternate their patrols with each other.

WHO PRODUCES PATROL SERVICES?

Most agencies conducting general area patrol in the 80 metropolitan areas are municipal police departments. Seventy-three percent of the patrol agencies in these areas are municipal police departments (Table 5–1) [2]. These departments contribute 70 percent of the total patrol force on the street during both the day shift (measured at 10 a.m.) and the evening shift (measured at 10 p.m.) (see Table 5–2). Because of the similarity between day shift and evening shift percentages, only the evening shift percentages are presented.

County police and sheriffs' departments account for another 8 percent of the patrol agencies and supply 14 percent of the on-street patrol force in the metropolitan areas. State police agencies do not usually supply patrol services in most of the metropolitan areas. In later chapters we discuss state agencies and their contributions to other direct services (particularly traffic patrol and accident investigation) and their major contributions to two auxiliary services: entry-level training and criminal laboratory analyses.

Several types of patrol producers are often ignored in discussions of metropolitan policing. They constitute about 18 percent of the agencies producing patrol and contribute about 14 percent of the officers on patrol in the 80 metropolitan areas. Military police and shore patrols account for 4 percent of these agencies and contribute 5 percent of the officers on patrol. College and university campus police agencies account for 8 percent of the agencies and contribute 6 percent of the patrol force. Other types of patrol agencies, like park police, Indian reservation police, local school district police, airport and hospital police, make up 6 percent of the agencies supplying patrol and contribute 3 percent of the patrol force.

In some regions of the United States, military, campus, and the other agencies mentioned above constitute 30 percent or more of the agencies patrolling in metropolitan areas. Such agencies contribute more than 20 percent of the patrol officers on the street during the evening shift in these regions. Where they are present in such numbers they substantially increase the supply of patrol services. Without their contributions the workload of the conventional patrol agencies would undoubtedly be increased.

Table 5–1. Patrol Agencies in the 80 Metropolitan Areas: Region and Type of Agency

Location	Number of SMSAs	Number of Patrol Agencies	Percent of General Area Patrol Agencies That Are					
			Municipal Police	County Sheriffs and Police	State Police	Campus Police	Military Police	Other Police[a]
Total	80	1,279	73	8	1	8	4	6
Northeast								
Region 1	8	72	82	0	3	13	0	3
Region 2	4	155	86	3	1	3	0	7
Region 3	6	132	84	1	1	6	2	5
Midwest								
Region 5	16	258	79	9	2	7	0	4
Region 7	4	47	72	8	2	4	2	11
South								
Region 4	15	268	71	10	0	12	4	4
Region 6	14	152	59	12	1	12	8	9
West								
Region 8	4	36	58	11	0	8	14	8
Region 9	7	133	55	6	1	12	12	14
Region 10	2	26	73	19	4	0	0	4

Note: Rows may not total 100 percent due to rounding errors.

[a] Other police includes nonmilitary federal police in this chapter.

Table 5–2.   Distribution of On-Street Patrol Force: Type of Producer

Location	Number of SMSAs	Number of Patrol Officers on the Street at 10 p.m.	Percent of On-Street Patrol Force (10 p.m.) Supplied By						
			Municipal Police	County Sheriffs and Police	State Police	Campus Police	Military Police	Other Police[a]	
Total	80	6,821	70	14	3	6	5	3	
Northeast									
Region 1	8	366	94	0	b	5	0	1	
Region 2	4	823	84	5	5	4	0	3	
Region 3	6	393	81	3	5	5	4	2	
Midwest									
Region 5	16	967	69	15	8	6	1	2	
Region 7	4	177	76	11	4	1	1	7	
South									
Region 4	15	1,769	67	21	b	7	4	1	
Region 6	14	987	65	15	2	7	9	3	
West									
Region 8	4	167	65	11	0	10	12	2	
Region 9	7	1,092	59	18	2	5	10	6	
Region 10	2	80	65	25	10	0	0	0	

Note: Rows may not total 100 percent due to rounding errors.
[a] Includes nonmilitary federal police
[b] Less than one half of one percent.

Regional variations in the types of agencies patrolling and their contributions to the patrol force are related to legal authorization for police patrol. In the heavily incorporated areas of the Northeast, municipal police departments dominate both in proportion of agencies and in share of the patrol force. In these densely populated metropolitan areas county sheriffs are not typically involved in patrol service delivery. Few county police departments (other than specialized ones such as county park police) have been established. In most Northeastern metropolitan areas only an occasional campus police force, or perhaps county park police or local school district police agency, is the exception to an otherwise uniform pattern of municipal patrol service delivery.

Outside the Northeast, patterns of patrol service production are more varied. County sheriffs' and county police departments supply a substantial part of the on-street patrol force. In Regions 4 and 10, sheriffs and county police supply over 20 percent of the patrol officers on the street. In the Southwest, the Mountain states, and the Far West (Regions 6, 8, and 9) military police and shore patrols also contribute substantially to the on-street patrol force. Many of the metropolitan areas in these regions have large military installations with resident populations and attendant support and entertainment facilities.

Municipal police departments are most prevalent, as a percentage of all patrol producers and in terms of their relative contribution to the on-street patrol force, in those metropolitan areas having 500,000 or more inhabitants (Table 5–3) [3]. County police and sheriffs' departments supply about 14 percent of the on-street patrol force in all SMSAs, but they constitute a larger share of all patrol producers in the smaller metropolitan areas. The picture is mixed for other types of patrol producers because the presence or absence of special enclaves, such as colleges and universities and military bases, is not directly related to SMSA size.

MEASURES OF PATROL SERVICE DIVISION

In this section we discuss the number of producers of general area patrol in each of 80 metropolitan areas. We use the measures "multiplicity," "relative multiplicity," and "relative dominance" to characterize the extent to which patrol service production is divided in each SMSA.

Multiplicity measures the number of patrol producers in a metropolitan area. It is the figure often quoted by critics of American policing when they argue that there are too many police agencies

Table 5–3. Patrol Producers and Patrol Force Composition: SMSA Population and Type of Producer

Metropolitan Population (1973 est.)	Number of SMSAs	Number of Patrol Producers	Percent of General Area Patrol Producers That Are					
			Municipal Police	County Sheriffs and Police	State Police	Campus Police	Military Police	Other Police[a]
50,000 to 124,999	20	127	61	15	6	8	5	6
125,000 to 249,999	26	317	74	8	4	8	2	3
250,000 to 499,999	21	406	66	6	2	9	6	11
500,000 and over	13	459	76	6	1	7	2	7

Metropolitan Population (1973 est.)	Number of SMSAs	Number of Patrol Officers on the Street at 10 p.m.	Percent of On-Street Patrol Force (10 p.m.) Supplied By					
			Municipal Police	County Sheriffs and Police	State Police	Campus Police	Military Police	Other Police[a]
50,000 to 124,999	20	618	68	16	4	6	4	1
125,000 to 249,999	26	1,184	69	14	5	6	5	1
250,000 to 499,999	21	2,055	66	14	2	6	8	4
500,000 and over	13	2,964	74	14	2	4	2	3

Note: Rows may not total 100 percent due to rounding errors.   [a]Includes nonmilitary federal police.

operating in a given area. But a simple count of producers does not characterize an industry adequately. For example, one metropolitan area might have 10 police agencies that produce patrol service for a population of one million, while another area might also have 10 producers, but a population of only 100,000. Both would have a multiplicity score of 10, but would critics find division of patrol services in these two metropolitan areas equally objectionable? Probably not.

The second measure, relative multiplicity, clarifies this issue. It measures the number of producing agencies per 100,000 metropolitan inhabitants. The two metropolitan areas mentioned above would now appear to be quite different. The first would have a multiplicity score of 10 and a relative multiplicity score of 1.0. The second, also scoring 10 on multiplicity, would have a relative multiplicity score of 10 as well. There are many more producers in relation to residents served in the second metropolitan area than in the first.

But with these two measures we still do not have a complete picture of the way in which patrol service is divided up among different agencies. One metropolitan area might have 10 producing agencies, each of which supplied patrol service to 10 percent of the population. In a second area there might also be 10 producers of patrol; however, one of them might supply 90 percent of the population while the other 9 producers supply the remaining 10 percent of the population. Once again, an observer would see two very different patterns.

While complex measures of the distribution of serviced population among the several producers in a metropolitan area would be required to completely clarify this aspect of service division, a simpler measure—relative dominance—captures important variations. Relative dominance for patrol service delivery measures the percent of the metropolitan population that receives patrol service from the producer that has the largest serviced population. In the example given above the first metropolitan area would have a relative dominance score of 10, while the second area's score would be 90.

In 64 of the 80 metropolitan areas studied the central city police department is the dominant patrol producer. In 12 SMSAs there are more residents in the unincorporated areas patrolled by the county sheriff or county police; therefore, in those SMSAs the county producer is dominant. In the four remaining SMSAs state police are the dominant patrol producers.

The number of patrol agencies in metropolitan areas ranges from a low of 1 in Meriden/Connecticut to a high of 91 in Paterson-Clifton-Passaic/New Jersey [4]. The median number of patrol producers in an area is 13 (Table 5-4), with an interquartile range of 7 to 20

Table 5–4. Multiplicity and Dominance in Patrol Service Production: Region and SMSA Population

Location	Number of SMSAs	Number of Patrol Producers in an SMSA		Number of Patrol Producers per 100,000 SMSA Population (1973 est.)		Percent of SMSA Population (1973 est.) Served By Dominant Producer	
		Median	Range[a]	Median	Range	Median	Range
Total	80	13	7 — 20	5.9	3.9 — 7.3	51	38 — 70
Northeast							
Region 1	8	6	3 — 9	3.9	2.5 — 6.4	51	46 — 65
Region 2	4	19	8 — 38	6.0	4.3 — 6.2	32	11 — 33
Region 3	6	14	10 — 32	6.6	3.3 — 13.6	44	42 — 48
Midwest							
Region 5	16	13	9 — 20	7.2	5.9 — 9.1	41	34 — 52
Region 7	4	7	4 — 17	4.6	4.2 — 7.1	68	67 — 77
South							
Region 4	15	18	6 — 25	5.3	3.4 — 7.0	54	38 — 68
Region 6	14	8	5 — 12	3.7	2.8 — 6.8	73	66 — 85
West							
Region 8	4	5	5 — 12	4.2	4.0 — 5.9	60	44 — 73
Region 9	7	20	19 — 22	4.8	2.6 — 7.2	38	27 — 53
Region 10	2	—	5 — 21	—	3.9 — 10.5	—	46 — 70

Metropolitan Population (1973 est.)						
50,000 to 124,999	20	5	4 — 8	5.9	4.0 — 7.6	71	49 — 81
125,000 to 249,999	26	10	7 — 16	6.4	4.2 — 10.3	50	44 — 64
250,000 to 499,999	21	19	12 — 21	6.0	4.2 — 7.1	52	37 — 68
500,000 and over	13	29	22 — 38	4.0	3.4 — 5.8	36	28 — 45

[a]Range is the interquartile range except for Region 10, where it is the full range of variation.

agencies. (This range accounts for about 50 percent of the 80 metropolitan areas. Twenty-five percent have 7 or fewer producers, and 75
percent have 20 or fewer.) The median relative multiplicity score for
metropolitan areas is 5.9 producers per 100,000 residents, with an
interquartile range of 3.9 to 7.3 producers per 100,000. The dominant patrol producer in the median SMSA serves 51 percent of the
metropolitan area residents. The interquartile range for relative dominance is from 38 to 70 percent.

The number of patrol producers per metropolitan area is generally
highest in New York and New Jersey (Region 2), the Southeast (Region 4), and California and Arizona (Region 9). Metropolitan areas in
New England (Region 1), Missouri and Iowa (Region 7), and the
Mountain states (Region 8) tend to have fewer patrol producers in
absolute terms.

However, when we look at the number of producers per 100,000
population the picture changes. Several regions that score high on
multiplicity have lower relative multiplicity scores. In relative terms
the areas with the largest numbers of producers are found in Pennsylvania and Virginia (Region 3) and the North Central states (Region 5). Both these regions have smaller police agencies than are
common in other regions. Areas with the lowest relative multiplicity
scores are New England (Region 1), the Southwest (Region 6), and
the Mountain states (Region 8).

There are some interesting regional variations in the relative dominance scores of metropolitan area patrol producers. SMSAs in the
Southwest and the Midwest (Regions 6 and 7) are more dominated
by single patrol producers than are the metropolitan areas in other
regions. This may be attributed to the annexation statutes in several
of the states in these two regions. For example, in Texas and Oklahoma (both in Region 6) it is relatively easy for a city to annex
adjoining territory, preempting the formation of another municipality that might form its own police agency. As the central city ex-
pands by annexation, its police department increases its dominance.

As one might expect, multiplicity is higher in larger metropolitan
areas and lower in the smaller areas (Table 5−4). But as the data
show, the number of police agencies producing patrol service in a
metropolitan area per 100,000 metropolitan inhabitants does not increase as rapidly as the number of inhabitants. The largest SMSAs
have the largest number of producing agencies, but they generally
have fewer producers per 100,000 inhabitants. The areas with the
highest relative multiplicity scores are those in the 125,000 to
249,999 population range. These areas, while typically having fewer
than half the number of producers of the largest SMSAs, have over

50 percent more producers relative to population. In terms of producers per 100,000 inhabitants we see that patrol is not most divided in the large metropolitan areas so often cited by critics. Rather, some smaller areas appear to be less "consolidated."

The figures for relative dominance shown in Table 5–4 suggest another view on consolidation, however. In the metropolitan areas with the most patrol producers per 100,000 residents a single large producer serves more of the residents than in the very large metropolitan areas. Relative dominance tends to decrease as metropolitan area size increases, indicating a proportionately smaller role for the central city police department in patrolling the large metropolitan areas. Obviously, all three measures—multiplicity, relative multiplicity, and relative dominance—must be considered in any description of the extent to which patrol service production is divided in a given metropolitan area.

The types of patrol producers found and the extent of their involvement in on-street patrol service delivery vary with the structure of the metropolitan areas (Table 5–5). As both multiplicity and relative multiplicity increase, municipal police departments constitute more of the patrol producers. Officers from municipal police departments tend to supply more of the on-street patrol force in these areas.

The trend is different for relative dominance, however. As dominance increases, proportionately fewer of the patrol producers are municipal police departments. But the reduction in percent of patrol force supplied is much less marked. Municipal police departments continue to supply a high percentage of the on-street patrol force as dominance increases. This is consistent with our finding that the dominant producer in a metropolitan area is generally the central city police department. Instead of there being a larger number of somewhat smaller municipal police forces in areas with high relative dominance scores, there is likely to be one large central city force.

THE OPERATIONAL ORGANIZATION OF PATROL AGENCIES

Agency Size and Patrol Production

Size distributions for the different kinds of local patrol producers across the 10 federal regions are shown in Table 5–6. Local patrol producers include municipal police departments, county sheriffs' and county police departments, and other agencies. We include here local agencies established by state governments and agencies established by private organizations, but statewide and federal agencies are not in-

Table 5-5.   Multiplicity and Dominance in Patrol Service Production:
Type of Producer

	Number of Patrol Producers in an SMSA			
	1 to 7	8 to 13	14 to 20	Over 20
Number of patrol producers	108	197	321	683
Percent of patrol producers that are				
Municipal police	53	58	70	78
County sheriffs and police	17	11	7	5
State police	5	5	2	1
Campus police	12	10	9	7
Military police	7	6	4	2
Other police	7	10	8	6
Number of patrol officers on the street at 10 p.m.	810	1,001	1,375	3,635
Percent of on-street force supplied by				
Municipal police	67	64	63	75
County sheriffs and police	15	15	15	13
State police	2	4	3	3
Campus police	6	6	9	4
Military police	10	7	6	2
Other police	1	3	3	3

Note: Columns may not total 100 percent due to rounding errors.

cluded in this discussion. Campus police agencies account for most of
the local patrol producers that are not municipal police departments
or county sheriffs or police. These include the police units of private
colleges and universities, municipal or county community colleges,
and state colleges and universities [5].

Patrol agency size varies considerably from region to region. There
are also large variations within each region and across agency types.
Sheriffs' and county police departments are usually larger than the
other types of local patrol producers, but municipal police departments dominate all size ranges due to their prevalence. For example,

Table 5—5. continued

Number of Patrol Producers per 100,000 SMSA Population (1973 est.)				Percent of SMSA Population (1973 est.) Served by Dominant Producer			
0 to 3.9	3.9 to 5.9	5.9 to 7.3	Over 7.3	0 to 38	39 to 51	52 to 71	Over 71
214	297	418	380	589	277	284	159
56	66	74	80	78	71	69	50
9	11	6	6	5	7	9	13
1	2	2	3	1	4	2	3
13	9	7	7	6	11	8	13
8	5	3	1	2	3	5	10
13	7	8	4	7	5	8	11
2,123	1,710	1,813	1,175	2,830	1,485	1,342	1,164
68	65	76	71	72	72	65	67
14	19	11	12	13	13	18	12
2	3	3	5	3	3	4	1
6	6	4	6	5	6	4	8
7	4	3	4	3	4	5	9
3	3	3	2	3	1	3	3

of the 67 local patrol producers having more than 150 full-time sworn officers, 48 (72 percent) are municipal police departments. Other local producers are generally smaller than either municipal or county producers.

The largest local producers of patrol are most common in California and Arizona (Region 9). Sheriffs' departments are particularly large in that region. New England, New York and New Jersey, and California and Arizona (Regions 1, 2, and 9) generally have larger municipal police departments than do other regions, while many municipal departments are very small in Virginia and Pennsylvania, the Midwest, and the Northwest (Regions 3, 5, 7, and 10). While

Table 5-6. Size of Local Patrol Producers

Type of patrol producer	Northeast Regions			Midwest Regions		Southern Regions		Western Regions		
	1	2	3	5	7	4	6	8	9	10
Municipal police (N)[a]	(59)	(133)	(110)	(187)	(34)	(187)	(89)	(21)	(73)	(19)
Full-time personnel										
Median	18	20	3	5	2	10	8	10	21	5
Range[b]	9–33	10–36	1–6	1–20	0–13	4–28	3–22	2–22	10–77	3–11
Full-time sworn										
Median	17	19	2	4	2	8	6	7	16	4
Range	8–30	9–35	1–6	1–16	0–9	4–22	3–17	1–18	8–51	2–10
County sheriffs and police (N)	(0)	(5)	(2)	(23)	(4)	(27)	(18)	(4)	(8)	(5)
Full-time personnel										
Median	—	56	—	55	66	67	34	34	228	31
Range	—	41–100	32–82[c]	34–79	27–67	23–174	21–125	32–65	118–480	7–66
Full-time sworn										
Median	—	54	—	36	49	36	34	25	166	17
Range	—	38–80	29–62	20–60	25–58	18–149	15–100	23–65	90–319	6–39
Other local producers (N)	(10)	(11)	(10)	(21)	(2)	(36)	(24)	(5)	(27)	(0)
Full-time personnel										
Median	8	18	3	9	—	12	12	7	10	—
Range	7–11	4–21	3–20	6–33	9–10[c]	7–22	6–30	5–13	5–20	—
Full-time sworn										
Median	8	15	3	8	2	10	9	7	8	—
Range	6–10	4–20	1–5	6–26	7–10	7–21	5–16	5–8	3–20	—

[a]Number reporting. [b]Range is interquartile range. [c]Full range of variation is reported.

SMSAs generally have agencies of many sizes, the smallest producers constitute a higher proportion of producers in the smaller SMSAs, and the largest producers are more prevalent in the larger SMSAs (Table 5−7).

Agency Size and Patrol Deployment

Table 5−8 provides perspective on the debate over eliminating small municipal police departments. As the table shows, these agencies are quite common throughout the country. Nearly 60 percent of the municipal agencies in the 80 metropolitan areas employ 10 or fewer full-time sworn officers. In some regions this percentage is 75 percent or even higher. But patrol officers from these small municipal departments are only about 11 percent of the patrol force on the street at 10 p.m. In many regions that proportion is even lower. In only two regions does it exceed 20 percent. These data indicate that complete elimination of all municipal patrol producers that employ 10 or fewer officers would have relatively little effect on the way in which most of the metropolitan area patrol force is organized.

Patrol Deployment and Citizen-to-Patrol Officer Ratios

While small producers contribute only a fraction of the patrol force in most SMSAs, their elimination would probably have a negative impact on the availability of patrol service to the residents of the parts of those metropolitan areas served by these smaller agencies. The larger the local police agency that produces patrol service, the lower the proportion of the agency's officers generally assigned to patrol duties (Table 5−9). This relationship is found for all types of local patrol producers. Larger departments tend to assign more officers to specific direct service duties other than patrol. Larger departments are also more likely to produce their own auxiliary services and to assign officers to these nonpatrol duties.

What is remarkable is the magnitude of the differences in assignment and deployment of officers. The largest local patrol producers generally have only about half as many officers on the street in proportion to their total number of sworn officers as do agencies with fewer than 10 officers. The very smallest departments achieve still higher ratios, but often do so by augmenting their full-time sworn personnel with part-time officers.

For the municipal patrol producers, variations in proportion of sworn officers actually deployed for street duty have a direct bearing on the availability of patrol officers to citizens as measured by a citizen-to-patrol officer ratio (Table 5−10). A patrol officer in the

Table 5–7.   Local Patrol Producer Size and SMSA Population

	Total	Metropolitan Population (1973 est.)			
		50,000 to 124,999	125,000 to 249,999	250,000 to 499,999	500,000 and Over
Municipal police (N)[a]	(916)	(77)	(222)	(267)	(350)
Percent with					
Part-time only	8	17	14	9	2
1 to 4 full-time officers	27	40	35	26	19
5 to 10 full-time officers	24	9	20	29	26
11 to 20 full-time officers	14	1	9	14	19
21 to 50 full-time officers	13	5	10	8	21
51 to 150 full-time officers	9	25	7	6	8
Over 150 full-time officers	5	3	5	6	5
County sheriffs and police (N)	(97)	(19)	(27)	(23)	(28)
Percent with					
1 to 4 full-time officers	3	0	11	0	0
5 to 10 full-time officers	5	0	11	0	7
11 to 20 full-time officers	17	26	15	17	11
21 to 50 full-time officers	29	47	41	9	21
51 to 150 full-time officers	28	26	19	44	25
Over 150 full-time officers	19	0	4	30	36

Other local producers (N)	(146)	(14)	(26)	(57)	(49)
Percent with					
Part-time only	4	7	4	5	2
1 to 4 full-time officers	20	21	27	21	12
5 to 10 full-time officers	36	43	42	35	33
11 to 20 full-time officers	19	7	12	18	27
21 to 50 full-time officers	19	21	12	18	25
51 to 150 full-time officers	3	0	4	4	2

Note: Columns may not total 100 percent due to rounding errors.
[a]Number reporting.

Table 5–8. Municipal Police: Size and Percent of On-Street Patrol Force (10 p.m.)

	Total	Northeast Regions			Midwest Regions		Southern Regions			Western Regions	
		1	2	3	5	7	4	6	8	9	10
Municipal police (N)[a]	(916)	(59)	(133)	(111)	(189)	(34)	(188)	(89)	(21)	(73)	(19)
Percent with											
No full-time officers	8	7	2	20	16	29	2	3	0	0	5
1 to 4 full-time officers	27	5	13	43	35	35	26	33	38	3	53
5 to 10 full-time officers	24	20	13	23	20	12	31	33	33	36	21
11 to 20 full-time officers	14	27	25	5	10	9	14	11	5	15	11
21 to 50 full-time officers	13	25	34	3	9	3	12	5	5	21	0
51 to 150 full-time officers	9	7	11	1	9	3	9	8	10	21	11
Over 150 full-time officers	5	9	2	5	3	9	6	8	10	6	0
Percent of on-street patrol force (10 p.m.) from municipal police departments with											
No full-time officers	1	1	0	5	2	3	0	0	0	0	0
1 to 4 full-time officers	4	1	3	14	6	6	2	3	4	0	14
5 to 10 full-time officers	6	6	4	12	7	4	6	5	7	5	10
11 to 20 full-time officers	6	13	12	4	7	9	5	3	2	3	5
21 to 50 full-time officers	10	24	27	5	8	2	8	2	3	7	0
51 to 150 full-time officers	15	15	19	3	21	14	14	10	12	18	36
Over 150 full-time officers	30	36	19	40	18	38	32	42	36	26	0
Percent of on-street patrol force (10 p.m.) from nonmunicipal patrol producers	30	6	16	19	32	24	33	35	35	41	35

Note: Columns may not total 100 percent due to rounding errors. [a] Number reporting.

Table 5-9.   Deployment of Sworn Officers for Patrol Duty in Local Patrol Producers: Size and Type of Producer

Type of Producer and Number of Full-Time Sworn Officers	Percent of Full-Time Sworn Officers Assigned To Patrol Duty		Ratio of Officers on the Street (10 p.m.) to Number Assigned to Patrol Duty		Ratio of Officers on the Street (10 p.m.) to Number of Full-Time Sworn	
	Median	Range[a]	Median	Range	Median	Range
Municipal police	85	67 – 100	.28	.21 – .39	.22	.16 – .33
1 to 4 full-time officers	100	100 – 100	.50	.33 – 1.0	.50	.33 – 1.0
5 to 10 full-time officers	100	83 – 100	.29	.20 – .38	.25	.20 – .33
11 to 20 full-time officers	74	67 – 85	.27	.22 – .33	.20	.16 – .25
21 to 50 full-time officers	68	62 – 74	.24	.21 – .29	.16	.14 – .19
51 to 150 full-time officers	63	56 – 70	.22	.18 – .27	.14	.12 – .17
Over 150 full-time officers	56	50 – 62	.21	.16 – .26	.12	.09 – .16
County sheriffs and police	52	40 – 66	.29	.19 – .38	.15	.09 – .20
1 to 4 full-time officers	100	75 – 100	.33	0 – .67	.33	0 – .50
5 to 10 full-time officers	80	75 – 83	.33	.25 – .40	.25	.20 – .29
11 to 20 full-time officers	56	43 – 76	.33	.23 – .43	.18	.17 – .22
21 to 50 full-time officers	56	50 – 66	.29	.19 – .40	.13	.10 – .21
51 to 150 full-time officers	45	37 – 55	.26	.19 – .32	.11	.08 – .15
Over 150 full-time officers	44	35 – 52	.22	.16 – .30	.10	.08 – .13
Other local patrol producers	100	80 – 100	.29	.20 – .43	.25	.18 – .39
1 to 4 full-time officers	100	75 – 100	.50	.33 – 1.0	.50	.33 – 1.0
5 to 10 full-time officers	100	86 – 100	.25	.20 – .43	.25	.17 – .40
11 to 20 full-time officers	93	75 – 100	.33	.22 – .38	.25	.21 – .33
21 to 50 full-time officers	82	69 – 95	.24	.20 – .37	.19	.13 – .28
51 to 150 full-time officers	66	42 – 86	.17	.13 – .23	.13	.10 – .14
Over 150 full-time officers	—	—	—	—	—	—

[a] Range is the interquartile range.

Table 5–10.   Patrol Deployment and Density in Local Patrol Producers: Size and Type of Producer

Type of Producer[a] and Number of Full-Time Sworn Officers	Number of Local Patrol Producers	Number of Officers on the Street (10 p.m.)		Number of Inhabitants per Officer on the Street (1973 Population est.)	
		Median	Range[b]	Median	Range
Municipal police					
1 to 4 full-time officers	209	1	1 – 1	1,623	886 – 2,396
5 to 10 full-time officers	209	2	1 – 2	2,383	1,533 – 3,594
11 to 20 full-time officers	124	3	2 – 4	2,877	2,141 – 4,047
21 to 50 full-time officers	121	5	4 – 6	3,244	2,364 – 4,482
51 to 150 full-time officers	77	13	10 – 16	3,985	2,926 – 5,718
Over 150 full-time officers	45	30	23 – 57	4,256	3,086 – 6,017
County sheriffs and police					
1 to 4 full-time officers	2	—	1 – 2	—	328 – 8,259
5 to 10 full-time officers	5	2	1 – 2	7,867	5,820 – 10,013
11 to 20 full-time officers	13	3	3 – 4	7,756	3,835 – 8,978
21 to 50 full-time officers	28	5	3 – 7	7,224	2,956 – 12,217
51 to 150 full-time officers	27	8	6 – 13	5,768	4,821 – 8,126
Over 150 full-time officers	17	22	18 – 30	5,985	4,039 – 7,191
Other local producers					
1 to 4 full-time officers	10	1	1 – 1	1,257	486 – 2,124
5 to 10 full-time officers	25	2	1 – 3	1,346	745 – 1,982
11 to 20 full-time officers	18	4	4 – 5	1,268	782 – 2,021
21 to 50 full-time officers	21	6	5 – 7	1,770	1,034 – 2,894
51 to 150 full-time officers	3	8	7 – 18	1,250	311 – 5,764

[a] Only producers assigning officers at 10 p.m. are included. Several small departments do not assign officers at 10 p.m.; these are excluded from this table.
[b] Range is interquartile range.

median municipal department of 5 to 10 sworn officers serves slightly fewer than 2,400 citizens, while a patrol officer in the median department with more than 150 full-time sworn officers must serve more than 4,200 citizens. When considering these figures it is important to remember that the larger departments generally have more sworn officers per 1,000 residents than do the smaller [6]. But the larger departments do not translate this relative personnel advantage into an on-street presence as well as the small- to medium-sized agencies do.

The finding that smaller municipal departments usually deploy more officers per 1,000 citizens suggests that consolidation of patrol agencies might increase rather than decrease costs. If the larger consolidated departments tried to achieve the citizen-to-patrol officer ratio of the smaller departments, more officers would need to be employed. Conversely, if the newly consolidated department failed to employ additional officers, the citizen-to-patrol officer ratio would increase, assuming the new department was organized like other large departments.

Variations in Patrol Practices

In addition to the variations in number and proportion of officers deployed for on-street patrol duty, patrol producers use a variety of patrol systems and patrol shift arrangements. The one-officer radio patrol car is by far the most commonly used patrol unit. Close to 80 percent of the patrol producers in the metropolitan areas rely on this arrangement exclusively, while 22 percent use some or all two-officer radio patrol cars. Over 80 percent use no foot patrols (Table 5–11). Half the military police agencies use some two-officer patrol cars. County sheriffs and county police use two-officer patrols more often than other types of local producers. Foot patrols are used most often by campus police.

Among the local patrol producers the use of two-officer patrols is closely related to the size of the agency. Large municipal police departments (those with over 150 sworn officers) are quite likely to use two-officer patrols. Two thirds of these departments use some two-officer patrols, and 7 percent use only two-officer patrols (Table 5–12). There is a similar tendency to use more two-officer patrols among county police and sheriffs' departments as their size increases, although this tendency is not as marked as among the municipal producers.

These findings regarding local patrol producer size and use of two-officer patrols shed further light on our earlier discussion of high citizen-to-patrol officer ratios found in areas served by the larger

Table 5–11.   Patrol Practices Among Different Types of Producers

Type of Patrol Producer	Use of Patrol Cars				Use of Foot Patrols			
	Number of Patrol Producers	Percent Using			Number of Patrol Producers	Percent Using		
		One-Officer Cars Only	One- and Two-Officer Cars	Two-Officer Cars Only		No Foot Patrol	Some Foot Patrol	Foot Patrol Only
Total	1,183	78	15	7	1,188	83	16	1
Municipal police	858	79	15	6	860	88	12	0
County sheriffs and police	94	63	20	17	97	98	2	0
State police	28	93	7	0	28	100	0	0
Campus police	97	81	16	3	98	29	61	10
Military police	38	50	42	8	38	74	26	0
Federal police	9	67	0	33	9	78	22	0
Other police	59	86	5	9	58	72	21	7

Note: Rows may not total 100 percent due to rounding errors.

Table 5–12. Patrol Practices and Local Producer Size

Type and Size of Patrol Producer	Use of Two-Person Patrols				Use of Foot Patrols			
	Number of Patrol Producers	Percent Using			Number of Patrol Producers	Percent Using		
		None	Some	All		None	Some	All
Municipal police								
No full-time officers	53	93	0	7	54	100	0	0
1 to 4 full-time officers	221	93	1	6	223	99	0	0
5 to 10 full-time officers	215	85	6	9	216	98	2	0
11 to 20 full-time officers	124	79	14	6	124	90	11	0
21 to 50 full-time officers	122	70	26	3	122	73	26	1
51 to 150 full-time officers	78	58	41	1	78	69	31	0
Over 150 full-time officers	45	27	67	7	43	40	60	0
County sheriffs and police								
1 to 4 full-time officers	3	100	0	0	3	100	0	0
5 to 10 full-time officers	5	100	0	0	5	100	0	0
11 to 20 full-time officers	15	60	13	27	16	100	0	0
21 to 50 full-time officers	27	63	19	19	28	100	0	0
51 to 150 full-time officers	27	56	22	22	27	100	0	0
Over 150 full-time officers	17	59	35	6	18	89	11	0
Other local producers								
No full-time officers	4	100	0	0	4	25	75	0
1 to 4 full-time officers	26	96	0	4	27	63	11	26
5 to 10 full-time officers	50	84	12	4	50	54	34	12
11 to 20 full-time officers	26	85	12	4	26	27	69	4
21 to 50 full-time officers	25	72	24	4	25	20	80	0
51 to 150 full-time officers	4	75	25	0	4	0	100	0

Note: Rows may not total 100 percent due to rounding errors.

municipal departments. When we consider the number of citizens that each patrol unit must serve, the larger municipal police departments are more thinly spread than already noted. Not only do they assign fewer officers to on-street patrol duty in relation to the number of citizens they must serve, but in assigning these officers to two-officer patrol units, the citizen-to-patrol unit ratio is further reduced. Given equivalent service demands we would predict longer response times in areas served by the larger municipal departments, a prediction consistent with earlier research findings [7].

Another patrol practice of interest is the staffing of shifts around the clock. Traditionally, departments have relied on three shifts of the same size in order to simplify scheduling of officers' days off and vacations. Recently, some departments have experimented with variations from this level loading of shifts in an attempt to fit the number of officers on duty at any particular time to an estimate of the demand for service on that shift. They use a peak patrol force, an extra shift, or a variable length shift to supplement the normal force on duty during periods of exceptionally high demands for service.

We focused our patrol analysis on two times of day (10 a.m. and 10 p.m.), which usually fall within the day and evening shifts. We gathered information on the number of officers actually on the street at these two times and the patrol arrangements used. We also determined whether there was some other time of day or specific day of the week when the department has a peak patrol force larger than the regular number of officers on duty on the two shifts we analyzed.

About one half the patrol producers assign the same number of officers to the day and evening shifts (Table 5-13). Where there is a different number of officers on duty on each of these two shifts, the evening shift generally has the greater number of officers assigned. County police and sheriffs' departments and military police agencies are the most likely to vary the number of officers on duty across shifts. Often this is done by adding a second officer to patrol units that are one-officer patrols during the day shift. County police and sheriffs' departments and state police agencies are most likely to employ a peak patrol force in addition to regular shifts.

Table 5-14 indicates that variation in shift staffing is related to the size of the producer for both municipal and county producers. Producer size bears little relationship to whether or not a peak patrol force is employed, however.

Table 5–13. Patrol Shift Staffing Among Different Types of Producers

Type of Patrol Producer	Variation in Staffing on Regular Shifts				Use of Peak Force	
	Number of Patrol Producers	Percent With			Number of Patrol Producers	Percent with Peak Force
		Same Day and Evening	More Day Than Evening	More Evening Than Day		
Total	1,219	49	9	42	1,128	39
Municipal police	883	49	7	44	822	38
County sheriffs and police	97	34	16	50	89	46
State police	28	54	7	39	23	52
Campus police	98	53	9	38	91	32
Military police	39	38	20	41	33	21
Federal police	10	60	10	30	10	40
Other police	64	59	19	22	60	32

Note: Rows may not total 100 percent due to rounding errors.

Table 5–14.   Patrol Shift Staffing and Local Producer Size

Type and Size of Patrol Producer	Variation in Staffing on Regular Shifts				Use of Peak Force	
	Number of Patrol Producers	Percent With			Number of Patrol Producers	Percent With Peak Force
		Same Day And Evening	More Day Than Evening	More Evening Than Day		
Municipal police						
No full-time officers	68	41	3	56	64	37
1 to 4 full-time officers	228	64	8	28	204	32
5 to 10 full-time officers	217	56	6	38	200	44
11 to 20 full-time officers	125	48	3	49	121	40
21 to 50 full-time officers	122	47	10	43	117	33
51 to 150 full-time officers	78	18	12	70	73	43
Over 150 full-time officers	45	13	13	73	43	47
County sheriffs and police						
1 to 4 full-time officers	3	67	0	33	1	0
5 to 10 full-time officers	5	40	60	0	5	60
11 to 20 full-time officers	16	56	19	25	14	50
21 to 50 full-time officers	28	32	11	57	25	36
51 to 150 full-time officers	27	30	4	67	26	38
Over 150 full-time officers	18	17	28	56	18	67
Other local producers[a]						
No full-time officers	5	40	20	40	5	20
1 to 4 full-time officers	27	82	4	15	27	26
5 to 10 full-time officers	50	58	12	30	45	33
11 to 20 full-time officers	26	46	12	42	24	21
21 to 50 full-time officers	27	44	7	48	25	40
51 to 150 full-time officers	4	50	0	50	4	0

Note: Rows may not total 100 percent due to rounding errors.
[a]Includes campus and other local special district police.

INDEPENDENCE AND AUTONOMY
IN PATROL SERVICE DELIVERY

A service area is "independent" with respect to patrol service delivery if patrol services in that area are supplied by an agency of the service area's local government. A service area is "autonomous" if the patrol services in that area are supplied exclusively by such an agency. Variations in independence and autonomy of patrol service areas are partially related to variations in the legal authorization for the supply of patrol services in incorporated areas by county police and sheriffs' departments, by state police and highway patrols, or by special district police agencies. Patrol autonomy is reduced by the presence of patrol units from these agencies operating within the service areas of other agencies.

Table 5—15 presents the variations in patrol service independence and patrol service autonomy throughout the country. Almost all SMSAs have an independence score of 100 percent because most service areas use their own producer to meet at least part of their patrol service needs. Contracting for all patrol services with an agency of another governmental unit accounts for cases where a service area is not independent.

There is a much wider range in autonomy scores for the 80 SMSAs. Many service areas receive some patrol service in addition to that supplied by their own producer. (A service area's "own producer" is defined as an agency that is a department of the service area's local government.) As we explain in the following section, this additional patrol service usually involves some alternation in service delivery, either in space, time, or clientele served. Such arrangements are more commonly found in larger SMSAs; consequently, autonomy is often lower in these areas.

ALTERNATION AND DUPLICATION
IN PATROL SERVICE PRODUCTION

Critics of American policing often contend that "duplication" results from the large number of police agencies found in metropolitan areas. To the extent that duplication exists in service delivery, it might result in redundancy (a good characteristic in terms of backup capability) or in inefficiency (a waste of resources). Critics take the latter view. In either case an important question is: Just how much duplication in service delivery actually exists in metropolitan areas?

We find very little duplication in the supply of patrol services in the 80 metropolitan areas we studied. Two or more patrol producers

Table 5–15.   Independence and Autonomy in Patrol Service Delivery: Region and SMSA Population

Location	Number of SMSAs	Percent of SMSA Population (1973 est.) Receiving Patrol Service From Own Producer		Percent of SMSA Population Receiving Patrol Service Exclusively From Own Producer	
		Median	Range[a]	Median	Range
Total	80	100	100 – 100	54	23 – 79
Northeast					
Region 1	8	100	100 – 100	95	51 – 100
Region 2	4	99	87 – 100	25	21 – 40
Region 3	6	96	81 – 100	42	27 – 66
Midwest					
Region 5	16	100	100 – 100	54	14 – 67
Region 7	4	100	98 – 100	13	13 – 23
South					
Region 4	15	100	100 – 100	63	46 – 87
Region 6	14	100	100 – 100	26	12 – 99
West					
Region 8	4	100	99 – 100	56	12 – 100
Region 9	7	100	97 – 100	26	19 – 38
Region 10	2	—	99 – 100	—	17 – 100

Metropolitan Population (1973 est.)					
50,000 to 124,999	20	100	100 – 100	75	62 – 100
125,000 to 249,999	26	100	99 – 100	62	36 – 75
250,000 to 499,999	21	100	99 – 100	23	18 – 42
500,000 and over	13	100	100 – 100	32	25 – 55

[a]Range is the interquartile range except for Region 10, where it is the full range of variation.

rarely supply patrol service to the same population with no attempt to alternate the supply in terms of time, space, or clientele served. In only 16 of the 80 areas do more than 10 percent of the inhabitants receive duplicate patrol service. There are, however, two metropolitan areas where more than half the population receives patrol services regularly from two or more producers without alternation.

When two or more patrol agencies operate in the same geographic area, the agencies usually have a division of labor that eliminates duplication. The most common division we have characterized as "alternation." Alternation occurs in time, in space, or with respect to specific clientele groups. For example, some small municipal police departments patrol the streets of their municipalities from 8 a.m. to midnight. When their officers are off duty, the county sheriff's department patrols those municipalities. This is alternation in time: no duplication is involved.

Alternation in space usually occurs when a special purpose patrol agency operates in the jurisdiction of another agency. Examples include municipal park police (who patrol exclusively in parks), school district or community college police, or special district agencies, such as airport or harbor police. The primary characteristic of alternation in space is the supply of patrol service to a part of another agency's jurisdiction where the part does not have a resident population. Officers from the larger jurisdiction may or may not patrol that part as well. Most often they do not.

An example of alternation in clientele is the relationship between a municipal police department and the military police or shore patrol in a municipality adjoining a large military base. In some cities military police or shore patrol officers patrol along with officers from the municipal police department. Their attention is limited, however, to military personnel. The municipal police deal with civilians and generally leave any problems involving military personnel to the military police or shore patrol. Alternation of this type is found in a number of the 80 metropolitan areas where there are large Army, Air Force, or Navy installations.

Table 5—16 summarizes the alternation and duplication measures for the 80 metropolitan areas. The data shown are relative measures (i.e., the percent of the metropolitan population that receives patrol service through alternation or duplication). In New York and New Jersey (Region 2) both state and county agencies supply patrol service to areas served primarily by municipal agencies. However, most of their patrol service is limited to such special areas as county roads and parks (for the county agencies) or state roads, parks, and rural townships (for both state and county agencies). The extent of duplication is not great. In Iowa and Missouri (Region 7) and California and Arizona (Region 9) the state police or highway patrols alternate with municipal and county agencies. Here, as in New York and New Jersey, there is virtually no strict duplication.

The North Central states from Ohio to Minnesota (Region 5) comprise the only region where duplication is present to any marked extent. This duplication is found mainly in the rural areas of the smaller SMSAs in these states, where state police patrols are present in addition to county sheriffs' departments. Alternation arrangements are more likely to have been worked out to avoid duplication in the larger metropolitan areas [8].

PATROL DIVERSITY: WHAT DOES IT MEAN?

Local police departments provide most of the patrol personnel in metropolitan areas. The largest local agencies provide the majority of these patrol personnel. Almost all SMSAs have more than one patrol producer. While this division of patrol responsibility has been criticized, our findings lead us to suggest that more research needs to be done on this subject.

The kinds of agencies supplying patrol service to a metropolitan area are related to the kinds of public jurisdictions within the SMSA. Municipal police departments are usually most numerous. Easy incorporation and annexation in some states, compared to the difficulties of incorporation and annexation in other states, account for some differences in the number of agencies patrolling SMSAs from region to region.

The existence of special jurisdictions within a metropolitan area is an important source of nonmunicipal police patrol agencies. College and university campuses and U.S. military installations are especially likely to have their own patrol forces. Another factor affecting the number of patrol producers is the size of the metropolitan area. We find, however, that when we control for population, the large metropolitan areas are *not* the most divided among patrol producers. Rather, it is smaller areas that are least "consolidated."

Consolidated patrol arrangements are not necessarily better, however. Our data show that consolidation of small municipal patrol suppliers might in fact have a negative impact on patrol service to residents of the consolidated areas [9]. We find that larger departments do not translate their relative personnel advantage into as high an on-street presence as do the small- and medium-sized agencies. We also find that when staffing of patrol units (i.e., one- or two-officer

Table 5–16.   Alternation and Duplication in Patrol Service Delivery: Region and SMSA Population

Location	Number of SMSAs	Percent of SMSA Population Receiving Patrol Service From Producers That Alternate in Space, Time, or Clientele		Percent of SMSA Population Receiving Patrol Service Regularly From More Than One Producer	
		Median	Range[a]	Median	Range
Total	80	37	2 – 68	0	0 – 8
Northeast					
Region 1	8	0	0 – 46	0	0 – 0
Region 2	4	60	0 – 74	3	0 – 13
Region 3	6	36	24 – 67	0	0 – 1
Midwest					
Region 5	16	24	2 – 51	18	3 – 33
Region 7	4	77	2 – 83	0	0 – 9
South					
Region 4	15	28	13 – 54	0	0 – 2
Region 6	14	34	0 – 88	0	0 – 0
West					
Region 8	4	0	0 – 13	0	0 – 0
Region 9	7	67	61 – 76	0	0 – 0
Region 10	2	—	0 – 37	—	0 – 46

Metropolitan Population (1973 est.)					
50,000 to 124,999	20	4	0 – 23	0	0 – 27
125,000 to 249,999	26	28	0 – 46	0	0 – 13
250,000 to 499,999	21	72	58 – 82	0	0 – 2
500,000 and over	13	60	41 – 75	0	0 – 3

[a] Range is the interquartile range except for Region 10, where it is the full range of variation.

patrols) is taken into account, the larger departments are even more thinly spread. We find that most apparent duplication of patrol service really involves alternate arrangements for providing police service to the particular areas. Rather than duplicating activities, these agencies characteristically supplement each other's service.

Before metropolitan police forces are consolidated or decentralized, we should look much more carefully at how patrol operations are conducted by agencies of different sizes and types. What differences are there in patrol officer activities in large departments contrasted with smaller agencies? Are citizens served by smaller departments more or less likely to cooperate with police? Are citizens aware of which agency is responsible for patrolling? With which agency do they feel more secure? Our preliminary findings suggest that arrangements that divide responsibility for metropolitan area patrol may have a more positive effect on general area police patrol than has often been supposed.

✻ *Chapter 6*

Traffic Control Services

Elaine Sharp

Traffic patrol and accident investigation are supplied by a
variety of producers in U.S. metropolitan areas. Municipal
police departments usually patrol traffic on city streets.
In most cases they investigate serious personal injury accidents
occurring within city limits. County police or sheriffs' departments
typically patrol traffic in unincorporated parts of metropolitan areas.
In some counties, however, all roads in unincorporated areas are
patrolled by state police.

Accident investigation is usually, but not always, the responsibility
of the patrolling agency. In most states a state agency patrols traffic
on major highways and investigates all serious personal injury accidents on such thoroughfares. Many metropolitan areas also contain
one or more special enclaves, such as parks, airports, campuses, and
military bases, where traffic is controlled by officers of the enclave.

Complex organizational arrangements for controlling traffic do
not generally, however, lead to confusion in the delivery of traffic
patrol and accident investigation services. Police agencies in most
metropolitan areas have well-established guidelines limiting each of
their activities. In this chapter we describe the traffic patrol and
accident investigation service delivery systems resulting from these
guidelines.

WHO PRODUCES TRAFFIC
CONTROL SERVICES?

Municipal police departments are the most numerous producers of
traffic patrol and accident investigation services in metropolitan

areas all across the country. They are least numerous in the South-west, the Mountain states, and the Far West (Regions 6, 8, and 9), where they make up only slightly more than half the producers of traffic patrol (Table 6-1). In each of these regions campus police, military base police, park and Indian reservation police, and other special enclave police agencies constitute over one fourth of the metropolitan traffic control producers. In New York, New Jersey, Pennsylvania, and Virginia (Regions 2 and 3) municipal police de-partments account for more than 80 percent of the traffic control producers, and special enclave police are less than 10 percent of the producers.

County police and sheriffs' departments as traffic control pro-ducers are relatively most numerous in the Northwest (Region 10), although our sample of only two SMSAs in that region makes gen-eralization difficult. In both the SMSAs we studied in Region 10, no campus, military, or other special enclave police were involved in traffic control. Greater participation of county agencies in these SMSAs reflects the absence of special district police agencies and also the relatively low number of incorporated municipalities in these metropolitan areas.

County agencies also control traffic in parts of each of the metro-politan areas in the Midwest (Regions 5 and 7). In most other regions county police and sheriffs' departments control traffic in some SMSAs, but not in others. In some states, North Carolina for ex-ample, county sheriffs' departments do not patrol traffic in any of the SMSAs studied. In New England (Region 1) county agencies have no role in traffic patrol or accident investigation.

A single state agency is involved in traffic control in the SMSAs of each state with one exception. In Massachusetts SMSAs the State Police patrol traffic and investigate' accidents on major highways, but the Registry of Motor Vehicles investigates fatalities. So, two state producers control traffic in each of the four Massachusetts SMSAs studied.

Separate Production of Traffic Patrol
and Accident Investigation

More than 90 percent of the 1,264 traffic patrol producers in the 80 SMSAs also investigate serious personal injury traffic accidents. Of the 1,206 producers who investigate serious personal injury acci-dents fewer than 5 percent do not also patrol traffic. So, separate production of each of these traffic control services is infrequent. Most of the agencies that patrol traffic, but do not investigate acci-dents, are usually small, municipal, campus, or special district police.

Table 6-1. Traffic Control Producers: Region and Type of Producer

			Percent of Traffic Control Producers That Are					
Location	Number of SMSAs	Number of Producers	Municipal Police	County Sheriffs and Police	State Police	Campus Police	Military Police	Other Police[a]
Total	80	1,290	71	6	6	8	3	6
Northeast								
Region 1	8	80	75	0	15	10	0	0
Region 2	4	152	86	3	3	3	0	5
Region 3	6	133	84	1	4	4	2	4
Midwest								
Region 5	16	263	74	9	6	6	b	4
Region 7	4	50	68	8	8	4	2	10
South								
Region 4	15	270	70	6	6	11	3	4
Region 6	14	150	59	5	9	12	7	7
West								
Region 8	4	39	54	8	10	8	13	8
Region 9	7	127	58	3	6	9	9	16
Region 10	2	26	73	19	8	0	0	0

Note: Rows may not total 100 percent due to rounding errors.
[a] Includes nonmilitary federal police.
[b] Less than half of one percent.

Investigation of traffic accidents in the areas they patrol is usually conducted by police from a larger, encompassing jurisdiction.

For example, the Blair Township and Greenfield Township Police Departments each patrol traffic in their respective service areas in the Altoona/Pennsylvania SMSA, but they do not investigate serious personal injury traffic accidents. The Pennsylvania State Police investigates accidents in both service areas. Similarly, the campus police at Oral Roberts University in Tulsa patrol traffic on the campus, but the Tulsa Police Department investigates serious personal injury accidents on campus.

The few producers of serious personal injury traffic accident investigation that do not also patrol traffic are mostly municipal police departments or special investigative agencies. The Massachusetts Registry of Motor Vehicles (described above) and the Bureau of Indian Affairs are examples of these special investigative agencies. The BIA investigates serious personal injury accidents on the Isleta Pueblo in the Albuquerque SMSA, but does not patrol traffic there. Traffic patrol on the Pueblo is conducted by tribal police.

Separate production of traffic patrol and accident investigation is uncommon for municipal, military, and state police agencies. Only 3 percent of the municipal police departments patrolling traffic do not also investigate accidents. Less than 2 percent of the municipal departments investigating serious personal injury accidents do not patrol traffic. All but one of the military producers of traffic patrol also investigate serious personal injury traffic accidents, and all military producers of accident investigation also patrol traffic. All state producers of patrol also investigate accidents. Except for the Massachusetts Registry of Motor Vehicles, all state traffic accident investigation agencies also patrol traffic.

County, campus, and special district police are more likely to patrol traffic, but not investigate traffic accidents. About 15 percent of county and campus producers of traffic patrol and about 50 percent of special district police producers of traffic patrol do not investigate serious personal injury traffic accidents.

The Number of Producers in SMSAs

The number of traffic control producers serving metropolitan areas varies widely. Both the Meriden/Connecticut and Midland/Texas SMSAs have only 2 producers of traffic patrol, while the Paterson-Clifton-Passaic/New Jersey SMSA has 90 producers of traffic patrol. The Meriden SMSA is a single city. The Meriden Police Department patrols traffic throughout the city, but the Connecticut State Police patrols the interstate highways. The Midland SMSA consists only of Midland County and includes a single city, Midland. The Midland Police Department patrols traffic within the city limits and also at the municipal airport, which is located in the unincorporated part of the county. The Texas Department of Public Safety patrols traffic in the rest of the county. The DPS also patrols on sections of the interstate highway that are within the Midland city limits.

Two counties are included in the Paterson-Clifton-Passaic metropolitan area. Each county is divided into many cities and townships. In all, 86 municipal agencies produce traffic patrol for the area. There are 73 city police departments and 12 township police departments patrolling traffic in this SMSA. The other municipal traffic patrol agency is the Clifton Fire and Public Safety Department. This agency patrols traffic during evening hours supplementing the traffic patrols of the Clifton Police Department that patrols round the clock.

Four other producers of traffic patrol include one county agency, one state agency, and two police departments associated with interstate authorities. The Bergen County Police Department patrols on county highways throughout Bergen County. The New Jersey State Police patrols traffic on state freeways, interstate highways, and toll roads crossing the metropolitan area. The Port Authority of New York and New Jersey has its own police department for traffic patrol on the approaches to the heavily travelled George Washington Bridge in Fort Lee. The Palisades Interstate Park Commission also has its own police department that patrols traffic in the park and along its parkway system.

Organizational arrangements for traffic accident investigation are similar to those for traffic patrol in each of these metropolitan areas. The single exception is in Clifton, New Jersey, where the Fire and Public Safety Department does not regularly investigate serious personal injury traffic accidents. The Clifton Police Department conducts traffic accident investigations in that city.

Most metropolitan areas have more traffic control producers than Meriden or Midland, but fewer than Paterson-Clifton-Passaic. For the 80 SMSAs studied the median number of producers of traffic patrol is 13. The median number of producers of traffic accident investigation for the 80 SMSAs is 11. That is, half the SMSAs have 13 or fewer producers of traffic patrol and 11 or fewer producers of serious personal injury accident investigation (Table 6–2).

The interquartile ranges are quite similar for the two services. One fourth of the SMSAs have fewer than seven producers of traffic patrol and fewer than six producers of accident investigation. Another fourth of the SMSAs have 20 or more traffic patrol producers and 19 or more accident investigation producers. Regional variation in the

Table 6–2. Multiplicity in Traffic Service Production: Region and SMSA Population

Location	Number of SMSAs	Number of Producers in an SMSA				Number of Producers Per 100,000 SMSA Population (1973 est.)			
		Traffic Patrol		Accident Investigation		Traffic Patrol		Accident Investigation	
		Median	Range[a]	Median	Range	Median	Range	Median	Range
Total	80	13	7 – 20	11	6 – 19	5.5	3.6 – 7.3	5.3	3.3 – 6.8
Northeast									
Region 1	8	6	4 – 9	7	4 – 9	4.2	3.5 – 6.4	4.2	3.5 – 6.4
Region 2	4	18	6 – 38	18	6 – 35	4.6	4.3 – 5.7	4.6	3.9 – 5.7
Region 3	6	13	9 – 32	11	9 – 30	5.5	3.2 – 13.6	5.5	3.2 – 12.8
Midwest									
Region 5	16	13	9 – 19	12	9 – 20	6.4	5.8 – 8.0	6.4	5.6 – 8.0
Region 7	4	7	5 – 17	7	5 – 15	5.8	4.2 – 6.8	5.8	4.2 – 5.8
South									
Region 4	15	17	6 – 21	16	6 – 21	4.3	3.3 – 6.7	4.1	3.3 – 6.5
Region 6	14	8	6 – 13	7	5 – 12	3.3	2.6 – 6.9	3.2	2.6 – 6.8
West									
Region 8	4	6	5 – 13	5	5 – 9	4.6	4.0 – 7.1	4.0	3.2 – 5.9
Region 9	7	18	14 – 21	16	12 – 17	3.8	2.6 – 5.4	2.9	2.4 – 5.3
Region 10	2	—	6 – 20	—	6 – 20	—	4.7 – 10.0	—	4.7 – 10.0

Metropolitan Population (1973 est.)									
50,000 to 124,999	20	5	4 – 7	5	4 – 7	5.8	3.5 – 7.2	5.8	3.5 – 6.9
125,000 to 249,999	26	10	7 – 16	10	7 – 15	6.4	4.6 – 9.5	6.4	4.6 – 8.5
250,000 to 499,999	21	16	10 – 20	16	9 – 18	5.3	3.6 – 6.7	5.1	2.9 – 5.9
500,000 and over	13	29	21 – 38	27	21 – 35	3.6	2.7 – 5.5	3.5	3.2 – 5.2

[a] Range is the interquartile range except for Region 10, where it is the full range of variation.

number of traffic control producers in metropolitan areas is considerable. Most SMSAs in New England, the Southwest, the Midwest, and the Mountain states (Regions 1, 6, 7, and 8) have fewer producers per SMSA than the nationwide median. Over half these SMSAs have eight or fewer traffic control producers. New York and New Jersey, Pennsylvania and Virginia, and California and Arizona (Regions 2, 3, and 9) tend to have more producers per SMSA than other parts of the country.

Much of the variation in number of traffic control producers is due to the difference in size of the resident populations of the various SMSAs. Examining the number of producers per 100,000 residents in each SMSA we see that the median for all 80 metropolitan areas is 5.5 for traffic patrol and 5.3 for accident investigation. The relationship between the size of an SMSA's population and the number of traffic control producers is quite strong. Table 6-2 shows that larger SMSAs generally have more producers of traffic control. The third quartile for the number of producers in SMSAs having fewer than 125,000 residents is seven. That is, 75 percent of the SMSAs of that size have seven or fewer producers. Ten producers is the median number for the next largest group of SMSAs. In each of the size groupings at least 75 percent of the SMSAs have fewer producers than the median for the next category.

At the same time, SMSAs with larger populations tend to have fewer traffic control producers for every 100,000 residents. The median relative number of traffic control producers in the larger SMSAs is smaller than in the SMSAs with fewer residents. So, while there are more producers of traffic control in the larger SMSAs, there are usually fewer producers per 100,000 residents. Relative multiplicity of traffic control producers tends to be greatest in the SMSAs with from 125,000 to 250,000 residents.

USE OF FULL-TIME TRAFFIC OFFICERS

With the exception of state police and highway patrols, use of full-time traffic officers is not common among producers of traffic control services in the 80 metropolitan areas. Nearly three fourths of the state producers assign officers full time to traffic control. In most other agencies the officers assigned to general area patrol also patrol traffic and investigate serious personal injury accidents. Traffic control services are conducted as a part of the patrol officer's regular assignment (Table 6-3).

Municipal police departments and county sheriffs' and police departments are most likely to assign officers to full-time traffic control duties in New York and New Jersey and in California and Arizona (Regions 2 and 9). Even in these states less than one third of the municipal and county producers of traffic control assign officers to traffic control full time. Forty-five percent of the military base police agencies assign personnel to full-time traffic control. Campus police and other special district police rarely have full-time traffic control assignments.

The population size of a metropolitan area has little relationship to the use of full-time traffic control officers. State and county producers are somewhat more likely to use full-time traffic control officers in the larger SMSAs, but no clear pattern is evident for municipal, military, campus, or other traffic control producers (Table 6-3). Rather, it is the size of the local agency that relates to the assignment of full-time officers to traffic duty. This is especially true for municipal police agencies.

Over two thirds of the municipal agencies with more than 50 full-time officers assign some officers to full-time traffic control duties (Table 6-4). And, the larger the department the larger the traffic control contingent is likely to be. County police and sheriffs' departments are less likely to assign officers to full-time traffic control duties, although in general it is the larger departments that are more likely to do so.

Only one county agency with fewer than 50 full-time sworn officers assigns personnel to full-time traffic duties. This is the LaCrosse (Wisconsin) County Traffic Department, an agency organized especially for traffic patrol and accident investigation. Other local agencies seldom assign officers to full-time traffic control duties, regardless of agency size.

Most metropolitan areas have full-time traffic control officers assigned from at least two of the agencies controlling traffic there (Table 6-5). In over 40 percent of the SMSAs the state police or highway patrol assigns the majority of full-time traffic control officers. A single municipal police department assigns the majority of the metropolitan area's full-time traffic control officers in another third of the SMSAs. Seven metropolitan areas have full-time traffic personnel only from the state agency serving them. Twelve have all their full-time traffic personnel located in a single municipal police department. On the other hand, more than one fourth of the 80 SMSAs have no state police officers assigned to full-time traffic duties, and 16 have no municipal police officers assigned to full-time traffic control.

The number of officers assigned to full-time traffic duties in each SMSA varies considerably. Four of the 80 metropolitan areas have

Table 6–3.   Assignment of Full-Time Officers to Traffic Control in Different Types of Agencies: Region and Size of SMSA

Location	Number Reporting	Municipal Police	County Sheriffs and Police	State Police	Campus Police	Military Police	Other Police[a]
				Percent of Producers of Each Type Assigning Officers To Full-Time Traffic Duties			
Total	1,222	17 (875)[b]	12 (68)	73 (84)	9 (91)	45 (38)	5 (66)
Northeast							
Region 1	76	23 (57)	— (0)	67 (12)	0 (7)	— (0)	— (0)
Region 2	151	32 (130)	20 (5)	100 (4)	25 (4)	— (0)	25 (8)
Region 3	127	.6 (109)	0 (1)	83 (6)	0 (5)	100 (2)	0 (4)
Midwest							
Region 5	225	12 (164)	14 (22)	37 (16)	8 (13)	100 (1)	0 (9)
Region 7	42	14 (28)	0 (4)	50 (4)	0 (1)	0 (1)	25 (4)
South							
Region 4	266	16 (187)	12 (17)	87 (15)	10 (30)	38 (8)	0 (9)
Region 6	146	10 (88)	13 (8)	79 (14)	12 (17)	80 (10)	0 (9)
West							
Region 8	38	19 (21)	0 (3)	100 (4)	33 (3)	25 (4)	0 (3)
Region 9	126	29 (72)	25 (4)	100 (7)	0 (11)	17 (12)	0 (20)
Region 10	25	0 (19)	0 (4)	50 (2)	— (0)	— (0)	— (0)

Metropolitan Population (1973 est.)							
50,000 to 124,999	114	26 (62)[b]	9 (11)	57 (21)	10 (10)	40 (5)	0 (5)
125,000 to 249,999	285	14 (205)	5 (20)	71 (28)	14 (21)	75 (4)	0 (7)
250,000 to 499,999	370	15 (260)	14 (14)	82 (22)	10 (29)	37 (19)	8 (26)
500,000 and over	453	18 (348)	17 (23)	85 (13)	3 (31)	50 (10)	4 (28)

[a]Includes nonmilitary federal police.
[b]Number of producers of each type is shown in parentheses.

Table 6–4. Assignment of Full-Time Officers to Traffic Duties: Size and Type of Local Producer

Type and Size of Local Producer	Total	Percent of Producers That Assign to Traffic Control					
		No Full-Time Officers	1–4 Full-Time Officers	5–10 Full-Time Officers	11–20 Full-Time Officers	21–50 Full-Time Officers	51–150 Full-Time Officers
Municipal police							
1 to 4 full-time officers	228	100	0	0			
5 to 10 full-time officers	219	98	2	0			
11 to 20 full-time officers	126	90	9	1	0		
21 to 50 full-time officers	121	68	28	4	0	0	
51 to 150 full-time officers	77	31	18	31	16	4	0
Over 150 full-time officers	47	15	2	11	19	32	21
County sheriffs and police							
1 to 4 full-time officers	6	100	0	0			
5 to 10 full-time officers	8	100	0	0			
11 to 20 full-time officers	20	95	0	0	5		
21 to 50 full-time officers	29	100	0	0	0	0	
51 to 150 full-time officers	27	85	11	4	0	0	0
Over 150 full-time officers	18	83	6	11	0	0	0
Other local producers[a]							
1 to 4 full-time officers	28	100	0	0			
5 to 10 full-time officers	54	100	0	4			
11 to 20 full-time officers	28	93	4	3	0		
21 to 50 full-time officers	36	86	11	0	0	0	
51 to 150 full-time officers	6	83	0	0	0	17	0
Over 150 full-time officers	2	100	0	0	0	0	0

Note: Rows may not total 100 percent due to rounding errors.
[a]Includes campus and other local special district police.

no full-time traffic control officers. Four of the 80 have more than 200 officers assigned full time to traffic. In general, metropolitan areas with larger resident populations have more officers assigned to traffic control full time. The percentage of an SMSA's sworn police personnel assigned to full-time traffic duties also varies widely across SMSAs. Metropolitan areas with more than 500,000 residents have from 2 to 12 percent of their sworn officers assigned full time to traffic control. Half these SMSAs have from 5 to 11 percent of their officers assigned to traffic patrol full time (Table 6–5).

For metropolitan areas with 50,000 to 125,000 residents the range is much broader—from no sworn officers assigned full time to traffic to 22 percent of all sworn officers assigned full time to traffic. Half the SMSAs of this size have from 2 to 11 percent of their officers assigned full time to traffic. Obviously, the size of the SMSA resident population is not the only factor that influences the assignment of officers to full-time traffic duties.

Among the other factors are those associated with region. North Central and Western SMSAs are likely to have more of their sworn officers assigned to traffic full time. Half the metropolitan areas in the Mountain and Far West states (Regions 7, 8, and 9) have more than 10 percent of their sworn personnel assigned full time to traffic. In contrast, half of the SMSAs in Pennsylvania and Virginia and in the Great Lake states (Regions 3 and 5) have fewer than 5 percent of their officers on such assignment (Table 6–5).

SERVICE DELIVERY PATTERNS

Each metropolitan area is divided into traffic control service areas. Meriden/Connecticut is the only 1 of the 80 SMSAs that has a single traffic patrol and accident investigation service area. In general, the number of service areas for traffic patrol is the same as for accident investigation (Table 6–6). The only exceptions are jurisdictions in which local police supply one service, but not the other. For example, in the Grand Rapids SMSA the Lowell Police Department investigates traffic accidents, but does not regularly patrol traffic. The Kent County Sheriff's Department patrols traffic in Lowell as well as in the unincorporated areas of the county. Lowell is, therefore, a service area for traffic accident investigation, but is merged into the Kent County service area for traffic patrol.

Decisions about which services to produce are usually made locally and reflect the resources of the departments involved. The decision of local officials not to purchase expensive speed monitoring equipment, such as that used by the department already patrolling in the

Table 6–5.   Officers Assigned Full-Time to Traffic Control: Region and SMSA Population

Location	Number of SMSAs	Number of Full-Time Sworn Officers Assigned to Traffic		Population per Full-Time Officers Assigned to Traffic		Percent of Full-Time Sworn Officers Assigned to Traffic	
		Median	Range[a]	Median	Range	Median	Range
Total	80	37	12 – 78	5,453[b]	3,733 – 9,314	8	3 – 11
Northeast							
Region 1	8	10	8 – 18	7,086	5,191 – 12,800	5	3 – 8
Region 2	4	61	23 – 99	5,635	3,187 – 6,334	6	4 – 8
Region 3	6	10	9 – 42	23,504	4,532 – 33,896	2	2 – 10
Midwest							
Region 5	16	17	3 – 38	8,184[c]	5,596 – 16,406	4	1 – 10
Region 7	4	23	21 – 54	3,778	2,587 – 5,453	10	9 – 11
South							
Region 4	15	60	33 – 120	4,672	3,733 – 7,507	9	5 – 11
Region 6	14	21	17 – 65	5,171	4,303 – 8,382	7	6 – 11
West							
Region 8	4	37	17 – 37	3,418	3,357 – 4,273	10	8 – 16
Region 9	7	117	103 – 155	2,661	2,246 – 4,199	12	11 – 18
Region 10	2	—	0 – 37	3,456[d]	—	—	0 – 18

Metropolitan Population (1973 est.)							
Total	80	37	12 – 78	5,453[b]	3,733 – 9,314	8	3 – 11
50,000 to 124,999	20	13	3 – 21	5,171[e]	3,778 – 9,314	7	2 – 11
125,000 to 249,999	26	21	10 – 38	6,962[f]	4,273 – 12,800	6	2 – 11
250,000 to 499,999	21	78	54 – 104	4,199	3,250 – 5,453	10	8 – 11
500,000 and over	13	129	83 – 204	5,859	4,672 – 7,507	9	5 – 11

[a] Range is the interquartile range.
[b] No sworn officers were reported as assigned to traffic control in 4 SMSAs, so this column is based on 76 cases.
[c] 13 cases.
[d] 1 case.
[e] 18 cases.
[f] 24 cases.

Table 6–6. Fragmentation in Traffic Service Production: Region and SMSA Population

Location	Number of SMSAs	Number of Service Areas in an SMSA				Number of Service Areas Per 100,000 SMSA Population (1973 est.)			
		Traffic Patrol		Accident Investigation		Traffic Patrol		Accident Investigation	
		Median	Range[a]	Median	Range	Median	Range	Median	Range
Total	80	12	6 – 19	11	6 – 20	5.0	3.3 – 6.4	4.9	3.2 – 6.3
Northeast									
Region 1	8	5	3 – 10	5	3 – 10	3.9	2.5 – 5.9	3.9	2.5 – 5.9
Region 2	4	15	6 – 38	15	6 – 35	4.6	4.3 – 4.8	4.6	3.9 – 4.8
Region 3	6	12	8 – 31	11	8 – 30	5.5	2.7 – 13.2	5.1	2.7 – 12.8
Midwest									
Region 5	16	12	8 – 19	11	8 – 19	6.3	5.0 – 7.6	6.2	4.9 – 7.6
Region 7	4	8	3 – 15	8	3 – 15	4.8	3.5 – 5.1	4.8	3.5 – 5.1
South									
Region 4	15	19	7 – 23	17	6 – 24	4.6	3.2 – 6.4	4.2	2.8 – 6.4
Region 6	14	7	4 – 11	7	4 – 11	3.2	2.3 – 5.7	3.2	2.3 – 5.7
West									
Region 8	4	5	5 – 12	5	5 – 8	4.2	4.0 – 5.9	4.0	2.8 – 5.9
Region 9	7	16	12 – 20	16	12 – 20	2.9	2.4 – 5.7	2.9	2.3 – 5.7
Region 10	2	—	5 – 21	—	5 – 21	—	3.9 – 10.5	—	3.9 – 10.5

Metropolitan Population (1973 est.)									
50,000 to 124,999	20	5	3 – 7	5	3 – 7	5.0	3.3 – 6.3	4.2	3.2 – 6.3
125,000 to 249,999	26	10	7 – 18	10	6 – 15	5.7	4.6 – 10.0	5.7	4.6 – 8.7
250,000 to 499,999	21	15	8 – 16	15	8 – 17	4.8	2.9 – 5.7	4.8	2.8 – 5.7
500,000 and over	13	27	20 – 38	26	21 – 35	3.6	3.0 – 5.0	3.8	3.0 – 5.0

[a] Range is the interquartile range except for Region 10, where it is the full range of variation.

area, was sometimes cited as a reason for not patrolling traffic. Also, local officials cited better officer training in traffic accident investigation by the agency already conducting this service as a reason for not investigating traffic accidents.

A service area can receive traffic patrol or accident investigation services from one or more producers. Many areas have a single producer for each service, but two or more producers are not uncommon, especially for traffic patrol. The several producers do not necessarily patrol traffic on the same thoroughfares in the service area, however. Freeways, parks, airports, and state capitol grounds are not service areas by our definition because they have no resident population. These special types of streets and roads are often patrolled by a different police agency from the one patrolling the surrounding service area's thoroughfares. We discuss these alternative arrangements for traffic control in more detail later in this chapter.

Traffic control producers are often more numerous than traffic control service areas in any given SMSA. About two thirds of the 80 metropolitan areas have more producers of traffic patrol than service areas for traffic patrol. Some metropolitan areas, such as San Antonio and Nashville, have several special district police agencies patrolling traffic, including airport and park police as well as police at commuter colleges and universities. More than half the 80 SMSAs also have more producers of traffic accident investigation than traffic accident investigation service areas.

Conversely, some metropolitan areas have fewer producers of traffic control than traffic control service areas. In Alabama a city police department may control traffic not only in its own municipality, but also in an adjoining "Police Jurisdiction"—an unincorporated area that under state law remits some sales tax revenues to the city. These municipal police departments have two service areas: the city itself and the "Police Jurisdiction" outside city limits. Service areas also may outnumber producers when a service area contracts with another government for traffic control services. In the Reading/Pennsylvania SMSA, for example, four townships have traffic patrol contracts with municipalities in the metropolitan area. The police departments of these municipalities patrol both their own municipal service area and the service area of the contracting township. About one fifth of the metropolitan areas have fewer traffic control producers than they have service areas for traffic control.

Metropolitan areas with more residents are likely to be divided into more service areas. There are, however, usually fewer service areas per 100,000 residents in the larger metropolitan areas. This is not because larger SMSAs do not have small service areas; they often have many more small service areas than smaller SMSAs have. It is because almost all larger metropolitan areas include two or three service areas with quite large populations, such as center cities or unincorporated county areas.

Independence in Traffic Control

Despite contracting and other arrangements for outside suppliers, most traffic control service areas have their own police agencies that patrol traffic and investigate accidents within the service area. Service areas without their own producers are often quite small in population. In more than half the 80 metropolitan areas almost all residents live in service areas with independent traffic control (Table 6−7). Unincorporated county areas, in which a state agency patrols traffic and investigates accidents, are the most common service areas with large populations and without their own traffic control producers. In these areas the county governing authority has no responsibility for setting day-to-day traffic control policy. Independence implies the presence of such responsibility. As with any local governmental authority, however, independence of a service area in traffic control is subject to applicable federal and state laws.

Autonomy in Traffic Control

Autonomy as used here does not imply the absence of state and federal legal constraints. Rather, it refers to the production of all traffic patrol or accident investigation services within a service area by the service area's own police agency. An autonomous service area is one that receives service only from its own police. Many cities receive traffic patrol from their own police department and, thus, are independent traffic patrol service areas; most of these cities also have some thoroughfares patrolled by other police, so they are not autonomous traffic patrol service areas. Only about one third of the traffic patrol service areas in the 80 SMSAs are autonomous (Table 6−8).

Slightly more of the traffic investigation service areas receive accident investigation exclusively from their own police. Autonomy in traffic control is most extensive in the South and Southwest (Regions 4 and 6), in Pennsylvania and Virginia (Region 3), and in California and Arizona (Region 9). Autonomy is least extensive in New York and New Jersey (Region 2). In the Mountain states (Region 8) many service areas that are not autonomous for traffic patrol are autonomous for accident investigation. A state agency patrols traffic in many of these service areas, but does not regularly investigate traffic accidents.

Autonomous traffic control service areas tend to be smaller than other service areas. So, the proportion of an SMSA's population

Table 6–7.   Independence in Traffic Service Production: Region

Location	Number of SMSAs	Percent of Service Areas Receiving Service From Own Producer				Percent of SMSA Population (1973 est.) Receiving Service From Own Producer			
		Traffic Patrol		Accident Investigation		Traffic Patrol		Accident Investigation	
		Median	Range[a]	Median	Range	Median	Range	Median	Range
Total	80	93	83 – 100	93	83 – 100	100	90 – 100	99	85 – 100
Northeast									
Region 1	8	100	96 – 100	100	96 – 100	100	99 – 100	100	99 – 100
Region 2	4	89	83 – 99	89	83 – 99	99	80 – 100	99	80 – 100
Region 3	6	88	80 – 94	91	88 – 93	88	81 – 96	85	77 – 90
Midwest									
Region 5	16	100	92 – 100	100	95 – 100	100	96 – 100	100	99 – 100
Region 7	4	88	83 – 100	100	82 – 100	99	98 – 100	100	98 – 100
South									
Region 4	15	87	76 – 100	87	82 – 100	100	61 – 100	100	62 – 100
Region 6	14	86	71 – 96	83	71 – 92	98	87 – 100	91	86 – 100
West									
Region 8	4	83	80 – 100	80	80 – 88	99	83 – 100	85	83 – 94
Region 9	7	95	88 – 100	88	80 – 94	100	88 – 100	82	63 – 97
Region 10	2	—	80 – 86	—	86 – 100	—	97 – 99	—	99 – 100

[a]Range is the interquartile range except in Region 10, where it is the full range of variation.

Table 6–8. Autonomy in Traffic Service Production: Region

Location	Number of SMSAs	Percent of Service Areas Receiving Service Exclusively From Own Producer				Percent of SMSA Population (1973 est.) Receiving Service Exclusively From Own Producer			
		Traffic Patrol		Accident Investigation		Traffic Patrol		Accident Investigation	
		Median	Range[a]	Median	Range	Median	Range	Median	Range
Total	80	33	17 – 50	38	13 – 59	12	3 – 42	17	3 – 62
Northeast									
Region 1	8	20	0 – 48	0	0 – 0	9	0 – 24	0	0 – 0
Region 2	4	13	0 – 13	13	0 – 13	4	0 – 12	4	0 – 12
Region 3	6	40	37 – 47	40	22 – 64	17	5 – 59	9	5 – 68
Midwest									
Region 5	16	25	14 – 40	25	13 – 40	31	2 – 56	24	0 – 54
Region 7	4	6	0 – 33	18	0 – 50	1	0 – 3	8	0 – 80
South									
Region 4	15	43	33 – 63	50	16 – 67	29	11 – 58	23	6 – 62
Region 6	14	33	27 – 50	50	40 – 75	9	8 – 21	27	12 – 81
West									
Region 8	4	17	14 – 60	71	38 – 80	7	5 – 22	79	8 – 83
Region 9	7	33	20 – 50	38	27 – 65	12	2 – 20	15	3 – 26
Region 10	2	—	0 – 38	—	0 – 43	—	0 – 12	—	0 – 12

[a] Range is the interquartile range except for Region 10, where it is the full range of variation.

residing in autonomous traffic control service areas is usually less than the proportion of the SMSA's service areas that are autonomous. The Great Lakes states (Region 5) and the South (Region 4) have the largest proportion of residents with autonomous provision of both traffic control services.

Alternation, Coordination, and Duplication in Traffic Control

Most service areas are not autonomous in traffic control because they are served by alternate producers. Few service areas have duplicate traffic patrol or accident investigation, however. Some college and university campuses and small towns receive traffic patrol from both their own police and the police from the surrounding city or county with no coordination or alternation, but this arrangement is infrequent. An arrangement by which a service area's own police patrol traffic on some roads while another agency patrols only other thoroughfares is more usual. Interstate highways are common traffic patrol enclaves. Other major highways, parkways and park drives, and airport access roads and parking areas are also often patrolled by special producers.

The several producers of traffic patrol in a service area do not usually coordinate their patrols in the way we have defined coordination in Chapter 3. Instead, a division of responsibility by type of thoroughfare is established. For traffic accident investigation the division of responsibility between agencies is often established by the seriousness of the accident. Property loss limits may determine which agency investigates a particular accident, or fatalities may be investigated by one agency and nonfatal personal injury accidents by another.

Alternation in traffic patrol is most common in the Northeast (Regions 1 and 2) and in California and Arizona (Region 9). Sixty percent or more of the service areas in half these metropolitan areas have alternative traffic patrol producers. In the South and the Mountain states (Regions 4 and 8) half of the metropolitan areas have alternate traffic patrol producers in no more than one third of their service areas. Alternate producers of traffic accident investigation are most common in New England (Region 1) and least common in the Mountain states (Region 8). In general, service areas with alternate producers of traffic control are larger than service areas without alternate producers. So, half the metropolitan areas have more than three fourths of their residents served by alternate traffic patrol agencies. Half the 80 SMSAs have 60 percent or more of their residents served by alternate accident investigation agencies (Table 6-9).

Table 6–9. Alternation in Traffic Service Production: Region

Location	Number of SMSAs	Percent of Service Areas Receiving Service From Producers That Alternate in Space, Time, or Clientele				Percent of SMSA Population (1973 est.) Receiving Service From Producers That Alternate in Space, Time, or Clientele			
		Traffic Patrol		Accident Investigation		Traffic Patrol		Accident Investigation	
		Median	Range[a]	Median	Range	Median	Range	Median	Range
Total	80	47	33 – 67	35	13 – 64	78	35 – 90	60	18 – 87
Northeast									
Region 1	8	67	42 – 80	100	80 – 100	88	69 – 95	100	91 – 100
Region 2	4	61	50 – 67	50	46 – 60	74	56 – 88	74	47 – 88
Region 3	6	40	38 – 53	38	14 – 64	59	32 – 82	35	24 – 81
Midwest									
Region 5	16	42	20 – 75	20	6 – 50	44	20 – 88	48	2 – 75
Region 7	4	47	44 – 67	33	0 – 33	82	82 – 92	2	0 – 84
South									
Region 4	15	33	20 – 45	29	8 – 76	58	14 – 77	31	19 – 83
Region 6	14	43	33 – 70	21	8 – 50	86	74 – 92	72	4 – 86
West									
Region 8	4	20	0 – 67	0	0 – 21	78	0 – 78	0	0 – 15
Region 9	7	60	50 – 63	50	25 – 53	85	80 – 90	65	47 – 79
Region 10	2	—	29 – 100	—	38 – 100	—	41 – 100	—	42 – 100

[a]Range is the interquartile range except for Region 10, where it is the full range of variation.

State producers of traffic control are quite likely to alternate with other producers. About 90 percent of the state producers limit their traffic patrol to major highway systems. Three fourths of the state accident investigation producers alternate investigations with local agencies (Table 6–10). Special district police are also more likely than not to be alternate producers of traffic control. Most of these producers have no service area of their own. Instead, they are responsible for traffic in nonresidential enclaves within surrounding service areas. Parks, airports, state capitol grounds, and nonresidential campuses are examples.

While most county agencies do not alternate traffic control with other agencies in the areas they serve, a substantial minority (about one third) do provide alternate traffic control services to other service areas in their counties. Military and municipal producers, on the other hand, are rarely involved in alternate arrangements outside their own service areas. Some municipal police patrol traffic on city property located outside the municipal boundaries. In a few instances military police patrol traffic off base in areas with high military personnel presence.

TRAFFIC CONTROL DIVERSITY:
WHAT DOES IT MEAN?

Metropolitan areas of the United States have a diversity of arrangements for producing and delivering traffic patrol and accident investigation services. Is the public well or ill served by this diversity? Adequate research is not yet available to support definitive answers. To assess the impact of organizational arrangements for traffic control services on traffic safety we will need comparable data on:

- Traffic incidence and flow patterns
- Street and highway safety design
- Traffic law enforcement practices
- Trial and sentencing practices
- Accident rates

We can offer some preliminary observations, however. Diversity, in and of itself, is neither useful nor harmful. It need not lead to confusion, but it may. Most police chiefs with whom we spoke expressed little concern over the existence of several or many traffic control producers in their metropolitan areas or even over the fact that there were other producers of traffic control serving their own service areas. At the same time, there were some chiefs who were concerned

Table 6-10.   Extent of Alternative Production of Traffic Services: Type of Producer

| Type of Producer | Number Reporting | Percent of Producers Conducting Alternative Services In | | | | | |
		No Service Areas	1 Service Area	2 Service Areas	3-5 Service Areas	6-10 Service Areas	Over 10 Service Areas
		Traffic Patrol					
Municipal	905	93	7	a	a	0	0
County	68	66	10	10	7	3	3
State	80	11	14	10	28	20	18
Campus	98	74	24	3	0	0	0
Military	42	95	5	0	0	0	0
Other[b]	71	23	60	6	10	1	0
		Traffic Investigation					
Municipal	894	91	9	a	0	0	0
County	62	69	11	6	8	2	3
State	82	24	18	10	18	17	12
Campus	81	79	20	1	0	0	0
Military	41	95	2	2	0	0	0
Other[b]	46	37	41	7	13	2	0

Note: Rows may not total 100 percent due to rounding errors.
[a] Less than half of one percent.
[b] Includes nonmilitary federal police.

about ambiguities in the division of traffic control responsibilities between their own departments and others operating in the same area. Clearly, some localities have not developed smooth working relationships that are understood and accepted by all the agencies affected. These localities are rare, however.

Some suggest that limited access highway traffic, park traffic, residential suburb traffic, and campus traffic necessitate special police departments because of the special traffic control problems involved. Others maintain that the needs for uniform law enforcement and clearcut authority and responsibility necessitate having a few easily identifiable police agencies responsible for traffic control.

Whether a particular metropolitan area needs more or less diversity in arrangements for traffic control is a question that can be answered only by thoughtful study of the conditions in that area. Consideration of traffic control operations throughout the metropolitan area would be important. Are the special requirements of different types of traffic areas being dealt with adequately, or are operations in all types of areas subject to the same routine? Are some areas receiving lax traffic law enforcement or accident investigation services? Is there confusion over traffic control responsibilities? Is there a lack of local involvement in formulating traffic control policy?

The problems of one area may not be those of another. Consequently, a system of traffic control agencies that is appropriate to one area may be quite inappropriate in another. An examination of the operation of a specific metropolitan traffic control delivery system is necessary to determine whether more or less organizational diversity would be beneficial for any particular area.

※ *Chapter 7*

Criminal Investigation

Criminal investigation is the collecting of information and evidence for identifying, apprehending, and convicting suspected offenders. Although investigating offenses against the general criminal code is a basic responsibility of many police agencies, not all police departments do so. Some police control traffic or patrol, but do no criminal investigation. These producers refer reported crimes to others for investigation. Nor do all criminal investigation producers deal with the same types of crime. Some investigate only major crimes, such as homicide, armed robbery, and rape. Others investigate only less serious crimes, like residential burglary, shoplifting, or purse snatching. But police producers that regularly investigate all types of reported offenses against the general criminal code are more common.

In this chapter we examine only departments investigating offenses against the general criminal code of the jurisdictions in which they operate. We do not discuss special agencies established to investigate violations of particular statutes, such as alcoholic beverage control laws, fish and game laws, or commercial and banking codes. Our focus is on police producers in each metropolitan area who investigate homicides and residential burglaries.

Investigation of these two crimes usually involves different levels of activity. Residential burglary investigation commonly entails interviewing the victim to obtain a list of the stolen goods and perhaps the time, means of forced entry, and other details concerning the incident. Unless a witness identifies a suspect or unless someone is found in possession of the stolen goods, further investigation is not usually pursued. Homicide investigation, on the other hand, often

131

entails extensive collection of physical evidence and interviewing of potential witnesses. These activities may be quite time consuming.

Differences between investigative activity associated with each of these crimes can be seen in the duration of active investigation of cases by the Kansas City, Missouri, Police Department, which keeps detailed records of its investigators' use of time. Homicide investigations averaged 144.6 detective hours of investigation per case during the period May–November 1973. Residential burglary cases averaged only 6.8 detective hours of investigation per case for that same period. Almost two thirds of the residential burglary investigations were suspended after a single day of investigation [1].

This chapter does not describe the criminal investigative activities of police producers in the 80 metropolitan areas. Rather, our concern is with the ways in which police are organized to undertake these activities. Notable differences exist between organization for homicide investigation and organization for residential burglary investigation. In some metropolitan areas there are police agencies that investigate homicides, but not burglaries. These producers are usually criminal investigation specialists and work primarily on major crimes. Their efforts are directed toward crimes that both police and citizens generally regard as most injurious. Other producers are responsible for burglary investigation in their jurisdictions.

In some metropolitan areas there are also police agencies that investigate residential burglaries, but not homicides. These departments rarely specialize in investigation, but commonly provide other police services—general area patrol and traffic control, for example—to the communities they serve. Generally, they are small departments whose officers are assigned a wide range of duties. For the investigation of major crimes their citizens rely upon other, more specialized agencies.

Another difference between organization for homicide investigation and organization for residential burglary investigation involves the kind of officers assigned to investigations. Investigative specialists are more likely to be assigned to homicide than to burglary investigation. Yet another difference is the extent of coordination of investigations. There is more coordination among producers of homicide investigation. Many departments that investigate burglary and homicide regularly coordinate their homicide investigations with other producers, while they rarely coordinate burglary investigations.

WHO INVESTIGATES RESIDENTIAL BURGLARY AND HOMICIDE?

Investigations of residential burglary are conducted by 1,104 producers in the 80 metropolitan areas. Homicide investigations are conducted by 940 producers. More than 200 of the producers of burglary investigation do not investigate homicides, but only 43 of the homicide investigation producers do not investigate burglaries. Most producers of criminal investigation investigate both kinds of crime.

Producers Conducting Both Burglary and Homicide Investigation

Many sizes and types of producers investigate both homicide and residential burglary. Most of these producers are not special investigations agencies. Instead, they are responsible for other services like general area patrol and traffic control. Federal agencies that investigate crimes on military reservations are important exceptions. The Army Criminal Investigations Division, the Air Force Office of Special Investigations, and the Naval Investigative Services Office investigate crimes committed on installations of their respective branches of the service. The Federal Bureau of Investigation becomes involved in these investigations if civilian offenders are suspected. These four agencies specialize in criminal investigation.

More often, producers investigating both residential burglary and homicide also control traffic and patrol. These producers include county police and sheriffs' departments, campus police, police of other special districts, and, most commonly, municipal police departments. Municipal police departments account for about three fourths of the producers conducting both residential burglary investigation and homicide investigation (Table 7–1).

In the Northeast (Regions 1, 2, and 3) 9 of every 10 producers of both types of investigation are municipal police departments. In the Southwest (Region 6) and Rocky Mountain states (Region 8) only about half the producers investigating both kinds of crime are municipal police. Military and federal law enforcement agencies are especially numerous producers of both types of investigation in these regions. Metropolitan areas in these regions have fewer municipalities than the SMSAs in other parts of the country.

County producers investigate both residential burglary and homicide in all parts of the country except New England (Region 1). They are much less numerous than municipal police departments, however. Throughout the Midwest (Regions 5 and 7), South and Southwest (Regions 4 and 6), Rocky Mountain states (Region 8), and Northwest (Region 10) they account for about 15 percent of the producers of both types of investigation. Campus and other types of special district police also report investigating both homicides and residential burglaries. Special districts with their own police investi-

Table 7–1.   Producers of Both Burglary and Homicide Investigation: Region and Type of Producer

Location	Number Reporting	Percent of Producers That Are						
		Municipal Police	County Sheriffs and Police	State Police	Campus Police	Military Police	Federal Police	Other Police
Total	897	74	11	2	5	4	3	1
Northeast								
Region 1	62	92	0	5	3	0	0	0
Region 2	128	91	4	2	2	0	0	1
Region 3	103	87	2	4	4	2	1	0
Midwest								
Region 5	170	75	14	3	7	1	1	1
Region 7	26	65	15	8	4	4	0	4
South								
Region 4	149	67	17	1	6	5	4	0
Region 6	107	52	17	2	11	8	7	3
West								
Region 8	26	46	15	0	8	15	12	4
Region 9	102	68	8	0	4	11	7	3
Region 10	24	75	21	4	0	0	0	0

Note: Rows may not total 100 percent due to rounding errors.

gating both types of crime include housing authorities, hospitals, parks, and Indian reservations.

The Tuscaloosa/Alabama SMSA is the only 1 of the 80 metropolitan areas without any producers conducting both burglary and homicide investigation. There, a special interagency homicide unit conducts all homicide investigations while residential burglaries are investigated by county, municipal, and campus police.

Producers of Burglary, but Not Homicide, Investigation

Most producers of burglary investigation, but not homicide investigation, also patrol and control traffic. They are usually, but not always, small agencies. About two thirds of these producers are municipal police departments (Table 7−2). In the South, the Midwest, and the Rocky Mountain states (Regions 4, 5, 7, and 8) more than one fourth of the municipal police departments that do any investigative work conduct burglary, but not homicide, investigations. In most instances the county police or sheriff's department conducts homicide investigations in these municipalities. Many campus police departments also investigate burglary, but not homicide. The county or municipal agency serving the jurisdiction in which the campus is located conducts homicide investigations. Campus police departments account for about 16 percent of the producers of burglary investigation that do not conduct homicide investigations.

Military police agencies account for another 14 percent. These are the base law enforcement agencies: Army Military Police, Naval Base Police, and Air Force Base Security. Homicides (as well as burglaries involving losses of more than $250) are investigated by the investigations division of the respective branch of the military.

Many of the other types of police producers investigating burglaries do not investigate homicides. Tribal police investigate only burglaries on some Indian reservations. Homicides there are investigated by the Bureau of Indian Affairs. Some park and hospital police investigate burglaries, but not homicides. State, county, or municipal police serving the area investigate homicides in these parks and hospitals.

Producers investigating burglary, but not homicide, are found in 62 of the 80 SMSAs. These producers are most numerous in the South and the Great Lakes states (Regions 4 and 5), although each of these regions has a few metropolitan areas with no such producer. Each of the metropolitan areas in New York and New Jersey, Virginia and Pennsylvania, and California and Arizona (Regions 2, 3, and 9) has at least one such producer. Only half the metropolitan areas in

Table 7–2.   Producers of Burglary, but Not Homicide, Investigation: Region and Type of Producer

Location	Number Reporting	Percent of Producers That Are						
		Municipal Police	County Sheriffs and Police	State Police	Campus Police	Military Police	Federal Police	Other Police
Total	207	64	1	0	16	14	0	7
Northeast								
Region 1	8	25	0	0	75	0	0	0
Region 2	12	75	0	0	17	0	0	8
Region 3	17	53	0	0	12	18	0	18
Midwest								
Region 5	48	88	0	0	6	2	0	4
Region 7	10	100	0	0	0	0	0	0
South								
Region 4	69	62	1	0	23	10	0	3
Region 6	15	60	0	0	13	27	0	0
West								
Region 8	7	71	0	0	0	29	0	0
Region 9	20	10	0	0	5	55	0	30
Region 10	1	100	0	0	0	0	0	0

Note: Rows may not total 100 percent due to rounding errors.

New England, the Southwest, and the Northwest (Regions 1, 6, and 10) have producers of burglary, but not homicide, investigation. Producers in these regions are more likely to conduct both types of investigation.

Producers of Homicide,
but Not Burglary, Investigation

Special agencies for homicide investigation are federal, state, county, or cooperative agencies (Table 7–3). State detective bureaus have been established to investigate homicides in Massachusetts and New Mexico. In several other states state police regularly investigate homicides in some metropolitan areas where local investigative resources need to be supplemented. County prosecutor's detectives investigate all homicides and other major crimes in the California and New Jersey SMSAs we studied.

Special major case units have been established as cooperative ventures by local police in 2 of the 80 SMSAs. The Tuscaloosa County, Alabama, Homicide Unit operates as an independent, full-time investigative agency under the general supervision of the county sheriff and the chiefs of police of the cooperating departments. The cooperating departments contribute personnel, and the agency investigates homicides, rapes, and other major crimes occurring in the county [2]. A similar producer is the Major Case Squad in the Springfield, Missouri, metropolitan area, although this squad does not assume responsibility for investigation of all homicides throughout its metropolitan area as does the Tuscaloosa unit. Both squads differ from the ad hoc investigative units found in several metropolitan areas (Des Moines, for example) in that they have regularly assigned staff and operate as permanent agencies [3].

Producers of homicide, but not burglary, investigation are not found in all metropolitan areas. Fewer than half of the 80 metropolitan areas have such producers. State agencies account for nearly two thirds of the producers of this type, while county agencies constitute over a fourth of such producers. Most special homicide investigations reflect state policy requiring investigation of homicides by state or county agencies or by state investigative agencies helping localities that lack homicide investigative specialists.

The Number of Producers in SMSAs

Investigative services are usually divided among several different producers in a metropolitan area. Of the 80 SMSAs studied, only the Meriden/Connecticut metropolitan area has a single regular producer of burglary investigation for the entire SMSA. At the other

Table 7–3. Producers of Homicide, but Not Burglary, Investigation: Region and Type of Producer

Location	Number Reporting	Percent of Producers That Are						
		Municipal Police	County Sheriffs and Police	State Police	Campus Police	Military Police	Federal Police	Other Police
Total	43	0	27	65	0	0	2	7
Northeast								
Region 1	5	0	0	100	0	0	0	0
Region 2	5	0	80	0	0	0	0	20
Region 3	1	0	0	100	0	0	0	0
Midwest								
Region 5	8	0	0	100	0	0	0	0
Region 7	4	0	0	50	0	0	25	25
South								
Region 4	7	0	14	71	0	0	0	14
Region 6	6	0	17	83	0	0	0	0
West								
Region 8	1	0	0	100	0	0	0	0
Region 9	5	0	80	20	0	0	0	0
Region 10	1	0	100	0	0	0	0	0

Note: Rows may not total 100 percent due to rounding errors.

extreme, the Paterson-Clifton-Passaic/New Jersey SMSA has a total of 86 regular producers of burglary investigation. Both the Meriden and Tuscaloosa/Alabama metropolitan areas have single producers of homicide investigation. The Paterson-Clifton-Passaic SMSA has 88 producers of homicide investigation.

In Meriden the city police department is the only agency regularly investigating residential burglaries and homicides. The Connecticut State Police provide investigatory assistance when requested. The Tuscaloosa Homicide Unit investigates homicides throughout Tuscaloosa County. Residential burglaries in that metropolitan area are investigated by two municipal police departments, one campus police department, and one county sheriff's department. The 86 burglary investigation producers in the Paterson area include 73 municipal police departments, 12 township police departments, and 1 county police department. The 88 producers of homicide investigation in that SMSA include the 86 producers of burglary investigation plus county prosecutor's detectives in each of the two counties in the metropolitan area.

Half the 80 metropolitan areas have 10 or fewer producers of burglary investigation and 8 or fewer producers of homicide investigation (Table 7−4). New York and New Jersey, the South, and California and Arizona (Regions 2, 4, and 9) have more SMSAs with higher numbers of producers than other regions. This is mainly due to the large populations of many of the metropolitan areas in these regions. In general, SMSAs with larger populations have more producers of both burglary and homicide investigation, but larger metropolitan areas also tend to have fewer producers of criminal investigation per 100,000 residents. In terms of producers per 100,000 residents the Midwest and part of the Northeast (Regions 3, 5, and 7) tend to have SMSAs with more producers of burglary investigation. Regions 3, 5, and 8 tend to have SMSAs with more producers of homicide investigation per 100,000 residents.

USE OF INVESTIGATIVE SPECIALISTS AND GENERALISTS

One important choice law enforcement administrators face is whether or not to use specialized criminal investigations personnel. The National Advisory Commission on Criminal Justice Standards and Goals, for instance, has recommended that agencies with fewer than 75 employees assign officers to criminal investigation full time only ". . . where specific needs are present" [4]. The Commission seems to presume that nonspecialists are generally adequate, but no specific

Table 7–4. Multiplicity in Criminal Investigation: Region and SMSA Population

| Location | Number of SMSAs | Number of Producers in an SMSA | | | | Number of Producers Per 100,000 SMSA Population (1973 est.) | | | |
| | | Burglary Investigation | | Homicide Investigation | | Burglary Investigation | | Homicide Investigation | |
		Median	Range[a]	Median	Range	Median	Range	Median	Range
Total	80	10	6 – 17	8	5 – 13	4.9	3.6 – 6.4	4.1	2.9 – 5.6
Northeast									
Region 1	8	6	3 – 9	6	3 – 9	3.9	2.5 – 6.3	3.9	2.5 – 6.3
Region 2	4	16	6 – 31	13	5 – 26	4.9	3.5 – 5.3	4.1	3.0 – 4.3
Region 3	6	12	11 – 27	7	7 – 26	5.7	3.7 – 11.5	4.9	2.8 – 11.1
Midwest									
Region 5	16	11	7 – 15	8	5 – 11	5.6	4.7 – 8.0	4.6	3.7 – 5.1
Region 7	4	8	5 – 9	6	5 – 6	5.2	4.9 – 5.5	3.9	3.7 – 4.5
South									
Region 4	15	15	7 – 21	10	5 – 15	4.5	3.6 – 5.7	3.7	2.5 – 4.0
Region 6	14	6	4 – 10	6	5 – 9	3.5	2.5 – 5.9	3.2	2.4 – 5.9
West									
Region 8	4	7	4 – 8	7	4 – 7	4.9	3.4 – 5.9	4.9	3.0 – 5.9
Region 9	7	17	13 – 19	16	11 – 17	3.8	2.9 – 6.8	3.4	2.3 – 6.0
Region 10	2	—	5 – 20	—	5 – 20	—	4.5 – 10.7	—	4.5 – 10.7

Metropolitan Population (1973 est.)									
Under 125,000	20	4	4 – 7	4	3 – 5	4.9	3.7 – 6.0	4.6	3.4 – 5.6
125,000 to 249,999	26	10	6 – 14	8	6 – 11	5.9	4.3 – 8.0	4.5	3.8 – 6.5
250,000 to 499,999	21	15	10 – 17	12	8 – 13	5.2	3.4 – 5.8	4.0	2.8 – 4.9
500,000 and over	13	28	21 – 32	22	17 – 28	3.6	2.9 – 4.7	3.0	2.5 – 4.0

[a] Range is the interquartile range except for Region 10, where it is the full range of variation.

guidelines are presented for determining when investigative specialists are desirable.

A recent study of criminal investigation operations in 150 of the nation's largest police departments also concluded that "... a significant reduction in follow-up investigative efforts would be appropriate for all but the most serious offenses in which public confidence demands some type of response" [5]. That same study suggests that generalist investigators, rather than investigative specialists, are suitable for assignment to all but the most serious cases. The seriousness of the offense being investigated, rather than size of the department, is suggested as a guideline.

We do not have data with which to compare the effectiveness of generalist and specialist investigators. Greenwood, Petersilla, and colleagues have recently addressed themselves to this question, and further work along the lines they suggest will help individual departments decide what type of personnel arrangements to adopt [6]. We present here data on the extent to which detectives and patrol officers and their supervisors are used by departments of all types and sizes in the investigation of residential burglary and homicide in medium-sized metropolitan areas.

More than 80 percent of the producers of burglary, but not homicide, investigation in the 80 SMSAs assign police generalists to investigate residential burglary. Of these generalists three fourths are patrol officers and one fourth are supervisory personnel who also have noninvestigative police duties. Detectives are assigned by about 20 percent of the producers of burglary, but not homicide, investigation. Only in the Rocky Mountain states and California and Arizona (Regions 8 and 9) is the use of detectives markedly more extensive among this group of criminal investigation producers. In these regions more than two fifths of the producers of burglary, but not homicide, investigation assign detectives to investigate residential burglaries (Table 7-5).

The use of detectives in residential burglary investigation is much more extensive among agencies investigating both burglary and homicide. Over half these producers assign only detectives to residential burglary investigation, and another 8 percent assign either detectives or patrol officers. Still, patrol officers are used exclusively by almost one third of the producers.

Producers of burglary and homicide investigation are somewhat more likely to assign detectives to homicide investigation than to burglary investigation. More than 60 percent of these producers in the 80 SMSAs assign only detectives to homicide investigation and another 4 percent assign both patrol officers and detectives. Use of detectives is especially pronounced in New York and New Jersey, the South, the Rocky Mountain states, and California and Arizona (Regions 2, 4, 8, and 9).

Almost all the producers of homicide, but not burglary, investigation assign only detectives. The exceptions are state highway patrols that do not have detectives and assign patrol officers to homicide investigation in the metropolitan areas where they conduct this service. In general, state agencies, other than state highway patrols, tend to assign detectives to homicide investigation as do county and special interagency investigative units. Not surprisingly, smaller local police producers are more likely to assign patrol officers. (Local police producers include municipal police, county law enforcement departments, campus police, and other special district police, such as housing authority, Indian reservation, or park police.)

Detectives are used most commonly by the larger departments. But, use of detectives is not confined to departments having more than 75 employees, as suggested by the Advisory Commission on Criminal Justice Standards and Goals. Ninety-six percent of all municipal police departments having 21 or more sworn officers assign only detectives to burglary and homicide investigation. The percentages are quite similar for county departments. Other local producers are somewhat less likely to use detectives, but more than half those having over 20 full-time sworn officers do so (Table 7-6).

Because of the differences in population size of metropolitan areas, wide variation exists in the number of sworn officers assigned full time to criminal investigation per SMSA. The median number of full-time detectives in an SMSA ranges from 23 to 120 across the 10 regions (Table 7-7). The national median is 43. Even controlling for population size, there is considerable difference in the number of investigative personnel, however. Regional medians range from 2,716 residents per detective to 5,080 residents per detective. The national median is 4,301. Less variation exists in the percentage of each metropolitan area's sworn police officers who are criminal investigation specialists. Regional medians for this figure range from 10 to 12 percent with a national median of 12.

SERVICE DELIVERY PATTERNS

Most metropolitan areas are divided into many distinct territorial units, each with its own arrangements for burglary and homicide investigation. Most metropolitan areas have more burglary investigation

Table 7–5. Use of Full-Time Investigators: Region and Crime Investigated

| Region and Crime Investigated | Number Reporting | Personnel Assignments in Producers of Burglary Investigation | | | |
| | | Percent Assigning | | | |
		Patrol Officers	Detectives	Both Patrol Officers and Detectives	Supervisory Personnel
Total					
Burglary, not homicide	182	62	18	1	20
Burglary and homicide	839	30	53	8	10
Homicide, not burglary	—	—	—	—	—
Northeast					
Region 1					
Burglary, not homicide	7	71	14	14	0
Burglary and homicide	60	47	40	10	3
Homicide, not burglary	—	—	—	—	—
Region 2					
Burglary, not homicide	10	70	0	0	30
Burglary and homicide	128	13	73	9	6
Homicide, not burglary	—	—	—	—	—
Region 3					
Burglary, not homicide	12	17	8	0	75
Burglary and homicide	100	24	20	5	51
Homicide, not burglary	—	—	—	—	—

Table 7–5. continued

Region and Crime Investigated	Number Reporting	Personnel Assignments in Producers of Burglary Investigation — Percent Assigning			
		Patrol Officers	Detectives	Both Patrol Officers and Detectives	Supervisory Personnel
Midwest					
Region 5					
Burglary, not homicide	41	76	5	0	20
Burglary and homicide	158	42	44	13	1
Homicide, not burglary	—	—	—	—	—
Region 7					
Burglary, not homicide	9	100	0	0	0
Burglary and homicide	23	30	52	17	0
Homicide, not burglary	—	—	—	—	—
South					
Region 4					
Burglary, not homicide	65	60	22	0	19
Burglary and homicide	141	26	67	4	4
Homicide, not burglary	—	—	—	—	—
Region 6					
Burglary, not homicide	13	69	23	0	8
Burglary and homicide	94	29	65	0	6
Homicide, not burglary	—	—	—	—	—

(Table 7-5. continued overleaf)

Table 7-5. continued

| Region and Crime Investigated | Number Reporting | Personnel Assignments in Producers of Burglary Investigation | | | |
| | | Percent Assigning | | | |
		Patrol Officers	Detectives	Both Patrol Officers and Detectives	Supervisory Personnel
West					
Region 8					
Burglary, not homicide	5	20	40	0	40
Burglary and homicide	21	19	76	0	5
Homicide, not burglary	—	—	—	—	—
Region 9					
Burglary, not homicide	19	42	47	5	5
Burglary and homicide	90	29	57	12	2
Homicide, not burglary	—	—	—	—	—
Region 10					
Burglary, not homicide	1	100	0	0	0
Burglary and homicide	24	50	29	8	13
Homicide, not burglary	—	—	—	—	—

Table 7–5. continued

Region and Crime Investigated	Number Reporting	Personnel Assignments in Producers of Homicide Investigation			
		Percent Assigning			
		Patrol Officers	Detectives	Both Patrol Officers and Detectives	Supervisory Personnel
Total					
Burglary, not homicide	—	—	—	—	—
Burglary and homicide	803	22	61	4	14
Homicide, not burglary	34	9	91	0	0
Northeast					
Region 1					
Burglary, not homicide	—	—	—	—	—
Burglary and homicide	58	35	47	5	14
Homicide, not burglary	5	0	100	0	0
Region 2					
Burglary, not homicide	—	—	—	—	—
Burglary and homicide	120	13	80	1	6
Homicide, not burglary	5	0	100	0	0
Region 3					
Burglary, not homicide	—	—	—	—	—
Burglary and homicide	92	10	22	4	64
Homicide, not burglary	0	0	0	0	0

(Table 7-5. continued overleaf)

Table 7–5. continued

Region and Crime Investigated	Number Reporting	Personnel Assignments in Producers of Homicide Investigation — Percent Assigning			
		Patrol Officers	Detectives	Both Patrol Officers and Detectives	Supervisory Personnel
Midwest					
Region 5					
Burglary, not homicide	—	—	—	—	—
Burglary and homicide	153	31	54	9	7
Homicide, not burglary	8	25	75	0	0
Region 7					
Burglary, not homicide	—	—	—	—	—
Burglary and homicide	24	29	63	8	0
Homicide, not burglary	2	50	50	0	0
South					
Region 4					
Burglary, not homicide	—	—	—	—	—
Burglary and homicide	136	21	74	2	4
Homicide, not burglary	6	0	100	0	0
Region 6					
Burglary, not homicide	—	—	—	—	—
Burglary and homicide	95	28	65	1	5
Homicide, not burglary	5	0	100	0	0

Table 7–5. continued

| | | Personnel Assignments in Producers of Homicide Investigation | | | |
| | | Percent Assigning | | | |
Region and Crime Investigated	Number Reporting	Patrol Officers	Detectives	Both Patrol Officers and Detectives	Supervisory Personnel
West					
Region 8					
Burglary, not homicide	—	—	—	—	—
Burglary and homicide	20	15	80	0	5
Homicide, not burglary	1	0	100	0	0
Region 9					
Burglary, not homicide	—	—	—	—	—
Burglary and homicide	84	11	73	4	13
Homicide, not burglary	2	0	100	0	0
Region 10					
Burglary, not homicide	—	—	—	—	—
Burglary and homicide	21	33	48	0	19
Homicide, not burglary	0	0	0	0	0

Note: Rows may not total 100 percent due to rounding errors.

Table 7–6.   Use of Investigative Specialists by Local Police Producers: Type and Size of Producer

Type and Size of Producer	Number Reporting	Percent of Producers Assigning			
		Patrol Officers	Detectives	Both Patrol Officers and Detectives	Supervisory Personnel
Municipal police					
No full-time officers	39	51	5	0	44
1 to 4 full-time officers	166	52	2	2	43
5 to 10 full-time officers	197	50	21	7	22
11 to 20 full-time officers	122	18	67	6	9
21 to 50 full-time officers	121	3	96	2	0
51 to 150 full-time officers	79	0	98	2	0
Over 150 full-time officers	48	0	98	2	0
County sheriffs and police					
1 to 4 full-time officers	3	67	33	0	0
5 to 10 full-time officers	7	14	57	0	29
11 to 20 full-time officers	15	20	73	0	7
21 to 50 full-time officers	30	10	90	0	0
51 to 150 full-time officers	27	0	100	0	0
Over 150 full-time officers	18	6	94	0	0
Other local producers					
No full-time officers	1	0	0	0	100
1 to 4 full-time officers	5	60	0	0	40
5 to 10 full-time officers	31	74	16	3	6
11 to 20 full-time officers	19	58	32	0	11
21 to 50 full-time officers	22	41	54	0	5
51 to 150 full-time officers	3	0	100	0	0

Note: Rows may not total 100 percent due to rounding errors.

service areas than homicide investigation service areas. This is because small municipalities, college and university campuses, and other special police districts are more likely to provide for their own investigation of burglaries than they are to provide for their own homicide investigation.

In these areas homicide investigation is supplied by the producers responsible for homicide investigation in a larger, encompassing district—the county in which the village is located or the city in which the campus is located. Table 7—8 presents the regional distribution of service areas per SMSA for burglary and homicide investigation. Fragmentation of metropolitan areas is greatest (in terms of service areas per 100,000 residents) in Pennsylvania and Virginia and the Great Lakes states (Regions 3 and 5) for burglary investigation and in Pennsylvania and Virginia (Region 3) for homicide investigation.

Independence and Autonomy in Criminal Investigation

In more than half the 80 metropolitan areas each of the burglary investigation service areas has its "own" producer of burglary investigation—a unit established under the authority of the service area's local governing authority (Table 7—9). Such independence of burglary investigation is least extensive in those parts of the country where federal and state agencies have sole investigative responsibility in parts of SMSAs and where contracting for investigative services from other municipalities occurs. Independence of investigative service does not mean that local jurisdictions function independently of federal and state laws. We use the term to indicate that the service area's governing authority has its own law enforcement producer for investigation.

Fewer service areas have their own homicide investigation producers than have their own burglary investigation producers. The national median for independence in homicide investigation is 88 percent. Because most of the homicide investigation service areas that are not independent are quite small, the percentage of metropolitan population served by own homicide investigation producers is close to that served by own burglary investigation units in most cases. Many service areas where investigation is conducted by the area's own producer are also served by one or more other producers of investigation.

Most SMSAs have some autonomous service areas for either burglary or homicide investigation; that is, service areas with regular and exclusive reliance on their own investigative producers. But in few SMSAs are all of the service areas autonomous. Larger service areas

Table 7–7. Assignment of Sworn Officers to Criminal Investigation: Region and SMSA Population

Location	Number of SMSAs	Number of Sworn Officers in Criminal Investigation		Population (1973 est.) per Sworn Officer in Criminal Investigation		Percent of Sworn Officers Assigned to Criminal Investigation	
		Median	*Range*[a]	*Median*	*Range*	*Median*	*Range*
Total	80	43	27 – 100	4,301	3,456 – 5,477	12	10 – 13
Northeast							
Region 1	8	30	14 – 53	4,049	3,798 – 4,835	11	8 – 13
Region 2	4	120	33 – 195	2,716	2,629 – 3,928	11	11 – 12
Region 3	6	42	36 – 43	4,699	4,426 – 6,529	10	10 – 15
Midwest							
Region 5	16	29	22 – 50	5,080	4,301 – 5,934	12	11 – 13
Region 7	4	29	24 – 38	4,358	3,621 – 4,749	12	11 – 12
South							
Region 4	15	91	41 – 167	4,122	2,592 – 5,477	12	9 – 14
Region 6	14	31	25 – 114	3,558	3,002 – 4,894	12	10 – 14
West							
Region 8	4	23	13 – 43	3,460	2,888 – 6,501	11	8 – 12
Region 9	7	89	64 – 295	3,921	3,718 – 4,199	11	8 – 12
Region 10	2	—	33 – 37	—	3,456 – 6,046	—	10 – 18

Metropolitan Population (1973 est.)							
Under 125,000	20	22	14 – 30	4,064	3,002 – 5,469	12	10 – 13
125,000 to 249,999	26	33	27 – 43	4,835	3,894 – 6,047	12	10 – 13
250,000 to 499,999	21	89	62 – 114	3,770	3,052 – 4,894	11	10 – 13
500,000 and over	13	180	144 – 277	4,122	3,718 – 4,686	12	12 – 13

[a] Range is the interquartile range except for Region 10, where it is the full range of variation.

Table 7–8. Fragmentation in Criminal Investigation: Region

Location	Number of SMSAs	Number of Service Areas in an SMSA				Number of Service Areas per 100,000 SMSA Population (1973 est.)			
		Burglary Investigation		Homicide Investigation		Burglary Investigation		Homicide Investigation	
		Median	Range[a]	Median	Range	Median	Range	Median	Range
Total	80	10	5 – 18	8	4 – 13	4.9	3.4 – 6.3	3.7	2.8 – 5.2
Northeast									
Region 1	8	5	3 – 10	5	3 – 10	3.9	2.5 – 6.3	3.9	2.5 – 5.8
Region 2	4	15	6 – 32	14	4 – 27	4.9	3.6 – 4.9	3.3	3.1 – 4.6
Region 3	6	12	8 – 28	7	7 – 26	5.3	2.8 – 12.0	4.9	2.8 – 11.1
Midwest									
Region 5	16	10	6 – 18	8	4 – 12	5.2	4.9 – 8.0	4.3	3.7 – 4.9
Region 7	4	8	3 – 11	4	3 – 5	4.5	3.5 – 5.2	3.1	2.6 – 3.5
South									
Region 4	15	15	6 – 20	11	3 – 14	4.6	2.8 – 5.7	3.5	2.3 – 3.8
Region 6	14	7	4 – 11	7	4 – 10	3.3	2.5 – 5.9	3.1	2.4 – 5.9
West									
Region 8	4	5	3 – 8	5	3 – 8	3.7	3.4 – 4.2	3.7	3.4 – 4.2
Region 9	7	16	13 – 20	15	13 – 20	3.6	2.5 – 6.0	3.5	2.4 – 6.0
Region 10	2	—	5 – 21	—	5 – 20	—	4.5 – 11.2	—	4.5 – 10.7

[a]Range is the interquartile range except for Region 10, where it is the full range of variation.

Table 7-9. Independence in Criminal Investigation: Region

Location	Number of SMSAs	Percent of Service Areas Receiving Service From Own Producer				Percent of SMSA Population (1973 est.) Receiving Service From Own Producer			
		Burglary Investigation		Homicide Investigation		Burglary Investigation		Homicide Investigation	
		Median	Range[a]	Median	Range	Median	Range	Median	Range
Total	80	100	86 – 100	88	75 – 100	100	97 – 100	99	93 – 100
Northeast									
Region 1	8	100	100 – 100	91	83 – 100	100	100 – 100	98	95 – 100
Region 2	4	84	83 – 99	85	79 – 99	95	80 – 100	97	96 – 100
Region 3	6	93	92 – 100	85	80 – 92	93	78 – 100	83	77 – 98
Midwest									
Region 5	16	100	86 – 100	90	82 – 100	100	95 – 100	100	91 – 100
Region 7	4	100	73 – 100	100	75 – 100	100	98 – 100	100	80 – 100
South									
Region 4	15	100	90 – 100	88	67 – 100	100	100 – 100	100	92 – 100
Region 6	14	100	75 – 100	80	64 – 100	100	99 – 100	98	96 – 100
West									
Region 8	4	67	63 – 100	67	50 – 80	92	90 – 100	84	77 – 90
Region 9	7	92	85 – 100	78	70 – 88	98	95 – 100	95	83 – 97
Region 10	2	—	81 – 100	—	85 – 100	—	88 – 100	—	98 – 100

[a] Range is the interquartile range except for Region 10, where it is the full range of variation.

tend to be autonomous. In at least half the SMSAs over 90 percent of the population lives in areas where burglaries are investigated solely by the area's own police producer. For homicide investigation the comparable figure is 71 percent (Table 7–10).

Alternation and Duplication in Criminal Investigation

Alternation, duplication, and coordination are the possible organizational patterns wherever several producers investigate the same kind of crime in the same service area. In almost all cases we found coordination rather than duplication or alternation. With very few exceptions two or more departments investigating the same kinds of crime in the same service area reported sharing leads, keeping a common case record, and working together during the course of the investigation.

Alternation of criminal investigation is found almost exclusively on military installations, where military law enforcement agencies have jurisdiction over cases involving military personnel and where the Federal Bureau of Investigation has responsibility for investigating cases that involve civilians. Even here, however, many investigations are coordinated between military investigative agencies and the FBI.

Duplication is the separate, uncoordinated investigation of the same crimes by two or more producers in the same service area. Duplication seldom occurs in the 80 metropolitan areas and only in a few cases where municipal and county law enforcement producers are in dispute over jurisdiction within municipal boundaries.

Coordination in Criminal Investigation

Coordination of criminal investigation occurs where two or more agencies combine their investigative efforts. For criminal investigation, it is the most widespread of the three types of service delivery involving multiple producers in a single service area. Regular coordination of criminal investigation typically involves two distinct kinds of activities. One is the screening of reports of crime, conducting initial inquiries, and providing contacts and background information regarding the service areas. The other kind of activity is the provision of detectives who conduct much of the investigation.

The first kind of activity is typically carried out by the service area's own police department. Departments performing only these aspects of criminal investigation usually coordinate investigations in a single jurisdiction. The second kind of investigation activity is typically performed by a state or county producer coordinating investigations in numerous service areas. Table 7–11 shows these different

Table 7–10.   Autonomy in Criminal Investigation: Region

Location	Number of SMSAs	Percent of Service Areas Receiving Service Exclusively From Own Producer				Percent of SMSA Population (1973 est.) Receiving Service Exclusively From Own Producer			
		Burglary Investigation		Homicide Investigation		Burglary Investigation		Homicide Investigation	
		Median	Range[a]	Median	Range	Median	Range	Median	Range
Total	80	67	47 – 81	40	5 – 57	91	69 – 99	71	17 – 94
Northeast									
Region 1	8	83	63 – 100	4	0 – 100	97	90 – 100	46	0 – 100
Region 2	4	50	47 – 67	0	0	74	51 – 93	0	0
Region 3	6	42	27 – 86	23	8 – 57	65	63 – 99	62	42 – 95
Midwest									
Region 5	16	50	21 – 81	40	0 – 50	75	51 – 90	51	0 – 80
Region 7	4	38	0 – 45	0	0	21	0 – 32	0	0
South									
Region 4	15	67	36 – 86	54	33 – 67	97	87 – 99	93	75 – 96
Region 6	14	60	50 – 73	47	38 – 67	94	76 – 99	90	8 – 99
West									
Region 8	4	67	50 – 71	40	11 – 50	91	90 – 93	90	17 – 91
Region 9	7	75	65 – 81	35	23 – 50	93	71 – 95	79	55 – 92
Region 10	2	—	40 – 76	—	5 – 40	—	54 – 94	—	34 – 94

[a] Range is the interquartile range except for Region 10, where it is the full range of variation.

Table 7–11. Coordination of Burglary Investigation: Region and Type of Producer

		Percent of Producers Coordinating on Burglary Investigation in			
Region and Type of Producer	*Number of Producers*	*No Service Areas*	*1 Service Area*	*2–5 Service Areas*	*6–10 Service Areas*
Northeast					
Region 1					
Municipal	59	86	12	2	0
State	3	33	0	67	0
Campus	8	13	88	0	0
Region 2					
Municipal	126	91	9	0	0
County	5	60	20	20	0
State	3	0	33	67	0
Campus	4	50	50	0	0
Other	2	100	0	0	0
Region 3					
Municipal	99	76	22	2	0
County	2	100	0	0	0
State	4	0	25	25	50
Campus	6	67	33	0	0
Military	5	100	0	0	0
Federal	1	100	0	0	0
Other	3	67	33	0	0
Midwest					
Region 5					
Municipal	169	81	17	2	0
County	23	52	30	13	4
State	5	60	20	20	0
Campus	15	67	33	0	0
Military	2	100	0	0	0
Federal	1	100	0	0	0
Other	3	100	0	0	0
Region 7					
Municipal	27	85	15	0	0
County	4	25	0	75	0
State	2	100	0	0	0
Campus	1	0	100	0	0
Military	1	100	0	0	0
Federal	1	100	0	0	0

Table 7-11. continued

Region and Type of Producer	Number of Producers	Percent of Producers Coordinating on Burglary Investigation in			
		No Service Areas	1 Service Area	2-5 Service Areas	6-10 Service Areas
South					
Region 4					
Municipal	143	71	25	4	1
County	26	38	23	31	8
State	1	100	0	0	0
Campus	25	52	48	0	0
Military	15	100	0	0	0
Federal	6	100	0	0	0
Other	2	100	0	0	0
Region 6					
Municipal	65	75	23	2	0
County	18	61	22	17	0
State	2	0	50	50	0
Campus	14	79	21	0	0
Military	13	100	0	0	0
Federal	8	100	0	0	0
Other	2	100	0	0	0
West					
Region 8					
Municipal	17	77	23	0	0
County	4	75	0	25	0
Campus	2	100	0	0	0
Military	6	100	0	0	0
Federal	3	100	0	0	0
Other	1	100	0	0	0
Region 9					
Municipal	71	97	3	0	0
County	8	75	25	0	0
Campus	5	80	20	0	0
Military	22	100	0	0	0
Federal	13	100	0	0	0
Other	3	33	67	0	0
Region 10					
Municipal	19	90	10	0	0
County	5	60	20	20	0
State	1	100	0	0	0

Note: Rows may not total 100 percent due to rounding errors.

levels of coordination for burglary investigation. About half the producers coordinating burglary investigation in more than one service area are county police departments. State police are the only type of agency coordinating burglary investigation in more than five service areas. Campus and special district police either do not coordinate burglary investigation or else coordinate with other producers only in investigations within their own service areas. No producer coordinates burglary investigation in more than 10 service areas in any of the 80 metropolitan areas.

Coordination in burglary investigation is found primarily in small towns and special districts, like university and college campuses. Each area's own producer for such areas is shown in Table 7–11 as coordinating investigation in only one service area. Most of the assistance to these producers comes from county and state investigation agencies—shown as producers coordinating investigation in several service areas. Less than one third of the service areas in 75 percent of the SMSAs receive coordinated burglary investigation (Table 7–12).

At the same time, over half the SMSAs have coordinated homicide investigations in at least one third of their service areas, and one fourth have coordinated homicide investigations in 70 percent or more of their service areas. Again, it is mostly municipal and special district police who receive assistance, although a small number of municipal agencies also provide assistance to other agencies in their metropolitan areas.

State and county law enforcement agencies are the only types of producers coordinating homicide investigation in more than five service areas (Table 7–13). County agencies predominate in the 6 to 10 service-area range. State agencies predominate in coordination of homicide investigation in more than 10 service areas. As with burglary investigation, campus and special district police either do not coordinate homicide investigations or else coordinate with other producers only within their own service areas. Some municipal and federal producers coordinate homicide investigation in two to five service areas, but many of these producers also coordinate only on investigations of homicides reported in their own service area.

Producers that investigate burglary, but not homicide, are more likely than producers that investigate both to coordinate their efforts with those of other producers in investigations within a single service area. Producers coordinating burglary investigations in several service areas are more likely to produce both burglary and homicide investigation, and these producers are more likely to have full-time criminal investigators.

Table 7-12. Coordination in Criminal Investigation: Region

Location	Number of SMSAs	Percent of Service Areas Receiving Service From Two or More Coordinating Producers				Percent of SMSA Population (1973 est.) Receiving Service From Two or More Coordinating Producers			
		Burglary Investigation		Homicide Investigation		Burglary Investigation		Homicide Investigation	
		Median	Range[a]	Median	Range	Median	Range	Median	Range
Total	80	6	0 – 27	33	13 – 70	0	0 – 6	6	1 – 44
Northeast									
Region 1	8	0	0 – 17	7	0 – 96	0	0 – 3	44	0 – 98
Region 2	4	9	0 – 33	100	33 – 100	2	0 – 6	100	5 – 100
Region 3	6	7	0 – 36	29	20 – 69	1	0 – 12	4	3 – 34
Midwest									
Region 5	16	3	0 – 25	33	7 – 80	0	0 – 22	20	2 – 67
Region 7	4	13	0 – 18	67	40 – 90	1	0 – 77	32	2 – 90
South									
Region 4	15	16	0 – 38	33	15 – 38	1	0 – 7	5	2 – 14
Region 6	14	10	0 – 25	25	0 – 50	0	0 – 3	0	0 – 15
West									
Region 8	4	0	0 – 21	0	0 – 40	0	0 – 0	0	0 – 5
Region 9	7	0	0 – 6	33	20 – 44	0	0 – 0	6	2 – 15
Region 10	2	—	0 – 60	—	60 – 70	—	0 – 6	—	6 – 20

[a] Range is the interquartile range except for Region 10, where it is the full range of variation.

Table 7–13. Coordination of Homicide Investigation: Region and Type of Producer

Region and Type of Producer	Number of Producers	Percent of Producers Coordinating on Homicide Investigation in				
		No Service Areas	1 Service Area	2-5 Service Areas	6-10 Service Areas	Over 10 Service Areas
Northeast						
Region 1						
Municipal	57	16	81	4	0	0
State	8	0	13	25	25	38
Campus	2	0	100	0	0	0
Region 2						
Municipal	117	9	89	2	0	0
County	9	0	44	22	0	33
State	3	0	33	67	0	0
Campus	2	0	100	0	0	0
Other	2	100	0	0	0	0
Region 3						
Municipal	90	32	62	6	0	0
County	2	100	0	0	0	0
State	5	0	20	20	20	40
Campus	4	0	100	0	0	0
Military	2	100	0	0	0	0
Federal	1	100	0	0	0	0

Midwest

Region 5

Municipal	127	62	32	6	0	0
County	23	22	22	39	13	4
State	13	23	8	46	15	8
Campus	12	42	58	0	0	0
Military	1	100	0	0	0	0
Federal	1	100	0	0	0	0
Other	1	100	0	0	0	0

Region 7

Municipal	17	18	82	0	0	0
County	4	25	25	50	0	0
State	4	25	0	50	25	0
Campus	1	0	100	0	0	0
Military	1	100	0	0	0	0
Federal	2	100	0	0	0	0
Other	1	50	0	50	0	0

South

Region 4

Municipal	100	60	36	4	0	0
County	26	27	35	35	4	0
State	6	0	50	50	0	0
Campus	9	11	89	0	0	0
Military	8	100	0	0	0	0
Federal	6	100	0	0	0	0
Other	1	100	0	0	0	0

(Table 7-13. continued overleaf)

Table 7–13. continued

Region and Type of Producer	Number of Producers	Percent of Producers Coordinating on Homicide Investigation in				
		No Service Areas	1 Service Area	2-5 Service Areas	6-10 Service Areas	Over 10 Service Areas
South (cont'd.)						
Region 6						
Municipal	56	64	34	2	0	0
County	19	42	21	26	11	0
State	7	29	29	14	29	0
Campus	12	50	50	0	0	0
Military	9	100	0	0	0	0
Federal	8	100	0	0	0	0
Other	2	100	0	0	0	0
West						
Region 8						
Municipal	12	33	58	8	0	0
County	4	75	0	0	25	0
State	1	0	100	0	0	0
Campus	2	50	50	0	0	0
Military	4	100	0	0	0	0
Federal	3	100	0	0	0	0
Other	1	0	100	0	0	0

Region 9

Municipal	69	48	52	0	0	0
County	12	8	25	50	18	0
State	1	0	0	100	0	0
Campus	4	50	50	0	0	0
Military	11	100	0	0	0	0
Federal	10	100	0	0	0	0

Region 10

Municipal	18	11	89	0	0	0
County	6	17	33	33	17	0
State	1	0	0	0	100	0

Note: Rows may not total 100 percent due to rounding errors.

Producers investigating homicide, but not burglary, usually have several full-time investigators on their staffs. More than 40 percent of the producers investigating both burglary and homicide coordinate homicide investigations in a single service area. Only about 10 percent of the producers investigating homicides, but not burglaries, coordinate investigations in only a single service area. About 40 percent of the producers investigating homicides, but not burglaries, coordinate homicide investigations in more than one service area.

In addition to these producers that regularly coordinate criminal investigations, there is also considerable temporary or special purpose cooperation among departments. Much criminal investigation is done cooperatively by several police departments. Occasional cooperation on investigations is practically universal. Few, if any, police departments, whatever their resources, find it possible to gather all the information and evidence they need for all cases without the assistance of other agencies. In many metropolitan areas special interagency task forces have been established to provide additional continuity to the cooperative efforts of the various criminal investigation producers working in the area [7].

DIVERSITY IN CRIMINAL INVESTIGATION: WHAT DOES IT MEAN?

The organizational patterns for investigation of residential burglaries are often quite different from the organizational patterns for the investigation of homicides. Many smaller municipal and special district police departments investigate burglaries, but do no homicide investigation. Other small municipal and special district producers investigate both types of crime, but receive assistance from large municipal, county, or state agencies in conducting homicide investigations. Some producers specialize in criminal investigation and work primarily on major crimes, like homicide. Producers of this kind include district attorney's police, local major case squads, and state bureaus of investigation.

Municipal police departments account for about three quarters of the producers supplying both types of investigation. Most county sheriffs' and county police departments also investigate both residential burglary and homicide. Producers that investigate both these crimes are also likely to control traffic and to patrol. Most producers assign detectives to both residential burglary and homicide investigation. Where patrol officers are assigned to investigations they are more likely to be assigned to residential burglary cases than to homicides.

With few exceptions we find little duplication of investigation services. Where two producers investigate the same crime in the same service area they typically divide their work into two kinds of activities. The service area's own police department screens reports of crime, conducts initial inquiries, and provides contacts and background information about the service area. The other (typically larger) producer provides detectives, who conduct much of the investigation. Under what conditions is this kind of coordinated investigation more effective than investigation by small local producers, on the one hand, or large SMSA-wide producers, on the other? Right now we do not know.

Different areas have different needs. In this respect the diversity of arrangements for investigation in metropolitan areas is neither surprising nor detrimental as such. Yet, much of the diversity that exists may also be the result of historical accidents, local traditions, and political compromises having little or no relation to the areas' current needs for burglary and homicide investigation. Evaluation of the impact of the different organizational arrangements for criminal investigation requires examination of the manner in which investigations are actually conducted in areas with these different service delivery systems. Only through such an evaluation can we learn whether a particular criminal investigations system is appropriate for any given metropolitan area.

✳ *Chapter 8*

An Overview of Direct Service Delivery Patterns

Metropolitan service delivery patterns differ considerably for police patrol, traffic control, and criminal investigation. By separately examining service delivery patterns for each direct police service we have been able to specify those differences.

Patrol is usually more fragmented than the other direct police services considered here. There are more separate service areas for patrol than for traffic control or for criminal investigation (Table 8–1). Most of these "patrol only" service areas are quite small—only a few thousand residents. They are organized as villages, townships, campuses, housing authorities, or hospitals. Residents of these areas receive other police services as part of a larger (usually city or county) service area. In most cases patrol in these "patrol only" service areas is provided by a small, local police department.

Consolidation of small police departments has been proposed, but one finding of this study is that areas served by small police departments are likely to have more patrol units on the street per thousand residents. Consolidation might well necessitate either reducing the level of patrol coverage or increasing the number of officers, and hence the cost of policing.

Service alternation for patrol occurs in about one fourth of the patrol service areas. Some of this is alternate patrol of service enclaves, such as parks, airports, or state capitols—places with no resident population that are part of a larger service area. In other cases alternate producers patrol the same places, but at different times of day. A third type of patrol alternation occurs where military agencies

Table 8–1.   Structure of Service Delivery for Direct Services in 80 Metropolitan Areas: Measures

| | Patrol | | | Traffic Control | | | | | |
| | | | | Patrol | | | Investigation | | |
	Mean	Median	Range	Mean	Median	Range	Mean	Median	Range
Fragmentation	15.9	12	7 – 21	15.4	12	6 – 19	14.9	11	6 – 20
Multiplicity	16.4	13	7 – 20	15.8	13	7 – 20	15.1	11	6 – 19
Independence	94.8	100	89 – 100	90.1	93	83 – 100	90.0	93	83 – 100
Autonomy	58.8	56	33 – 83	34.8	33	17 – 50	37.3	38	13 – 59
Duplication	12.2	0	0 – 14	11.2	0	0 – 13	12.5	0	0 – 7
Coordination	2.5	0	0 – 0	2.0	0	0 – 0	5.2	0	0 – 7
Alternation	25.3	21	4 – 38	49.5	47	33 – 67	41.5	35	13 – 64
Dominance	18.3	13	6 – 22	23.8	14	7 – 32	36.2	20	9 – 52

Table 8–1. continued

| | Criminal Investigation | | | | | |
| | Burglary | | | Homicide | | |
	Mean	*Median*	*Range*[a]	*Mean*	*Median*	*Range*
Fragmentation	13.9	10	5 – 18	11.8	8	4 – 13
Multiplicity	13.8	10	6 – 17	11.8	8	5 – 13
Independence	91.8	100	86 – 100	84.5	88	75 – 100
Autonomy	63.0	67	47 – 81	38.5	40	5 – 57
Duplication	4.0	0	0 – 0	3.4	0	0 – 0
Coordination	15.0	6	0 – 27	43.1	33	13 – 70
Alternation	13.1	7	0 – 25	9.9	0	0 – 15
Dominance	23.4	17	8 – 25	46.3	33	17 – 81

[a] Range is the interquartile range.

patrol off base to supplement the efforts of local police patrols. The military patrol effort is directed toward military personnel only.

More service alternation occurs in traffic patrol and accident investigation than in the other direct services studied. Quite commonly the highway patrol or state police patrols traffic and investigates accidents on major highways throughout a metropolitan area, while traffic on other streets and roads is patrolled by local police agencies, each serving separate service areas. Park police and transportation authority police commonly patrol traffic and investigate accidents only on certain roadways within the metropolitan areas they serve. Often these agencies are specialists and do not conduct general area patrol or criminal investigations. Those services are supplied by the police serving the city or county in which the enclave is located. Almost half the service areas for traffic patrol and accident investigation have alternate producers of these services.

Alternation of service may reflect the belief that different kinds of service areas have characteristically different sorts of policing requirements—that campuses should be policed by campus police, hospitals by hospital police, state capitol grounds by state capitol police, and so on. An opposing point of view is that uniform enforcement and clear-cut delineation of authority are more important than special purpose policing. Which of these views is appropriate to any particular metropolitan area or service area depends upon conditions in the specific area. What, for example, are the different traffic patrol requirements of the system of thoroughfares in a given area? Does confusion exist among police departments over division of responsibility for service delivery? In-depth study of service conditions and service delivery practices is needed to determine the appropriateness of service alternation in any particular area.

Coordination of service is more common in criminal investigation than in patrol or traffic control. Four of every 10 homicide investigation service areas have coordinated investigation. One sixth of all burglary investigation service areas have coordinated investigation. Many of the smaller burglary investigation service areas are subsumed in larger homicide investigation service areas—their local police do not participate in homicide investigation. Most small, local departments do participate in both homicide and burglary investigation, however. Especially for homicide investigation they coordinate their efforts with those of an agency employing investigative specialists. In some cases this is a district attorney's police department or an interagency major case squad. More commonly it is a state or county police department or the police department of a nearby large city.

Departments that coordinate criminal investigations in several service areas typically contribute specialized investigative personnel to the investigation. They supply technical assistance and investigative expertise to the departments with which they cooperate. The departments receiving the assistance supply initial inquiries, contacts, and background information regarding the service area. Whether the contributions of these independent, local police agencies are valuable is a question that must be left to further research. Independent service delivery—production of the service by the service area's own police agency—is almost as common for homicide investigation as for patrol, but the extensive coordination of homicide investigation results in considerably fewer autonomous service areas for homicide investigation.

The relative impact of a single producer of a direct service in most metropolitan areas can be seen by comparing the extent of producer dominance of service delivery for the various direct services. Almost half the homicide investigation service areas receive investigatory services from the dominant homicide investigation agency in their SMSA. This compares to an average dominance of about one third for traffic accident investigation—the next most dominated service. For general area patrol, which is least dominated by a single producer in most SMSAs, the average dominant producer serves one fifth of the patrol service areas in the SMSA.

It is common to cite the large number of police agencies serving most metropolitan areas as evidence of disorganization. A classic statement of this conclusion is Bruce Smith's:

> There is therefore no such thing in the United States as a police system, nor even a set of police systems within any reasonably accurate sense of the term. Our so-called systems are mere collections of police units having some similarity of authority, organization, or jurisdiction; but they lack any systematic relationship to each other [1].

We have found, however, considerable organization. Metropolitan policing in the United States is systematic when viewed service by service. Police departments know—with very few exceptions—where their responsibilities begin and end, both geographically and with regard to the delivery of various kinds of direct police service.

Although much more intensive examination of the practices and impacts of police service delivery is needed to assess the value of current organizational arrangements for patrol, traffic control, and criminal investigation, the patterns that exist are, in most cases, systematic. Interagency coordination and alternation of service in time, space, or clientele are patterns of working relationships among the varied producers of metropolitan police services.

※ *Chapter 9*

An Introduction
to Auxiliary Services

Auxiliary services are used by police agencies in the production of direct police services to citizens. Radio communications, adult pretrial detention, entry-level training, and crime labs are designed primarily to serve police agencies and indirectly the citizens they serve. The organization of auxiliary services is generally different from the organization of direct police services.

Except for radio communications, the proportion of direct service producers that also produce their own auxiliary services is low. Of the 1,454 direct police service producers serving the 80 SMSAs, only 11 percent produce adult pretrial detention, 15 percent produce entry-level training, and 8 percent produce crime laboratory analyses (Table 9−1). Two thirds of all producers of patrol, traffic control, and/or criminal investigation services also produce radio communications.

AGENCIES PRODUCING AUXILIARY SERVICES

The number of agencies producing auxiliary services is smaller than for direct services. The variety of agencies producing auxiliary services is greater (Figure 9−1). Of the 985 agencies that produce radio communications, only 63 percent are municipal police departments. County sheriffs and campus police each constitute about 10 percent of the agencies producing radio communications. About 3 percent are specialized communications centers. Many of these dispatch centers are municipal communications bureaus organized to dispatch

175

Table 9–1.   Auxiliary Services Supplied by Direct Service Producers: Type of Producer

Type of Direct Service Producer	Number of Direct Police Producers	Percent of Direct Producers That Supply			
		Radio Communications	Adult Pretrial Detention	Entry-Level Training	Chemical Laboratory Analysis
Total	1,454	68	11	15	8
Municipal police	936	66	6	6	1
County sheriffs and police	108	87	81	7	7
State police	97	88	0	86	60
Campus police	108	84	0	8	0
Military police	81	58	17	42	12
Federal police	40	32	8	75	65
Other police producers	84	56	0	10	0

Figure 9–1.   Types of Agencies Producing Auxiliary Services in 80 SMSAs

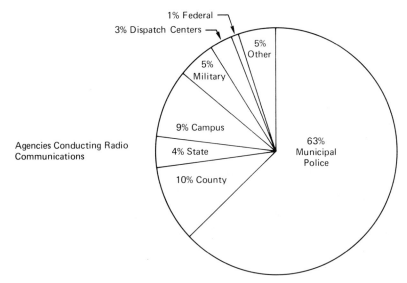

Agencies Conducting Radio
Communications

1% Federal
3% Dispatch Centers
5% Other
5% Military
9% Campus
4% State
10% County
63% Municipal Police

Total Number of Agencies = 985

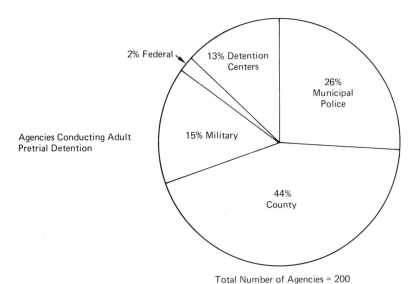

Agencies Conducting Adult
Pretrial Detention

2% Federal
13% Detention Centers
26% Municipal Police
15% Military
44% County

Total Number of Agencies = 200

Figure 9–1. (continued) Types of Agencies Producing Auxiliary Services in 80 SMSAs

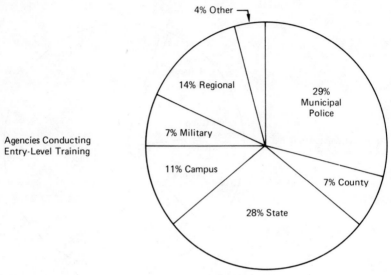

Agencies Conducting Entry-Level Training

4% Other

14% Regional

7% Military

11% Campus

29% Municipal Police

7% County

28% State

Total Number of Agencies = 226

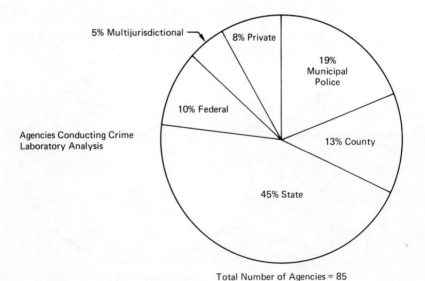

Agencies Conducting Crime Laboratory Analysis

5% Multijurisdictional

8% Private

19% Municipal Police

10% Federal

13% County

45% State

Total Number of Agencies = 85

for both police and fire departments. Some are regional communications centers organized to serve several neighboring police agencies.

The pattern for the 200 detention-producing agencies is quite different. County sheriffs maintain 44 percent of the jails, while municipal police departments maintain 26 percent. Specialized detention centers account for 13 percent. Most military bases have their own detention facilities. They constitute another 15 percent of the agencies producing this service. These units detain only military personnel, and we did not study them in depth. We did obtain data on the detention facilities of the nonmilitary producers, however. Although county sheriffs constitute less than half the civilian detention agencies in the 80 SMSAs, they supply more than 70 percent of the locally produced detention capacity in these areas.

All levels of government are involved in the production of entry-level training. Municipal agencies constitute nearly 30 percent of the 226 agencies conducting entry-level training, while state agencies constitute about the same percentage. Fourteen percent are regional training academies. Most of these academies are organized through interjurisdictional arrangements in which a number of local direct service producers in a metropolitan area organize one academy to serve their combined needs. Colleges also offer entry-level training for direct service producers in several SMSAs. They account for 11 percent of the producers of police recruit training. County academies and military and civilian federal agencies are the other suppliers of entry-level training.

The number of agencies regularly producing crime laboratory analyses for the 80 SMSAs is small—only 85. State agencies constitute 45 percent of these, municipal departments represent nearly 20 percent, and county sheriffs 13 percent. Ten percent are federal agencies. There are seven private producers and four multijurisdictional agencies conducting chemical analysis of evidence. Most of these agencies supply crime laboratory analyses to more than a single metropolitan area.

AUXILIARY SERVICE PRODUCERS
IN EACH SMSA

The number of producers of auxiliary services in each SMSA is much lower than that for direct services (Table 9–2). The median number of radio communications producers in an SMSA is nine, four for entry-level training, and two for detention and for laboratory analysis. There is no more than one jail and one crime lab for approximately every seven patrol or investigation producers in half of the

Table 9–2. Multiplicity in Auxiliary Service Producers: SMSA Population

Metropolitan Population (1973 est.)	Number of SMSAs	Median Number of Auxiliary Service Producers in an SMSA				Median Number of Auxiliary Service Producers in an SMSA per Direct Service Producers Who Utilize Service			
		Radio Communi- cations	Entry- Level Training	Adult Pretrial Detention	Chemical Laboratory Analysis	Radio Communi- cations	Entry- Level Training	Adult Pretrial Detention	Chemical Laboratory Analysis
Total	80	9	4	2	2	.86	.33	.15	.14
50,000 to 124,999	20	5	2	1	2	1.00	.50	.22	.25
125,000 to 249,999	26	8	3	1	1	.81	.33	.11	.11
250,000 to 499,999	21	16	7	2	3	.88	.35	.15	.15
500,000 and over	13	23	8	4	3	.82	.29	.11	.09

SMSAs. There is no more than one training academy for every three direct service producers. The median is less than one radio communications producer for each police agency using radio communications.

The number of auxiliary service producers increases in larger SMSAs, while the number relative to the number of direct service producers falls. So, in the median SMSA of those over 500,000 in population, there is approximately one jail and one lab per 10 direct service producers, while in the median SMSA of those under 125,000 there is one jail per five direct service producers and about one chemical lab per four direct service producers.

When we examine local direct service producers we see some additional differences. The size of the local direct service producer significantly affects the likelihood that it will produce auxiliary services. Even for radio communications, smaller agencies—particularly municipalities—are much less likely to dispatch their own officers than are larger agencies (Table 9—3).

A very small proportion of municipal police departments with 50 or fewer full-time sworn officers produce their own entry-level training, adult pretrial detention, or laboratory analyses. Because of their constitutional and/or statutory responsibilities, most county police and sheriffs' departments do produce adult pretrial detention, regardless of agency size. None of the other local direct service producers, such as park district police and airport police, produce detention or laboratory analyses.

AUXILIARY SERVICE SPECIALISTS

Agencies that produce one and only one of the auxiliary services (and none of the direct services) are auxiliary service specialists. In some metropolitan areas municipal dispatch centers or detention centers produce auxiliary services for local police departments. County dispatch and detention centers have been established in other areas. Private answering services and chemical laboratories supply communications and crime lab analyses to some direct service police agencies. State specialists in auxiliary services are mostly training academies. Most interjurisdictional specialists are also training academies, although a few joint dispatch centers do serve police in the 80 SMSAs. Federal agencies produce auxiliary services and none of the direct services in some SMSAs.

Table 9–3.   Auxiliary Service Production by Local Direct Service Producers: Type and Size of Producer

Type of Local Direct Producer and Number of Full-Time Sworn Officers	Number Reporting	Percent of Local Direct Producers That Also Produce			
		Radio Communications	Adult Pretrial Detention	Entry-Level Training	Chemical Laboratory Analysis
Total	1,174	69	12	6	1
Municipal police	920	66	6	6	1
No full-time officers	77	25	0	0	0
1 to 4 full-time officers	246	38	0	0	0
5 to 10 full-time officers	220	67	6	0	0
11 to 20 full-time officers	126	90	6	0	0
21 to 50 full-time officers	124	96	10	1	0
51 to 150 full-time officers	79	95	17	15	4
Over 150 full-time officers	48	94	15	81	10
County sheriffs and police	107	88	80	7	7
1 to 4 full-time officers	4	75	75	0	0
5 to 10 full-time officers	8	63	50	0	0
11 to 20 full-time officers	18	83	72	0	0
21 to 50 full-time officers	31	90	87	3	10
51 to 150 full-time officers	28	96	82	18	0
Over 150 full-time officers	18	89	89	11	28
Other local radio communications producers	147	73	0	5	0
No full-time officers	6	50	0	33	0
1 to 4 full-time officers	28	54	0	7	0
5 to 10 full-time officers	54	70	0	0	0
11 to 20 full-time officers	27	89	0	7	0
21 to 50 full-time officers	28	86	0	4	0
51 to 150 full-time officers	4	100	0	0	0

THE "FULL–SERVICE" POLICE DEPARTMENT

Some of the discussion of police agency size has centered around the notion of the "full-service" police department. Small departments are viewed as inadequate because they lack the resources to provide themselves with crime labs and detention facilities. They may have too few officers to justify their own training programs or full-time radio communications staff. Or, they may have too few serious crimes reported to justify the employment of investigative specialists.

The inability of small departments to supply such services, however, should not be interpreted as indicating that the services are not available to small departments and the communities they serve. With few exceptions, all direct police service producers in the 80 metropolitan areas not supplying their own auxiliary services have arrangements with other agencies to supply them with entry-level training, chemical analysis of evidence, pretrial detention of suspected offenders, and radio communications.

As we have seen in Chapter 7, the assistance of investigative specialists from other agencies is also common. Reliance on other agencies for auxiliary services is not limited to small departments. In fact, there is only one department in the 80 metropolitan areas producing *all* the services we studied. Like the smaller agencies, most large departments obtain some auxiliary services from other producers. In terms of the services discussed in this volume, "full-service" departments are very few, indeed.

✳ *Chapter 10*

Radio Communications

Radio communications is the relaying of requests for police assistance to officers in the field and the receipt of radioed requests for information or assistance from officers in the field. It is a key link between a citizen's need for emergency assistance and a police agency's immediate response capability. Departments without radio communications are not able to respond as quickly as agencies with this capability.

Radio communications systems also handle requests for information that do not require immediate response by a patrol unit. The way radio communications systems are operated may make important differences to the citizens being served and to the officers dependent upon a radio communications system for their own back-up and safety.

Radio communications systems are organized within and among police agencies in a variety of ways throughout the country. Most direct service producers—especially those that produce general area and traffic patrol—also produce their own radio communications. However, a substantial number of direct service producers obtain radio communications services from other agencies. Most often the agencies obtaining radio communications services from others are smaller agencies contracting with a county police or sheriff's department for these services. Many other arrangements exist also.

TYPES OF AGENCIES THAT PRODUCE
RADIO COMMUNICATIONS

Over 1,000 producers supply radio communications in the 80 SMSAs included in this study. Local direct service producers predominate. Of the 1,044 producers 59 percent are municipal police departments, 9 percent are county police or sheriffs, and another 9 percent are campus police (Table 10–1).

Most state producers dispatch for themselves. State police usually have separate dispatch facilities at various regional headquarters located near metropolitan areas and are not dispatched by a central state dispatch unit. So, the number of state police producers (81) is a better reflection of the actual number of individual state radio communications units serving the 80 SMSAs than is the number of state agencies (33) serving the 80 SMSAs.

Table 10–1.   Producers of Radio Communications: Type of Agency

Type of Agency	Number of Producers	Percent	Number of Agencies	Percent
Total	1,044	100	985	100
Local direct service producers				
Municipal police	615	59	615	62
County sheriffs and police	93	9	93	9
Campus police[a]	91	9	90	9
Other local producers	26	2	26	3
State direct service producers				
State police	81	8	33	3
Other state producers	28	3	22	2
Federal direct service producers				
Military	47	5	47	5
Civilian	13	1	9	1
Dispatch specialists				
Municipal	28	3	28	3
County	9	1	9	1
Private	8	1	8	1
Interjurisdictional	3	0	3	0
Other	2	0	2	0

Note: Columns may not total 100 percent due to rounding errors.

[a]Includes all campus police.

There are 50 "dispatch specialists" producing radio communications, but no direct police services, in these metropolitan areas. Many of these dispatch specialists are municipal communications bureaus organized to dispatch for both the police and fire departments. In some cases such bureaus also dispatch for a city utility company, municipal engineers, or other city employees who require radio communications. Nine dispatch specialists are county agencies. They dispatch for county departments and in some cases for other police agencies located in the county. In the San Jose SMSA the Santa Clara County Communications Center dispatches for 10 police agencies. The Monterey County Communications Center, located in the Monterey SMSA, dispatches for 12 agencies there.

In the 80 SMSAs studied we located three dispatch specialists specifically created by interjurisdictional arrangements: the Blair Radio Network dispatches for 9 agencies located in the Altoona/Pennsylvania SMSA, the Berks County Police Radio Network dispatches 40 police departments in the Reading/Pennsylvania SMSA, and the Tri-Boro Public Safety Corporation dispatches 3 police agencies located in the Paterson-Clifton-Passaic/New Jersey SMSA. Eight private agencies also dispatch police in the 80 SMSAs. These usually serve only a single police agency. The major exception to this is the Telephone Answering Exchange that dispatches 11 police agencies located in the Scranton/Pennsylvania SMSA.

Two thirds of the dispatch specialists are located in the Northeast (Regions 1, 2, and 3). Eighteen dispatch specialists serve metropolitan areas located in Virginia and Pennsylvania (Region 3); most of these are located in the three Pennsylvania metropolitan areas where county sheriffs do not produce direct police services or radio communications. Twelve dispatch specialists are located in New York and New Jersey (Region 2) where nine serve the Rochester/New York SMSA; the other three are located in New Jersey. Ten dispatch specialists are located in California and Arizona (Region 9); most of these supply metropolitan areas in California.

Direct Service Producers

Most direct police service producers produce their own radio communications services (Table 10-2). Of the more than 1,400 direct service producers we studied, 68 percent produce their own radio communications. About 85 percent of all sheriffs' and county police departments, state police, and campus police departments produce radio communications. In many regions the proportion of county departments producing their own radio communications approaches 100 percent. (The average for the 80 SMSAs is lowered by the rela-

Table 10–2. Percent of Direct Producers Who Produce Radio Communications: Region and Type of Producer

Types of Producers	Number Reporting	Northeast Regions			Midwest Regions		Southern Regions		Western Regions		
		1	2	3	5	7	4	6	8	9	10
Total	(1,454) 68	(87) 84	(162) 76	(143) 46	(275) 64	(54) 72	(305) 72	(182) 69	(48) 60	(170) 71	(28) 75
Municipal police	(936) 66	(60) 88	(133) 78	(112) 36	(204) 55	(35) 74	(190) 72	(89) 72	(21) 52	(73) 74	(19) 68
County sheriffs and police	(108) 87	(0) —	(9) 56	(2) 100	(24) 96	(4) 100	(28) 96	(19) 95	(4) 75	(12) 58	(6) 83
State police	(97) 88	(16) 69	(4) 100	(6) 100	(17) 100	(4) 100	(20) 75	(16) 87	(5) 100	(7) 100	(2) 100
Military police	(81) 58	(0) —	(0) —	(5) 60	(2) 50	(1) 0	(18) 56	(20) 60	(9) 56	(26) 61	(0) —
Campus police	(108) 84	(9) 89	(4) 100	(8) 100	(17) 100	(2) 50	(31) 81	(18) 78	(3) 100	(16) 69	(0) —
Other police[a]	(124) 48	(2) 50	(12) 58	(10) 60	(11) 46	(8) 50	(18) 28	(20) 20	(6) 33	(36) 69	(1) 100

Note: Numbers in parentheses equal number reporting.
[a]Other police includes nonmilitary federal police.

tively fewer county radio communications producers in New York, New Jersey, California, and Arizona—Regions 2 and 9—where half the dispatch specialists are found.)

About two thirds of all municipal police departments produce radio communications. This proportion falls to one third in Virginia and Pennsylvania (Region 3), another region with numerous dispatch specialists. Of the military police departments producing direct services, 58 percent produce radio communications, while 48 percent of the other direct service producers also produce radio communications.

THE STRUCTURE OF RADIO COMMUNICATIONS DELIVERY

A recurrent criticism of police organization is that there are far too many individual police radio systems in metropolitan areas. While not all direct service producers produce radio communications (about one third do not), the number of radio communications producers in each SMSA is considerably higher than the number of producers of other auxiliary services discussed in this volume (Table 10—3).

One measure of relative multiplicity for radio communications is the number of radio communications producers in a metropolitan area per 100 patrol units on the street in the area. The range of variation across regions for this ratio is less than the variation in relative multiplicity measured by the ratio of communications producers to direct service producers that use radio communications. The 10 p.m. average in metropolitan areas in all regions is between five and eight cars dispatched per radio communications producer.

Metropolitan areas from 125,000 to 500,000 population are more likely to have a higher ratio of producers to patrol units than are the smallest or largest SMSAs. In metropolitan areas over 500,000 the median for radio communications producers per 100 units on patrol is 12 (or, on the average, 8 patrol units are being dispatched per radio communications producer).

Independence and Autonomy

While measures of multiplicity provide information about the number of radio communications producers, they do not provide information about the proportion of agencies that dispatch for themselves either exclusively or at least for some hours each week. This information is conveyed by our measures of independence and autonomy (Table 10—4). Median SMSA independence for radio communications is 83; that is, 83 percent of the direct service producers in an

Table 10–3.   Multiplicity in Radio Communications Production: Region and SMSA Population

Location	Number of SMSAs	Number of Radio Communications Producers in an SMSA		Number of Radio Communications Producers per Consuming Agency		Number of Radio Communications Producers per 100 Patrol Units on the Street at 10 p.m.	
		Median	Range[a]	Median	Range	Median	Range
Total	80	9	6 – 17	.86	.67 – 1.0	17	12 – 23
Northeast							
Region 1	8	7	4 – 9	1.0	1.0 – 1.0	18	12 – 23
Region 2	4	15	8 – 31	.77	.75 – .88	17	11 – 18
Region 3	6	10	10 – 17	.71	.50 – 1.0	18	14 – 28
Midwest							
Region 5	16	8	5 – 13	.64	.50 – .78	17	13 – 24
Region 7	4	8	5 – 11	.80	.65 – .89	21	16 – 24
South							
Region 4	15	18	6 – 18	.92	.78 – 1.0	12	10 – 19
Region 6	14	7	5 – 10	.88	.73 – 1.0	13	8 – 30
West							
Region 8	4	8	4 – 8	.67	.53 – .75	17	14 – 18
Region 9	7	19	14 – 23	1.0	.79 – 1.0	18	8 – 19
Region 10	2	—	4 – 17	—	.67 – .81	—	16 – 31

Metropolitan Population (1973 est.)							
Nationwide	80	9	6 – 17	.86	.67 – 1.0	17	12 – 23
50 000 to 124,999	20	5	4 – 6	1.0	.65 – 1.0	15	13 – 28
125,000 to 249,999	26	8	7 – 11	.81	.65 – 1.0	18	16 – 33
250,000 to 499,999	21	16	9 – 20	.88	.75 – 1.0	18	11 – 20
500,000 and over	13	23	18 – 31	.82	.77 – .87	12	8 – 17

[a] Range is the interquartile range except for Region 10, where it is the full range of variation.

Table 10–4.   Independence and Autonomy in Radio Communications Production: Region and SMSA Population

Location	Number of SMSAs	Percent of Consuming Agencies per SMSA Who			
		Produce Their Own Communications		Use Only Their Own Communications Facilities	
		Median	Range[a]	Median	Range
Total	80	83	65 – 100	73	50 – 92
Northeast					
Region 1	8	100	96 – 100	100	96 – 100
Region 2	4	65	65 – 86	65	40 – 84
Region 3	6	50	31 – 100	29	28 – 83
Midwest					
Region 5	16	64	50 – 78	50	38 – 63
Region 7	4	80	65 – 100	45	33 – 47
South					
Region 4	15	92	78 – 100	81	63 – 100
Region 6	14	86	73 – 100	83	56 – 100
West					
Region 8	4	67	53 – 75	50	40 – 67
Region 9	7	90	63 – 95	77	46 – 80
Region 10	2	—	50 – 81	—	50 – 62

Metropolitan Population (1973 est.)					
50,000 to 124,999	20	100	65 – 100	83	56 – 100
125,000 to 249,999	26	81	57 – 100	62	42 – 100
250,000 to 499,999	21	86	75 – 96	78	60 – 83
500,000 and over	13	82	64 – 86	61	54 – 77

[a] Range is the interquartile range except for Region 10, where it is the full range of variation.

SMSA dispatch their own officers for at least some hours during each week.

In the median SMSA, 73 percent of the direct service producers are solely responsible for their own dispatching (autonomy). As would be expected, independence and autonomy are lower in those regions where a large proportion of dispatch specialists operate and where county and other large producers supply radio communications to smaller local agencies. Both independence and autonomy are highest in the smaller SMSAs and lower in the larger SMSAs. The median level of independence falls from 100 percent to 82 percent; that for autonomy falls from 83 percent to 61 percent.

Alternation, Duplication, and Coordination

Alternation is one form of multiple production of radio communications. Alternate arrangements exist for dispatching at different times of day. Small agencies are often dispatched by their own employees during the daytime hours. In the evening the agency's officers are dispatched by a county sheriff, a neighboring city, or private answering service.

Much alternation is found in only three regions (Table 10–5). It is highest in the Plains states, the Rocky Mountain states, and California and Arizona (Regions 7, 8, and 9). Even in these regions the absolute levels are low. Twenty percent of the agencies located in the median SMSA of the Plains states (Region 7) have alternate producers, while 13 percent alternate in the median SMSA of California and Arizona (Region 9). The level of alternation is related to size of metropolitan areas, rising somewhat in the larger metropolitan areas. While alternation is low across the country, duplication and coordination are almost nonexistent in all regions and all sizes of metropolitan areas.

THE ORGANIZATION OF RADIO COMMUNICATIONS OPERATIONS

Producers of radio communications must make several important decisions about the operation of that service. One of these involves the personnel assigned to operate the radio system. A second concerns the policies under which they operate.

Personnel

While a large proportion of local direct service producers supply some form of radio communications, many do not assign full-time personnel on a regular basis. Across the country over one fourth of the local agencies who do some dispatching for themselves do not assign full-time personnel to dispatching.

All the part-time patrol agencies with their own radio communications are dispatched during the daytime by a civilian who does not work exclusively for the police department. In some cases the police phone is answered by a clerk or secretary who also handles non-police business; in other cases we found the police phone and a radio in the home of the mayor. Such arrangements are also frequently used by local police agencies employing fewer than five full-time sworn officers.

For all types of local direct producers the number of full-time personnel assigned to radio communications duties is strongly related to the size of the agency (Table 10−6). County sheriffs, as a group, are more likely than municipal departments and other producers to assign more than four full-time personnel to radio communications. This reflects both the fact that county sheriffs' departments tend to be larger than other local direct service producers, and that county sheriffs are more likely to dispatch for other police departments as well as their own.

While the total number of employees assigned to radio communications is greater for larger direct producers, the ratio of full-time employees assigned to radio communications to full-time employees assigned to patrol is smaller (Table 10−7). This means that larger direct producers use their radio communications personnel to dispatch a proportionately larger patrol force than do smaller agencies. This relationship gives support to the assumption that there are economies of scale in the production of radio communications; that is, the larger dispatching units may be able to provide the service more efficiently in terms of personnel deployment.

Use of civilians for radio communications work has been urged to decrease the costs of producing police services and to free trained officers for other assignments. Fifty-three percent of the local direct service agencies that produce radio communications assign only civilian employees to communications duties (Table 10−8). As a group, municipal agencies are more likely to use only civilian dispatchers than are county sheriffs, but other types of local direct agencies that produce radio communications are even more likely than the city departments to use only civilians. Smaller agencies are more likely than larger agencies to rely exclusively on civilian personnel for radio communications. Frequently small agencies employ civilians to handle both radio communications and clerical work.

Table 10—5. Alternation and Duplication in Radio Communications Production: Region and SMSA Population

Location	Number of SMSAs	Percent of Consuming Agencies per SMSA Who			
		Utilize Alternate Communications Producers		Use More Than One Communications Producer Without Alternation	
		Median	Range[a]	Median	Range
Total	80	5	0 – 17	0	0 – 0
Northeast					
Region 1	8	0	0 – 0	0	0 – 0
Region 2	4	0	0 – 2	0	0 – 0
Region 3	6	3	0 – 8	0	0 – 0
Midwest					
Region 5	16	0	0 – 19	0	0 – 0
Region 7	4	20	20 – 35	0	0 – 11
South					
Region 4	15	0	0 – 10	0	0 – 0
Region 6	14	3	0 – 17	0	0 – 0
West					
Region 8	4	8	0 – 13	0	0 – 0
Region 9	7	13	7 – 20	0	0 – 0
Region 10	2	—	17 – 19	—	0 – 0

Metropolitan Population (1973 est.)					
50,000 to 124,999	20	0	0 – 11	0	0 – 0
125,000 to 249,999	26	0	0 – 19	0	0 – 0
250,000 to 499,999	21	7	3 – 13	0	0 – 0
500,000 and over	13	10	3 – 23	0	0 – 3

[a]Range is the interquartile range except for Region 10, where it is the full range of variation.

Table 10—6.   Local Radio Communications Producers Who Are Also Local Direct Producers: Number of Full-Time Personnel Assigned to Radio Communications

Type of Producer and Number of Full-Time Sworn Officers	Number Reporting	Percent of Agencies Assigning			
		No Full-Time Personnel	1-3 Full-Time Personnel	4 Full-Time Personnel	More Than 4 Full-Time Personnel
Total	768	28	22	25	25
Municipal police	571	25	20	30	25
No full-time officers	14	100	0	0	0
1 to 4 full-time officers	80	72	25	1	1
5 to 10 full-time officers	142	37	34	25	4
11 to 20 full-time officers	112	11	21	53	16
21 to 50 full-time officers	112	4	18	53	26
51 to 150 full-time officers	73	4	5	19	71
Over 150 full-time officers	38	3	0	3	95
County sheriffs and police	90	18	17	17	49
1 to 4 full-time officers	2	50	50	0	0
5 to 10 full-time officers	5	40	20	40	0
11 to 20 full-time officers	15	33	27	13	27
21 to 50 full-time officers	28	25	29	18	29
51 to 150 full-time officers	26	4	4	19	73
Over 150 full-time officers	14	0	0	7	93
Other radio communications producers	107	50	38	7	6
No full-time officers	3	67	33	0	0
1 to 4 full-time officers	15	87	13	0	0
5 to 10 full-time officers	38	61	34	3	3
11 to 20 full-time officers	23	30	52	9	9
21 to 50 full-time officers	24	29	46	13	13
51 to 150 full-time officers	4	25	50	25	0

Note: Rows may not total 100 percent due to rounding errors.

Table 10–7. Ratio of Full-Time Employees Assigned to Radio Communications to Full-Time Employees Assigned to Patrol By Local Direct Producers

Type of Producer and Number of Full-Time Sworn Officers	Number Reporting	Ratio of Full-Time Employees Assigned to Radio Communications to Full-Time Employees Assigned to Patrol	
		Median	Range [a]
Municipal police	426	.25	.14 – .39
1 to 4 full-time officers	22	.33	.25 – 1.00
5 to 10 full-time officers	89	.50	.33 – .67
11 to 20 full-time officers	100	.36	.30 – .40
21 to 50 full-time officers	108	.22	.15 – .29
51 to 150 full-time officers	70	.12	.09 – .16
Over 150 full-time officers	37	.12	.09 – .15
County sheriffs and police	73	.18	.12 – .30
1 to 4 full-time officers	1	1.00	—
5 to 10 full-time officers	3	.67	.50 – .67
11 to 20 full-time officers	9	.40	.20 – .67
21 to 50 full-time officers	21	.19	.15 – .26
51 to 150 full-time officers	25	.17	.12 – .29
Over 150 full-time officers	14	.10	.07 – .16
Other radio communications producers	53	.18	.10 – .25
No full-time officers	1	.07	—
1 to 4 full-time officers	2	—	.33 – .67
5 to 10 full-time officers	15	.20	.14 – .33
11 to 20 full-time officers	15	.20	.12 – .27
21 to 50 full-time officers	17	.16	.07 – .20
51 to 150 full-time officers	3	.08	.06 – .10

[a] Range is the interquartile range.

Table 10-8. Local Direct Radio Communications Producers Who Assign Full-Time Personnel to Radio Communications by Utilization of Civilian Dispatchers: Type and Size of Producer

Type of Producer and Number of Full-Time Sworn Officers	Number Reporting	Percent of Producers With		
		No Civilians Assigned to Radio Communications	Some Civilians Assigned to Radio Communications	Only Civilians Assigned to Radio Communications
Total	554	28	19	53
Municipal police	426	26	20	54
1 to 4 full-time officers	22	9	0	91
5 to 10 full-time officers	89	10	1	89
11 to 20 full-time officers	100	25	17	58
21 to 50 full-time officers	108	49	19	32
51 to 150 full-time officers	70	19	30	51
Over 150 full-time officers	37	19	70	11
County sheriffs and police	74	43	19	38
1 to 4 full-time officers	1	0	0	100
5 to 10 full-time officers	3	0	33	67
11 to 20 full-time officers	10	60	0	40
21 to 50 full-time officers	21	38	5	57
51 to 150 full-time officers	25	52	32	16
Over 150 full-time officers	14	36	29	36
Other radio communications producers	54	22	9	69
No full-time officers	1	0	0	100
1 to 4 full-time officers	2	0	0	100
5 to 10 full-time officers	15	13	0	87
11 to 20 full-time officers	16	31	19	50
21 to 50 full-time officers	17	24	6	71
51 to 150 full-time officers	3	33	33	33

Note: Rows may not total 100 percent due to rounding errors.

Radio Communications Policies

Large amounts of federal funds have been allocated in recent years to encourage the development of joint dispatching arrangements and the interagency monitoring of police radio frequencies in metropolitan areas. We find that joint dispatching is common for county police and sheriffs' departments. More than 60 percent of the county producers employing more than 20 full-time sworn officers produce radio communications on a regular basis for at least one other agency. If we add responsibilities for "backup" dispatching, three out of four county departments do some dispatching for other police agencies (Table 10—9).

Municipal agencies are not as likely to produce radio communications for other police departments. Nor is size of agency related to the likelihood of municipal agencies producing radio communications for other departments. Few other direct producers (park police, campus police, etc.) produce radio communications for other departments.

Internal radio communications policies vary a great deal. In some agencies formal written procedures have been established for how calls of differing types are to be handled. Each call is given a priority number, and cars are dispatched according to the urgency of the calls. In most agencies there are no formal procedures for dispatching, although most agencies have an unwritten understanding of how to handle urgent calls.

Written procedures are used by only 8 percent of the municipal departments and 11 percent of the county police and sheriffs (Table 10—10). State and military police are more likely than local police to have written procedures for priority ordering of calls. Agencies with more than 150 full-time sworn officers are more likely to have written procedures than are smaller agencies.

When we asked if some calls for service would be routinely handled without the dispatch of a patrol car, about one fourth of the agencies responded that they do handle some calls that way. Forty percent of the county police and sheriffs' departments handle some calls without dispatching a patrol car. More than half the local agencies with over 150 full-time sworn officers handle some calls without dispatching a car.

Interagency monitoring and sharing of radio frequencies are common within the 80 SMSAs. Agencies sometimes share either a regular or an alternate frequency. When they share the same regular frequency all radio communications made by any of the participating agencies are received automatically by the other agencies. Sharing an

Table 10—9.   Direct Producers Who Produce Radio Communications for Other Police Agencies: Type and Size of Producer

	Percent of Producers Who		
Type of Direct Radio Communications Producers	Regularly Dispatch for Other Police	Do Backup Dispatching for Other Police	Dispatch for Other Police Agencies Either Regularly or as Backup
Municipal police	10 (583)	26 (467)	27 (600)
No full-time officers	0 (15)	9 (11)	6 (17)
1 to 4 full-time officers	1 (81)	24 (70)	20 (88)
5 to 10 full-time officers	16 (141)	26 (123)	32 (146)
11 to 20 full-time officers	15 (109)	27 (84)	32 (111)
21 to 50 full-time officers	6 (119)	34 (76)	25 (119)
51 to 150 full-time officers	11 (74)	27 (63)	32 (75)
Over 150 full-time officers	7 (44)	13 (40)	16 (44)
County sheriffs and police	60 (92)	50 (86)	76 (94)
1 to 4 full-time officers	50 (2)	100 (2)	67 (3)
5 to 10 full-time officers	60 (5)	25 (4)	60 (5)
11 to 20 full-time officers	47 (15)	47 (15)	73 (15)
21 to 50 full-time officers	67 (27)	61 (26)	82 (28)
51 to 150 full-time officers	63 (27)	48 (25)	81 (27)
Over 150 full-time officers	56 (16)	36 (14)	62 (16)
State police	10 (62)	24 (58)	23 (78)
Military police	3 (39)	5 (38)	7 (42)
Campus police	1 (82)	8 (73)	8 (89)
Other police[a]	0 (51)	9 (45)	7 (54)

Note: Number in parentheses equals number reporting.
[a] Other police includes federal police.

Table 10–10.   Internal Procedures for Handling Radio Communications: Type and Size of Producer

| | Producers Who | | | |
| | Have Written Procedures for Dispatching | | Handle Some Calls Without Dispatching Car | |
Type of Producer and Number of Full-Time Sworn Officers	Number Reporting	Percent	Number Reporting	Percent
Municipal police	391	8	368	25
No full-time officers	14	7	14	0
1 to 4 full-time officers	58	0	51	10
5 to 10 full-time officers	106	2	92	17
11 to 20 full-time officers	61	7	62	27
21 to 50 full-time officers	60	10	59	29
51 to 150 full-time officers	56	16	56	38
Over 150 full-time officers	36	25	34	53
County sheriffs and police	74	11	74	40
No full-time officers	1	0	1	0
1 to 4 full-time officers	2	0	2	100
5 to 10 full-time officers	2	0	4	0
11 to 20 full-time officers	15	0	14	21
21 to 50 full-time officers	21	5	20	30
51 to 150 full-time officers	21	5	22	54
Over 150 full-time officers	12	50	11	64
State police	33	15	22	36
Military police	31	13	27	15
Campus police	55	6	49	22
Other police[a]	48	8	38	5

[a]Other police includes federal police.

alternate frequency involves the establishment of a "backup" frequency that several agencies can use to communicate directly with each other.

County police and sheriffs' departments are more likely than other types of direct producers to share both regular and alternate radio frequencies. State and campus police departments are far more likely to share alternate frequencies than regular frequencies. Military police and other police are not likely to share either regular or alternate frequencies (Table 10-11).

Whether or not a producer shares a regular or alternate radio frequency with other agencies, other agencies' radio traffic can be monitored. Agencies often monitor an adjacent jurisdiction's radio to be alerted to any problems that might be "coming their way." Often local agencies monitor the state patrol or other agencies within whose larger jurisdiction they serve.

The majority of all local radio communications producing agencies monitor at least one other agency. County police and sheriffs' departments are most likely to monitor other police radios. Over three quarters of all county agencies employing more than 10 full-time sworn officers monitor at least one other police radio frequency.

While state agencies are less likely than local agencies to share regular or alternate frequencies, they are as likely as county sheriffs to monitor other agencies. This often involves monitoring radio communications of the larger local agencies. More than half the campus police and close to one third of the military police monitor other police radio frequencies.

When we examine the percent of agencies that either share a radio frequency with another agency or monitor another department's radio communications, we find that four out of five agencies have some capacity to hear the radio communications of at least one other agency. Almost all county sheriffs are able to listen to the radio communications of at least one other agency in their SMSA, and 89 percent of all municipal departments have similar capabilities. The charge that many agencies work side by side in metropolitan areas without knowing what is going on in adjacent territories is suspect, given these findings.

RADIO COMMUNICATIONS: SUMMARY

In our survey of the patterns of radio communications production in the 80 SMSAs we have found that large numbers of agencies produce radio communications. Sixty-eight percent of all direct service producers also produce radio communications. There are also radio

Table 10–11. Direct Producers Who Produce Radio Communications by Sharing or Monitoring Radio Frequencies: Type and Size of Producer

Type of Producer and Number of Full-Time Sworn Officers	*Percent of Producers Who*			
	Share Regular Radio Frequency	*Share Alternative Radio Frequency*	*Monitor Other Agency*	*Share Frequency or Monitor Radio*
Total	42 (912)	45 (772)	64 (861)	80 (990)
Municipal police	50 (589)	47 (487)	65 (562)	89 (612)
No full-time officers	54 (13)	67 (12)	31 (13)	63 (19)
1 to 4 full-time officers	71 (87)	51 (66)	50 (74)	87 (94)
5 to 10 full-time officers	56 (144)	49 (120)	66 (133)	93 (147)
11 to 20 full-time officers	56 (109)	42 (90)	71 (109)	92 (113)
21 to 50 full-time officers	54 (117)	38 (93)	73 (115)	91 (119)
51 to 150 full-time officers	23 (74)	52 (65)	72 (74)	91 (75)
Over 150 full-time officers	4 (45)	54 (41)	54 (44)	78 (45)
County sheriffs and police	55 (93)	63 (84)	78 (86)	96 (94)
1 to 4 full-time officers	67 (3)	50 (2)	50 (2)	100 (3)
5 to 10 full-time officers	20 (5)	60 (5)	50 (4)	100 (5)
11 to 20 full-time officers	53 (15)	40 (15)	77 (13)	93 (15)
21 to 50 full-time officers	59 (27)	75 (24)	75 (24)	96 (28)
51 to 150 full-time officers	63 (27)	67 (24)	81 (27)	96 (27)
Over 150 full-time officers	44 (16)	64 (14)	86 (16)	94 (16)
State police	12 (58)	43 (47)	77 (51)	56 (84)
Military police	17 (41)	13 (39)	31 (39)	43 (47)
Campus police	18 (84)	39 (74)	56 (79)	67 (91)
Other police[a]	17 (47)	29 (41)	45 (44)	48 (60)

Note: Number in parentheses equals number reporting. [a]Other police includes federal police.

communications specialists in some SMSAs. Although some police departments have alternating communications producers, there is very little duplication of radio communications services.

Three quarters of all local direct service producers that also produce radio communications assign four or fewer full-time employees to dispatch duties. Civilian employees are used extensively for radio communications assignments, particularly in smaller municipal departments. Larger patrol agencies achieve some economies of scale in radio communications. They have fewer communications personnel per patrol officer.

Eighty percent of county police or sheriffs' departments dispatch for other departments either on a regular or on a backup basis. Widespread interagency sharing of radio frequencies and monitoring radios of other police agencies in the metropolitan areas exists. Most police agencies are able to listen to radio traffic in adjacent or surrounding jurisdictions.

�✳ *Chapter 11*

Adult Pretrial Detention

Frances Bish

Many study groups and commissions have proposed
changes in the organization of adult pretrial detention
services [1]. Transfer of responsibility for pretrial detention to local or state correctional agencies, a more active role on the
part of states in regulating local detention facilities, and a reduction
in the number of local detention facilities are all examples of changes
that, it is assumed, will lead to improvements in adult pretrial detention services.

The relationships between organizational arrangements and policy
outcomes in the delivery of adult pretrial detention services, however, have not been systematically examined. In this chapter we
describe the arrangements currently used for pretrial detention in
small- to medium-sized metropolitan areas. Included are city, county,
tribal, state, and military facilities identified by police agencies as
holding suspects from the time of arraignment to final court disposition. Facilities used solely for holding prisoners prior to arraignment
or solely for incarceration of convicted offenders were not studied.

STATE REGULATION OF LOCAL
DETENTION FACILITIES

In most states adult pretrial detention is a local, rather than a state,
responsibility. States, however, have been urged to take a more active
role in the delivery of adult detention services. The National Advisory
Commission on Criminal Justice Standards and Goals, for example,
recommends that states assume full responsibility for this function

by 1982. Short of assuming responsibility for this function, the Commission recommends that states:

- Establish statewide standards for local jail construction and operation.
- Implement statewide jail inspection programs.
- Provide agencies responsible for such inspections with specific enforcement powers [2].

The most recent survey of statewide minimum jail standards was conducted by the American Bar Association in 1974 [3]. Their findings are summarized in Table 11–1. At that time only four states— Connecticut, Delaware, Rhode Island, and Vermont—had assumed full responsibility for pretrial detention. Twenty-three states had established statewide minimum jail standards, and 26 states had statewide inspection programs. Of the states with statewide standards, 12 had also provided their respective regulatory agencies with specific enforcement powers.

The proportion of states having statewide jail standards or inspection programs and specific enforcement powers varies by region. All of the four states that had assumed full responsibility for pretrial detention by 1974 are located in the Northeast (Regions 1, 2, and 3). All but two of the other states in the Northeast—New Hampshire and West Virginia—had either statewide standards or inspection programs. In the South and the Midwest a somewhat lower proportion of states reported that they had statewide standards and/or inspection programs. The South, however, had the largest proportion of states reporting specific enforcement powers for agencies overseeing minimum jail standards. Proportionately, the West had the fewest states with statewide standards and inspection programs. No western states had given their respective regulatory agencies specific enforcement powers.

TYPES OF AGENCIES THAT PRODUCE PRETRIAL DETENTION

A total of 200 agencies produce adult pretrial detention in the 80 SMSAs (Table 11–2). This is a much smaller number than for any of the services previously discussed. About 70 percent of the agencies that produce detention are local direct service agencies—municipal police departments and county sheriffs that also produce general area patrol, traffic control, and/or criminal investigation. County sheriffs are the most prevalent of the local detention-producing agencies, both in terms of the number of SMSAs served and their contribution to local detention capacity. County sheriffs produce pretrial detention in 62 SMSAs and contribute 74 percent of local detention capacity. Municipal police agencies, in contrast, produce pretrial detention in 17 SMSAs and contribute only 8 percent of total local detention capacity.

Twenty-five of the 200 agencies that produce detention are "detention specialists." Detention specialists are nonmilitary agencies that produce detention, but do not produce any of the direct police services examined in the study [4]. Ten of the detention specialists are county sheriffs who operate local jails and perform other court-related duties, but do not patrol or investigate crime. Three are city sheriffs located in the state of Virginia, and two are county jailers (an elective constitutional office in Kentucky) serving the Owensboro and Lexington SMSAs [5]. The remaining local detention specialists are independent, nonlaw enforcement agencies of various types [6]. One specialist is a state agency—the Connecticut State Department of Corrections—responsible for all adult institutional care in that state.

Detention specialists serve 24 of the SMSAs in the study and account for 18 percent of local detention capacity. Thirty-three federal agencies also produce pretrial detention in the 80 SMSAs. Most of these (30) are military facilities used exclusively for military personnel. (Civilians arrested on base are detained in civilian detention facilities.) The other three federal agencies are tribal facilities located in the Phoenix/Arizona SMSA.

Regional Variations in Types of Detention Producers

Considerable regional variation exists in the types of agencies that produce pretrial detention. In the Northeast (Regions 1, 2, and 3) police in most SMSAs rely on detention specialists to hold prisoners before trial (Table 11−3). In the Midwest (Regions 5 and 7) and West (Regions 8, 9, and 10) all nonmilitary detention is provided by direct service producers. Most of these are county sheriffs, but in one third of the SMSAs in these regions municipal police departments also supply pretrial detention.

In the South (Regions 4 and 6), county sheriffs produce detention in a majority of the SMSAs, but some SMSAs are also served by detention specialists and/or municipal police. Most of the southern municipal police departments that supply detention are located in two SMSAs: Birmingham/Alabama, where 16 municipal police departments produce detention; and West Palm Beach/Florida, where 8 municipal police agencies produce detention.

Table 11–1.   Minimum Jail Standards and Their Enforcement in the 50 States, 1973–74

| | Level of Government Responsible for[a] | | | | Statutory Enforcement Powers | |
| | Standards | | Inspection | | | |
States[b]	State	Local	State	Local	General	Specific
Northeast						
Connecticut	Adult Detention Facilities Operated by the State					
Delaware	Adult Detention Facilities Operated by the State					
Maine	●		●			●
Maryland	●		●			
Massachusetts	●		●		●	●
New Hampshire				●		
New Jersey			●			
New York	●		●			●
Pennsylvania	Adult Detention Facilities Operated by the State					●
Rhode Island	Adult Detention Facilities Operated by the State					
Vermont	Pretrial Detention Provided by the State					
Virginia	●		●			
West Virginia		●		●	●	
Midwest						
Illinois	●		●			●
Indiana	●		○			●

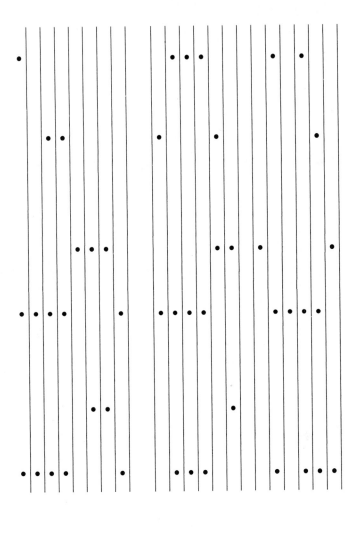

(Table 11-1. continued overleaf)

Table 11–1. continued

| States[b] | Level of Government Responsible for[a] | | | | Statutory Enforcement Powers | |
| | Standards | | Inspection | | | |
	State	Local	State	Local	General	Specific
West						
Alaska						
Arizona						
California	•			•		
Colorado				•		
Hawaii						
Idaho				•		
Montana				•		
Nevada				•		
No. Dakota		•				
Oregon	•		•			
So. Dakota			•			
Utah			•			
Washington	•					
Wyoming						

Source: American Bar Association, Commission on Correctional Facilities and Services, Statewide Jail Standards and Inspection Systems Project, *Survey and Handbook on State Standards and Inspection Legislation for Jails and Juvenile Detention Facilities* (Washington, D.C.: August 1974, pp. 10–16). Some changes have been made in this table by Workshop staff, reflecting statutes not identified by the ABA and revisions that took place during 1974.

[a] To the extent possible, we have attempted to indicate the level of government with primary regulatory responsibility. In most states a number of local agencies (e.g., grand juries, courts, fire marshals, and health departments) are also authorized and/or required to inspect local detention facilities.

[b] States left blank had no statutory powers in 1973–74, according to the ABA survey.

Table 11-2.   Producers of Adult Pretrial Detention: Type of Agency

Type of Agency	Number Reporting	Percent[a]	Number of SMSAs Served per Type	Percent[a] of Local Capacity[b]
Total	200	100	—[c]	—
Local direct service producers				
Municipal police	53	27	17	8
County sheriffs	89	45	62	74
Detention centers				
County sheriffs	10	5	8	7
Other local[d]	14	7	12	11
State[e]	1	1	4	—
Federal agencies				
Military	30	15	25	—
Tribal	3	2	1	—

[a]Columns may not total 100 percent due to rounding errors.
[b]Percent of locally supplied capacity; data on federal and state producers are insufficient to permit inclusion.
[c]Sum is greater than 80 because some SMSAs are served by more than one type of agency.
[d]Includes three Virginia city sheriffs.
[e]Connecticut State Department of Corrections.

Jail Standards and Types of Detention Producers

There are, thus, clear regional variations in the types of pretrial detention producers. It is conceivable that the types of detention producers would also vary by state law. As states adopt and enforce minimum jail standards, for example, agencies not required by law to produce detention (e.g., municipal police departments) might be unwilling to bear the costs of bringing existing jails up to standard. The number of SMSAs with municipal police jails would, thus, be lower in states with statewide jail standards and specific enforcement powers than those without. Alternatively, states with larger numbers of municipal jails may have a greater incentive to adopt statewide standards for local jail facilities. Were this the case, we might initially expect to find more SMSAs with municipal police department jails in states with standards than in those without.

Using data from the 1974 ABA survey we find little systematic relationship between detention laws and types of agencies that pro-

Table 11–3. Number of SMSAs Served by Different Types of Detention Producers: Region

Location	Number of SMSAs	SMSAs Served by the Following Types of Producers							
		County Sheriffs		Municipal Police		Detention Centers		Federal Agencies	
		Number	Percent	Number	Percent	Number	Percent	Number	Percent
Total	80	62	78	17	21	24	30	25	31
Northeast									
Region 1	8	0	0	0	0	8	100	0	0
Region 2	4	1	25	0	0	3	75	0	0
Region 3	6	2	33	0	0	6	100	1	17
Midwest									
Region 5	16	16	100	5	31	0	0	1	6
Region 7	4	4	100	1	25	0	0	1	25
South									
Region 4	15	13	87	5	33	5	33	5	33
Region 6	14	13	93	1	7	2	14	7	50
West									
Region 8	4	4	100	0	0	0	0	3	75
Region 9	7	7	100	3	43	0	0	7	100
Region 10	2	2	100	2	100	0	0	0	0

Note: Rows total more than 100 percent because some SMSAs are served by more than one type of producer.

duce detention. For example, municipal police departments produce detention in about the same proportion of SMSAs in states without any jail standards as in states with statewide jail standards (Table 11−4). The same patterns are evident with respect to jail inspection laws. On the other hand, a higher proportion of SMSAs in states with specific enforcement powers have municipal police department jails than do those without.

Because county sheriffs and detention specialists are generally required by law to provide detention, we would expect the adoption of minimum jail standards to have little impact on the number of SMSAs served by these types of producers. However, it is noteworthy that 18 of the 24 SMSAs served by detention specialists are located in states with statewide standards and 20 in states where jail inspection is conducted by a state agency. Proportionately fewer of the SMSAs in these states have detention produced by county sheriffs.

It is likely that the effects of state laws are complicated or obscured by regional variations in the types of agencies that produce pretrial detention—variations that themselves reflect historical patterns of law and policy. It is also possible that simply having or not having standards and/or enforcement powers means little. We may need to know more about the types of standards adopted and state inspection and enforcement policies before any judgments can be made about their effects.

AGENCY CHARACTERISTICS AND PERSONNEL POLICIES

The size of a detention-producing agency is thought by some to have a bearing on its ability to operate an adequately staffed and well-maintained detention facility—larger agencies presumably having more resources and personnel available for detention purposes than smaller agencies. In our study the largest agencies (in terms of number of full-time employees) that produce detention are county sheriffs (Table 11−5). Municipal police are the smallest detention-producing agencies. Municipal police departments that produce detention, however, are much larger than those that do not. The median number of full-time employees in municipal police departments producing detention is 37, compared to a median of 10 full-time employees in municipal police departments not producing detention.

In comparison to county sheriffs and detention specialists, municipal police agencies also operate relatively small detention facilities (Table 11−6). Fifty percent of the municipal police jails have capacity for fewer than 20 inmates. Only 5 percent of the direct service

Table 11–4.   Number of SMSAs Served by Different Types of Nonfederal Detention Producers: Type of State Law

| | Number of SMSAs | SMSAs Served by | | | | | |
| | | County Sheriffs | | Municipal Police | | Detention Centers | |
		Number	Percent	Number	Percent	Number	Percent
Total	80	62	78	17	21	24	30
Level of Government Responsible for Jail Standards in 1973							
None	19	13	68	4	21	6	32
Local	5	5	100	2	40	0	0
State	56	44	79	11	20	18	32
Level of Government Responsible for Jail Inspections in 1973							
None	2	2	100	1	50	0	0
Local	29	26	90	5	17	4	14
State	49	34	69	11	22	20	41
Type of Enforcement Powers in 1973							
None	44	35	80	7	16	12	27
General	12	7	58	2	17	6	50
Specific	24	20	83	8	33	6	25

Note: Rows total more than 100 percent because some SMSAs are served by more than one type of producer.

county sheriffs and none of the detention specialists have jails this small.

The number of full-time employees assigned to detention also varies by type of agency (Table 11–7). Twenty-four percent of the agencies that produce pretrial detention assign no full-time personnel to jail duties. In these agencies jail duties are performed by officers whose major responsibilities are the production of other police services or by part-time jail personnel. Municipal police agencies and small jails are most likely to assign no full-time personnel; 68 percent of the detention-producing municipal police agencies and 89 percent of all jails holding 20 or fewer inmates assign no full-time personnel. Only 2 percent of the direct service county sheriffs and none of the detention specialists assign no full-time employees to detention. All jails holding more than 100 persons assign at least one full-time employee to this function.

County sheriffs tend to assign a higher percentage of their total personnel to jail duties than do municipal police agencies (Table 11–8). About half the county sheriffs assign more than 20 percent of their total personnel to this function; no municipal police agency assigns this high a percentage.

There are also major differences among types and sizes of detention facilities in the ratio of full-time jail employees to detention capacity (Table 11–9). Fifty percent of the detention specialists assign 21 or more full-time employees per 100 units of capacity. The

Table 11–5. Number of Full-Time Personnel Employed in Local Agencies That Produce Detention: Type of Agency

| | | Number of Full-Time Personnel | |
Type of Agency	Number Reporting	Median	Range[a]
Municipal police			
Full-time employees	53	37	14 – 114
Full-time sworn	53	30	10 – 101
County sheriffs			
Full-time employees	85	58	32 – 125
Full-time sworn	86	46	22 – 98
Detention centers[b]			
Full-time employees	20	45	27 – 58
Full-time sworn	20	22	8 – 46

[a] Range is the interquartile range.
[b] Local agencies only; excludes state and federal producers and agencies for which data are not available.

Table 11–6.   Capacity of Local Detention Facilities: Type of Agency

| Type of Agency | Number Reporting | Capacity of Detention Facility[a] | | | | |
| | | Percent of Detention Facilities of This Size | | | | |
		0–20	21–50	51–100	101–250	Over 250
Total	156	18	14	28	19	21
Municipal police	48	50	23	17	6	4
County sheriffs	86	5	12	37	22	24
Detention centers	22	0	5	18	36	41

Note: Rows may not total 100 percent due to rounding errors.
[a]Refers to number of inmates that can be held in detention facility at a given time.

Table 11–7. Number of Full-Time Employees Assigned to Detention by Local Agencies: Type of Agency and Capacity of Detention Facility

Type of Agency	*Number Reporting*	*Number of Full-Time Employees in Detention*				
		Percent of Detention Facilities With				
		0	*1 to 4*	*5 to 19*	*20 to 39*	*40 or more*
Total	157	24	11	33	15	17
Municipal police	53	68	9	19	0	4
County sheriffs	82	2	15	48	16	19
Detention centers	22	0	0	14	45	41
Capacity of Detention Facility (Number of Inmates[a])						
Total	152	22	10	34	15	18
1 to 20	27	89	11	0	0	0
21 to 50	22	36	32	32	0	0
51 to 100	43	5	9	72	12	2
101 to 250	30	0	7	43	37	13
251 and over	30	0	0	3	23	73

Note: Rows may not total 100 percent due to rounding errors.

[a] Refers to the number of inmates that can be held in detention facility at a given time.

Table 11–8.   Percentage of Full-Time Employees Assigned to Jail Duties by Local Direct Service Agencies: Type of Agency

Producing Detention and Direct Service	Number Reporting	Percent of Agencies Assigning				
		No Full-Time Employees to Jail Duties	1 to 10 Percent Full-Time Employees to Jail Duties	11 to 20 Percent Full-Time Employees to Jail Duties	21 to 30 Percent Full-Time Employees to Jail Duties	More Than 30 Percent Full-Time Employees to Jail Duties
Municipal police	53	68	25	7	0	0
County sheriffs	82	2	9	40	28	21

Table 11–9. Ratio of Local Full-Time Jail Employees to Detention Capacity: Type of Agency and Capacity of Detention Facility

	Number Reporting	Full-Time Jail Employees per 100 Inmates	
		Median	Range
Total	152	9	3 – 18
Type of Agency			
Municipal police	48	0	0 – 6
County sheriffs	82	10	8 – 18
Detention centers	22	21	16 – 36
Capacity of Detention Facility (Number of Inmates[a])			
1 to 20	27	0	0 – 0
21 to 50	22	5	0 – 23
51 to 100	43	10	8 – 18
101 to 250	30	10	6 – 21
251 and over	30	15	9 – 22

[a]Refers to number of inmates that can be held in detention facility at a given time.

median ratio for direct service county sheriffs (10 jail employees per 100 units of capacity) is less than half that of detention specialists. For municipal police agencies the median ratio is zero. The ratio of full-time jail employees to capacity also varies with size of detention facility—larger facilities assigning more full-time personnel per 100 units of capacity than smaller facilities.

It is often suggested that civilian rather than sworn personnel be assigned to jail duties [7]. In the 80 SMSAs detention specialists are more likely to use all sworn personnel in their detention facilities than are municipal police or direct service county sheriffs (Table 11–10). Municipal police agencies that assign full-time employees to detention are most likely to use at least some civilian personnel. They are also more likely than direct service county sheriffs or detention specialists to employ a relatively high percentage of civilians (Table 11–10).

Jail Standards, Agency Characteristics, and Personnel Policies

Differences in state laws and standards may account for some of the variations in agency characteristics and personnel policies. A number of states, for example, now require local detention facilities to maintain sufficient staff to provide 24-hour supervision of inmates

Table 11-10. Percentage of Nonmilitary Jails Using Civilian and Sworn Personnel: Type of Agency and Capacity of Detention Facility

	Number Reporting	Percent of Agencies Whose Detention Personnel Include			
		No Civilians	1 to 50 Percent Civilians	51 to 99 Percent Civilians	All Civilians
Total[a]	117	35	33	11	21
Type of Agency					
Municipal police	16	31	6	31	31
County sheriffs	79	34	40	8	18
Detention centers	22	41	27	9	23
Capacity of Detention Facility[b]					
1 to 20	3	33	0	33	33
21 to 50	14	50	29	0	21
51 to 100	41	34	29	17	20
101 to 250	30	37	30	7	27
250 and over	29	28	48	10	14

Note: Rows may not total 100 percent due to rounding errors.

[a]Includes only agencies that assign full-time personnel to detention.

[b]Refers to the number of inmates that can be held in detention facility at a given time.

and inmate educational and vocational training programs. Some also require detention personnel to undertake specialized training. These and other regulations, if enforced, might influence the characteristics and personnel policies of detention-producing agencies.

As indicated in Tables 11–11 through 11–14, however, there appear to be few systematic relationships between state legislation regarding jail standards and agency characteristics and personnel policies. A few points might be noted. The first is that municipal police and county sheriffs' departments producing detention tend to be larger in states with state or local standards than in states without any mandated standards. Municipal police departments producing detention in states with specific enforcement powers also tend to be somewhat larger than such agencies in states with general or no enforcement powers.

Second, jail standards appear to have some effect on the size of local detention facilities. Municipal police departments producing detention in states with jail standards (state or local) generally have larger facilities than such agencies in states without standards. County sheriffs and detention specialists, on the other hand, have smaller facilities in states with, than in states without, standards. Finally, there is some tendency for municipal police departments and sheriffs' agencies in states with state or local standards to assign a higher ratio of full-time personnel to inmates and proportionately more civilian personnel than in states without standards. Beyond these trends few systematic relationships between state laws and agency characteristics and personnel policies can be identified.

METROPOLITAN INDUSTRY STRUCTURE
FOR PRETRIAL DETENTION

Proposals for change in the organization of pretrial detention services have also addressed the metropolitan area industry structure for delivering these services. One recommendation, for example, would reduce the number of locally operated jail facilities and consolidate existing jails into regional facilities or service networks [8]. Localities have also been encouraged to develop cooperative arrangements for the production of this service.

In terms of the number of detention producers per SMSA, we find that a majority of the 80 SMSAs are served by two or more detention facilities (Table 11–15). When military producers of detention are excluded, however, slightly more than half the SMSAs are served by one and only one nonmilitary facility (Table 11–16). The effect of excluding military producers is greatest in the South and West, where military bases are most numerous.

Table 11–11.　Number of Full-Time Employees in Local Agencies That Produce Detention: Type of State Law

Type of Agency	Level of Government Responsible for Jail Standards in 1973			Types of Enforcement Powers in 1973			Level of Government Responsible for Jail Inspections in 1973		
	None	Local	State	None	General	Specific	None	Local	State
Total	(49)	(9)	(102)	(65)	(34)	(59)	(7)	(39)	(112)
Median	27	100	54	55	25	55	32	87	45
Range[a]	15–70	55–132	30–125	30–121	15–67	32–125	12–120	34–135	21–90
Municipal police	(25)	(3)	(27)	(15)	(17)	(21)	(5)	(7)	(41)
Median	18	116	53	37	15	72	19	94	30
Range	11–41	94–132[b]	24–163	12–120	11–26	32–194	12–41	37–132	15–94
County sheriffs	(18)	(6)	(61)	(41)	(12)	(32)	(2)	(28)	(55)
Median	34	55	58	65	57	56	—	66	56
Range	22–90	51–150	32–130	31–125	22–69	36–167	32–480[b]	34–150	26–92
Detention centers	(6)	(0)	(14)	(9)	(5)	(6)	(0)	(4)	(16)
Median	58	—	39	58	39	25	—	30	45
Range	30–87	—	27–51	50–87	30–58	21–45	—	7–87	27–58

Note: Number in parentheses equals number reporting.
[a] Range is the interquartile range.
[b] Full range of variation.

Table 11–12. Capacity of Local Detention Facilities[a]: Type of State Law

Type of Agency	Level of Government Responsible for Jail Standards in 1973			Types of Enforcement Powers in 1973			Level of Government Responsible for Jail Inspections in 1973		
	None	*Local*	*State*	*None*	*General*	*Specific*	*None*	*Local*	*State*
Total	(46)	(9)	(101)	(64)	(33)	(59)	(7)	(39)	(110)
Median	64	136	80	90	70	75	42	123	75
Range[b]	18 – 145	40 – 222	41 – 170	44 – 268	16 – 125	39 – 158	18 – 77	60 – 342	38 – 150
Municipal police	(21)	(3)	(24)	(13)	(15)	(20)	(5)	(7)	(36)
Median	16	16	26	18	15	38	22	16	25
Range	12 – 40	15 – 170[c]	15 – 54	15 – 22	11 – 40	20 – 75	18 – 42	15 – 20	12 – 54
County sheriffs	(18)	(6)	(62)	(41)	(12)	(33)	(2)	(28)	(56)
Median	104	136	80	104	97	85	—	126	80
Range	64 – 200	75 – 310	55 – 202	60 – 300	60 – 180	55 – 160	64 – 598[c]	65 – 373	52 – 160
Detention centers	(7)	(0)	(15)	(10)	(6)	(6)	(0)	(4)	(18)
Median	228	—	150	150	124	120	—	325	145
Range	135 – 325	—	100 – 299	135 – 285	112 – 310	90 – 299	—	88 – 342	112 – 268

Note: Number in parentheses equals number reporting.

[a]Refers to number of inmates that can be held at a given time.

[b]Range is the interquartile range.

[c]Full range of variation.

Table 11–13. Ratio of Full-Time Jail Employees per 100 Local Inmates: Type of State Law

Type of Agency	Level of Government Responsible for Jail Standards in 1973			Types of Enforcement Powers in 1973			Level of Government Responsible for Jail Inspections in 1973		
	None	Local	State	None	General	Specific	None	Local	State
Total	(46)	(9)	(97)	(63)	(33)	(56)	(7)	(39)	(106)
Median	6	7	10	11	6	9	0	10	9
Range[a]	0 – 15	6 – 11	5 – 21	6 – 21	0 – 12	5 – 18	0 – 9	6 – 18	3 – 19
Municipal police	(21)	(3)	(24)	(13)	(15)	(20)	(5)	(7)	(36)
Median	0	0	0	0	0	3	0	0	0
Range	0 – 0	0 – 6[b]	0 – 6	0 – 0	0 – 0	0 – 6	0 – 0	0 – 6	0 – 6
County sheriffs	(18)	(6)	(58)	(40)	(12)	(30)	(2)	(28)	(52)
Median	9	10	12	11	8	11	—	11	10
Range	6 – 15	7 – 18	8 – 21	8 – 18	6 – 10	8 – 21	9 – 22[b]	8 – 16	7 – 18
Detention centers	(7)	(0)	(15)	(10)	(6)	(6)	(0)	(4)	(18)
Median	27	—	20	26	17	16	—	9	21
Range	9 – 40	—	16 – 26	21 – 37	9 – 38	15 – 23	—	8 – 21	17 – 37

Note: Number in parentheses equals number reporting.
[a] Range is the interquartile range.
[b] Full range of variation.

Table 11–14. Percent of Jail Employees Who Are Civilians: Type of Local Agency and State Law[a]

Type of Agency	Level of Government Responsible for Jail Standards in 1973			Types of Enforcement Powers in 1973			Level of Government Responsible for Jail Inspections in 1973		
	None	Local	State	None	General	Specific	None	Local	State
Total	(28)	(7)	(83)	(52)	(20)	(46)	(3)	(32)	(83)
Median	15	20	30	30	8	15	58	36	16
Range[b]	0–83	0–25	0–89	0–74	0–45	0–100	17–100	0–60	0–91
Municipal police	(4)	(1)	(12)	(4)	(2)	(11)	(1)	(2)	(14)
Median	67	91	80	100	—	80	100	—	67
Range	15–100	—	0–100	91–100	15–67[c]	0–100	—	91–100[c]	0–100
County sheriffs	(17)	(6)	(56)	(38)	(12)	(29)	(2)	(26)	(51)
Median	3	3	30	27	29	15	—	25	27
Range	0–58	0–22	0–60	0–50	0–45	0–100	17–58[c]	0–50	0–75
Detention centers	(7)	(0)	(15)	(10)	(6)	(6)	(0)	(4)	(18)
Median	7	—	8	16	0	8	—	100	7
Range	0–100	—	0–94	0–94	0–8	0–100	—	0–100	0–22

Note: Number in parentheses equals number reporting.
[a] Includes only those agencies that assign some full-time employees to detention.
[b] Range is the interquartile range.
[c] Full range of variation.

Table 11–15. Multiplicity in Detention Production: Region, SMSA Population, and Number of Counties

	Number of SMSAs	Number of Detention Producers in an SMSA		Number of Producers per 10 Consuming Agencies		Number of Producers per 1,000 Sworn Officers	
		Median	Range[a]	Median	Range	Median	Range
Total	80	2	1 – 3	1.5	.9 – 2.5	5	2 – 7
Northeast							
Region 1	8	1	1 – 1	1.7	1.1 – 2.5	4	2 – 7
Region 2	4	1	1 – 2	.5	.2 – 1.1	1	1 – 2
Region 3	6	1	1 – 2	.6	.3 – 3.3	3	2 – 6
Midwest							
Region 5	16	2	1 – 3	1.0	.8 – 1.6	6	4 – 7
Region 7	4	1	1 – 2	.9	.6 – .9	4	3 – 4
South							
Region 4	15	3	2 – 4	2.0	1.4 – 2.5	6	3 – 7
Region 6	14	2	1 – 2	1.7	1.1 – 2.5	3	2 – 8
West							
Region 8	4	2	1 – 2	1.3	.7 – 2.2	5	2 – 6
Region 9	7	3	2 – 5	1.8	.8 – 2.0	4	2 – 6
Region 10	2	—	2 – 7	—	3.3 – 3.3	—	10 – 22

Metropolitan Population (1973 est.)						
50,000 to 124,999	20	1	1 – 2	2.2	1.3 – 2.5	7	5 – 9
125,000 to 249,999	26	1	1 – 3	1.1	.8 – 2.5	5	3 – 8
250,000 to 499,999	21	2	2 – 4	1.5	.8 – 2.0	3	2 – 6
500,000 and over	13	4	2 – 5	1.1	.9 – 1.5	2	2 – 4

Number of Counties						
One	54	1	1 – 2	1.3	.8 – 2.5	5	3 – 7
Two	16	3	2 – 4	1.5	1.0 – 2.0	5	2 – 6
Three or more	6	4	3 – 4	1.5	1.1 – 3.1	3	3 – 12
Connecticut	4	1	1 – 1	1.7	1.1 – 2.5	3	2 – 4

a Refers to interquartile range except for Region 10, where it is the full range of variation.

Table 11–16. Multiplicity in Nonmilitary Detention Production: Region, SMSA Population, and Number of Counties

	Number of SMSAs	Number of Nonmilitary Producers in an SMSA		Number of Producers per 10 Consuming Agencies		Number of Producers per 1,000 Sworn Officers	
		Median	Range^a	Median	Range	Median	Range
Total	80	1	1 – 2	1.3	.8 – 2.0	4	2 – 7
Northeast							
Region 1	8	1	1 – 1	1.7	1.1 – 2.0	4	2 – 6
Region 2	4	1	1 – 2	.5	.2 – 1.1	1	1 – 2
Region 3	6	1	1 – 2	.6	.3 – 3.3	3	2 – 5
Midwest							
Region 5	16	2	1 – 3	1.0	.8 – 1.6	6	4 – 7
Region 7	4	1	1 – 1	.9	.6 – 1.0	4	3 – 4
South							
Region 4	15	2	1 – 4	1.7	1.4 – 2.2	4	3 – 7
Region 6	14	1	1 – 2	1.1	1.0 – 2.2	3	1 – 7
West							
Region 8	4	1	1 – 1	.9	.7 – 1.4	3	2 – 5
Region 9	7	2	1 – 3	1.4	.5 – 1.7	3	1 – 4
Region 10	2	—	2 – 7	—	3.2 – 3.3	—	10 – 22

Metropolitan Population (1973 est.)						
50,000 to 124,999	20	1 – 1	1.4	1.1 – 2.5	6	4 – 7
125,000 to 249,999	26	1 – 2	1.1	.8 – 2.2	5	3 – 8
250,000 to 499,999	21	1 – 3	1.0	.6 – 1.7	2	1 – 4
500,000 and over	13	2 – 5	1.1	.7 – 1.5	2	1 – 4
Number of Counties						
One	54	1 – 1	1.1	.7 – 1.7	4	2 – 7
Two	16	2 – 4	1.5	.7 – 2.0	4	2 – 6
Three or more	6	3 – 4	1.5	1.1 – 3.1	3	3 – 12
Connecticut	4	1 – 1	1.7	1.1 – 2.5	3	2 – 4

[a] Refers to interquartile range except for Region 10, where it is the full range of variation.

The number of nonmilitary producers of detention in an SMSA reflects the number of counties in the SMSA and the role of municipal police agencies. Twenty-two of the 35 SMSAs with more than one nonmilitary producer of pretrial detention are multicounty SMSAs. Multicounty SMSAs account for most of the variation in the number of detention producers per SMSA in the Northeast and the South. Municipal police departments producing pretrial detention account for most of the variation in the number of detention producers per SMSA in the Midwest and West.

The number of detention producers per SMSA does not take account of variations in the number of agencies or sworn personnel using pretrial detention facilities. To compare across SMSAs it is more appropriate to look at relative multiplicity measures—the number of detention producers relative to the number of agencies and sworn personnel that use these services.

The number of detention producers relative to the number of police agencies using detention is highest in New England, the South, and the Far West (Regions 1, 4, 9, and 10) (see Table 11-16). The number of detention producers relative to sworn personnel in agencies that use detention facilities is highest in the Great Lakes states (Region 5). However, differences in relative multiplicity among regions for detention are not large. Although larger SMSAs characteristically have more detention producers than smaller SMSAs, they have fewer detention facilities relative to the number of agencies and sworn personnel using this service.

Table 11-17 presents data on the extent to which direct service producers in each SMSA supply their own detention (independence). It also shows the percentage of direct service producers per SMSA using only their own detention facilities. Nationwide only about 10 percent of the direct service police departments produce this service for themselves. The proportion of direct service producers supplying this service for themselves is lowest in the Northeast and highest in the South and West.

Direct service producers generally obtain pretrial detention from some other agency. Table 11-18 shows the number of agencies per SMSA regularly served by different types of detention producers. From this table it is evident that municipal police departments with their own jails generally do not detain prisoners for other agencies. Most direct service police producers in the study are served by county sheriffs and detention specialists.

A number of the SMSAs included in the study have more than one jail. In these SMSAs it is possible that police agencies would use the services of more than one detention facility. However, we find little

Table 11–17. Independence and Autonomy in Detention Production Among Direct Service Producers: Region, SMSA Population, and Number of Counties

| | | Percent of Consuming Agencies per SMSA Who | | | |
| | | Produce Their Own Detention | | Use Only Their Own Detention Facilities | |
	Number of SMSAs	*Median*	*Range[a]*	*Median*	*Range*
Total	80	10	2 – 16	8	0 – 13
Northeast					
Region 1	8	0	0 – 0	0	0 – 0
Region 2	4	0	0 – 2	0	0 – 2
Region 3	6	0	0 – 7	0	0 – 7
Midwest					
Region 5	16	10	8 – 14	10	5 – 12
Region 7	4	9	6 – 9	6	0 – 9
South					
Region 4	15	13	8 – 20	9	0 – 10
Region 6	14	11	8 – 25	11	8 – 25
West					
Region 8	4	11	7 – 13	11	7 – 13
Region 9	7	15	4 – 18	8	4 – 13
Region 10	2	—	29 – 33	—	14 – 17
Metropolitan Population (1973 est.)					
50,000 to 124,999	20	13	0 – 18	11	0 – 18
125,000 to 249,999	26	8	0 – 17	6	0 – 10
250,000 to 499,999	21	9	0 – 15	7	0 – 11
500,000 and over	13	10	8 – 15	9	7 – 11
Number of Counties					
One	54	9	4 – 16	8	0 – 13
Two	16	10	7 – 18	10	7 – 12
Three or more	6	11	10 – 31	10	7 – 11
Connecticut	4	0	0 – 0	0	0 – 0

[a] Refers to interquartile range except for Region 10, where it is the full range of variation.

Table 11–18. Number of Agencies per SMSA Regularly Served by Detention Producers: Type of Detention Producer

Type of Producer	Number Reporting	Median	Interquartile Range
Total	(208)	5	2 – 11
Direct service producers			
Municipal police	(53)	1	1 – 2
County sheriffs	(89)	10	7 – 14
Detention centers	(30)	9	5 – 18
Federal police agencies	(36)	2	2 – 3

use of multiple detention facilities (Table 11–19). Where police agencies do use more than one jail, they generally use them in alternation (Table 11–19).

Three types of alternation are common. In some SMSAs male and female prisoners are housed in separate facilities. In others county facilities may be used for felony defendants and municipal facilities for prisoners charged with offenses against the municipal code. Another type of alternation occurs in multicounty SMSAs where some direct service producers serve more than one county. State police serving a two-county SMSA, for example, may use detention facilities in both counties—selecting one or the other on the basis of where an individual was arrested or is to be tried.

Most direct service agencies using adult pretrial detention are, thus, served by one and only one detention facility. In many SMSAs most agencies are also served by the same detention facility. The median percentage of agencies in an SMSA served by the "largest" producer is 88 percent (Table 11–19). Dominance in detention is highest in New England, Virginia and Pennsylvania, and the Midwest (Regions 1, 3, 5, and 7) and lowest in the South and Rocky Mountain states (Regions 4 and 8).

Variations in dominance reflect differences in the number of municipal producers, multicounty SMSAs, and military agencies. Except in the Connecticut SMSAs, the dominant producers of pretrial detention are county sheriffs or other county agencies. Typically these agencies are required by state law to supply pretrial detention for other police agencies in the county. In Connecticut the State Department of Corrections supplies detention to all direct service agencies.

USE OF METROPOLITAN AREA RESOURCES
FOR PRETRIAL DETENTION

Data presented earlier suggest that different types of agencies vary somewhat in their use of agency resources for pretrial detention. We now describe variations among SMSAs in the use of metropolitan area resources for this service. Three measures of resource use are discussed: the ratio of total SMSA jail capacity to SMSA population; the percentage of all SMSA police employees assigned to detention; and the ratio of total SMSA jail employees to total SMSA jail capacity. These measures have been computed using data on nonmilitary agencies. Data were sufficiently complete in 70 of the 80 SMSAs.

The ratio of total jail capacity to SMSA population and the ratio of total SMSA jail employees to capacity varies considerably among SMSAs located in different regions of the country and among different-sized SMSAs (Table 11-20). Less variation exists in the proportion of total SMSA personnel assigned to detention. In most SMSAs, from 4 to 8 percent of all police employees are assigned to jail duties.

SMSAs with low independence and low relative miltiplicity have lower ratios of jail capacity to population, but higher ratios of jail employees to jail capacity, than do SMSAs with higher relative multiplicity and independence. Relationships between the absolute number of detention producers per SMSA (multiplicity) and these measures of resource use are less clear—although the ratio of jail employees to jail capacity is lowest in those SMSAs with three or more producers of detention (Table 11-21). The lower ratios of jail employees to jail capacity in SMSAs with high relative multiplicity may be due to the presence of municipal police jails that have low ratios of jail employees to capacity.

IMPLICATIONS OF FINDINGS

In this chapter we have described the organizational arrangements used for adult pretrial detention in metropolitan areas. None of the data presented in the chapter allows us to draw conclusions about the quality of detention services provided in metropolitan areas or the performance of detention-producing agencies. Some of our findings, however, do have implications for proposals to reorganize adult pretrial detention services.

Our findings on the metropolitan industry structure for pretrial detention indicate that this service is already highly consolidated in most SMSAs. A majority of the SMSAs in the study are currently

Table 11–19. Duplication, Alternation, and Dominance in Detention Production Among Direct Service Producers: Region, SMSA Population, and Number of Counties

| | Number of SMSAs | Percent of Consuming Agencies per SMSA Who | | | | Percent of SMSA Consumers Served by Dominant Detention Producer | |
| | | Use More Than One Jail | | Utilize Alternate Jails | | | |
		Median	Range^a	Median	Range	Median	Range
Total	80	0	0 – 11	0	0 – 12	88	75 – 100
Northeast							
Region 1	8	0	0 – 0	0	0 – 0	100	75 – 100
Region 2	4	0	0 – 1	0	0 – 1	78	38 – 100
Region 3	6	0	0 – 14	0	0 – 14	100	83 – 100
Midwest							
Region 5	16	5	0 – 6	0	0 – 5	100	73 – 100
Region 7	4	0	0 – 20	0	0 – 20	100	100 – 100
South							
Region 4	15	11	0 – 35	7	0 – 35	70	56 – 100
Region 6	14	0	0 – 0	0	0 – 0	82	75 – 100
West							
Region 8	4	0	0 – 0	0	0 – 0	75	75 – 78
Region 9	7	8	0 – 15	6	0 – 15	82	76 – 88
Region 10	2	—	17 – 19	—	14 – 17	—	67 – 100

Metropolitan Population (1973 est.)							
50,000 to 124,999	20	0 – 0	0	0 – 0	0	100	80 – 100
125,000 to 249,999	26	0 – 17	0	0 – 17	0	100	75 – 100
250,000 to 499,999	21	0 – 14	4	0 – 14	4	82	75 – 100
500,000 and over	13	5 – 11	7	5 – 8	5	64	55 – 73
Number of Counties							
One	54	0 – 5	0	0 – 4	0	100	82 – 100
Two	16	5 – 22	9	5 – 22	9	67	55 – 73
Three or more	6	8 – 19	10	8 – 19	8	50	38 – 56
Connecticut	4	0 – 0	0	0 – 0	0	100	100 – 100

[a]Refers to interquartile range except for Region 10, where it is the full range of variation.

Table 11–20.   Use of Metropolitan Area Nonmilitary Resources for Detention: Region, SMSA Population, and Number of Counties

	Number of SMSAs	Units of Capacity per 100,000 SMSA Population (1973 est.)		Percent of SMSA Police Employees Assigned to Jail Duties		Ratio of SMSA Jail Employees to Total SMSA Capacity (per 100 Units of Capacity)	
		Median	Range[a]	Median	Range	Median	Range
Total	70	91	62 – 126	5	4 – 8	15	9 – 21
Northeast							
Region 1	2	–	74 – 157	–	14 – 14	–	20 – 45
Region 2	4	46	37 – 60	5	5 – 11	38	27 – 40
Region 3	6	62	38 – 126	8	5 – 9	16	16 – 24
Midwest							
Region 5	14	67	48 – 87	4	4 – 6	11	8 – 18
Region 7	4	53	44 – 63	4	2 – 6	15	8 – 21
South							
Region 4	14	118	91 – 185	5	4 – 8	10	8 – 15
Region 6	14	103	91 – 140	5	4 – 7	12	6 – 19
West							
Region 8	4	71	40 – 106	6	3 – 7	13	9 – 16
Region 9	6	90	76 – 142	7	5 – 10	16	16 – 39
Region 10	2	–	63 – 98	–	3 – 5	–	11 – 13

Metropolitan Population (1973 est.)

50,000 to 124,999	17	103	71 – 148	5	4 – 6	13	7 – 16
125,000 to 249,999	21	67	48 – 111	5	3 – 8	11	9 – 21
250,000 to 499,999	20	92	74 – 126	7	5 – 9	16	10 – 24
500,000 and over	12	76	45 – 86	5	4 – 7	18	15 – 24

Number of Counties

One	53	92	58 – 131	6	4 – 8	15	9 – 21
Two	13	86	68 – 98	5	4 – 7	15	11 – 19
Three or more	4	71	60 – 91	4	4 – 6	10	2 – 15

[a]Refers to interquartile range except for Regions 2 and 10, where it is the full range of variation.

Table 11–21. Use of Metropolitan Area Nonmilitary Resources for Detention: Level of Independence, Relative Multiplicity, and Multiplicity

	Number of SMSAs	Units of Capacity per 100,000 SMSA Population (1973 est.)		Percent of SMSA Police Employees Assigned to Detention		Ratio of SMSA Jail Employees to Total SMSA Capacity (per 100 Units of Capacity)	
		Median	Range	Median	Range	Median	Range
Total	70	91	62 – 126	5	4 – 8	15	9 – 21
Independence							
Low	21	67	44 – 104	7	4 – 11	20	16 – 39
Medium	25	87	63 – 118	6	5 – 7	15	10 – 24
High	24	99	70 – 164	5	3 – 6	11	6 – 15
Relative Multiplicity[a]							
Low	19	48	40 – 90	5	4 – 9	19	16 – 40
Medium	28	92	71 – 113	7	4 – 8	15	10 – 21
High	23	108	70 – 185	5	4 – 8	11	8 – 13
Multiplicity (number of producers)							
One	41	91	55 – 111	6	4 – 8	16	9 – 23
Two	12	78	53 – 142	7	4 – 8	15	10 – 19
Three or more	17	91	71 – 131	5	4 – 6	11	8 – 15

[a]Number of detention producers per 10 consuming agencies.

served by one and only one nonmilitary producer of pretrial detention. Exceptions are of two types. In multicounty SMSAs there
are generally separate detention facilities for each county. In some
SMSAs municipal police agencies also produce detention.

Even in SMSAs with more than one detention facility we find little duplication in the provision of pretrial detention. In multicounty
SMSAs the responsibilities for detention are clearly delineated by
county boundaries. In SMSAs where municipal police departments
provide this service they generally do so only for their own agencies.
Nearly *90 percent* of the agencies in a majority of the SMSAs are
served by the dominant (county or state) detention producer. Proposals to reduce the number of local detention facilities and/or to
consolidate these into larger facilities may, thus, be relevant only to a
relatively small proportion of the SMSAs in the United States. If
consolidation of facilities is to be considered in other places, it must
be addressed on a multicounty or a multi-SMSA basis.

Our documentation of regional variations in the types of agencies
that produce pretrial detention is also of interest. In the Northeast,
most SMSAs are served by detention specialists; few direct service
police agencies and no municipal police agencies are involved in the
production of this service. In the South, pretrial detention is provided by a number of different types of agencies—county sheriffs,
municipal police departments, and detention specialists. In the Midwest and West, on the other hand, detention in all the SMSAs is
provided by direct service producers, notably county sheriffs and
municipal police departments.

These regional variations suggest that alternative organizational
arrangements for pretrial detention are already in use. The availability of these alternatives means that comparative analysis could be
undertaken on the implications of proposals to reorganize pretrial
detention services—including proposals to transfer responsibility for
pretrial detention to specialized correctional agencies at the local or
state levels.

Comparative analysis of the consequences of alternative organizational arrangements would focus upon what difference, if any, different ways of organizing makes for various outcomes in the delivery of
pretrial detention services. Within this context, our finding that different types of agencies have different organizational characteristics
and personnel policies may also be relevant.

County sheriffs, detention specialists, and municipal detention-
producing agencies, for example, vary significantly in inmate capacity, the ratio of full-time employees to inmate capacity, the number
of full-time employees assigned to detention, the proportion of total

agency employees assigned to detention, and the use of civilian and sworn personnel for detention duties. These differences in personnel policies and agency characteristics suggest that different organizational arrangements *are* associated with different patterns of resource use at an agency level. The implications of different patterns of resource use for agency performance and quality of detention services is a question that needs to be addressed in future research.

In contrast to these variations among regions and types of agencies, we found few systematic relationships between types of minimum jail standards laws and organizational arrangements at the agency or metropolitan area level. This finding suggests either that variations in state laws make little difference in organizational arrangements, or that studies of the effects of minimum jail standards and their enforcement need to account more carefully for the types of standards adopted and state and local enforcement policies, or both. Merely having or not having statewide jail standards or inspection programs seems to make relatively little difference in organizational arrangements or patterns of resource use.

Our findings are, thus, of some interest to those proposing changes in the organization of adult pretrial detention services. The variety of arrangements we encountered suggests that opportunities currently exist for systematic evaluation of the relationships between organizational arrangements and outcomes in the delivery of adult pretrial detention services. Such evaluation can better our understanding of the consequences of alternative organizational arrangements. With such knowledge our choices will be more likely to lead to improvements in the quality of local detention services than might otherwise be the case.

❊   *Chapter 12*

Entry-Level Training

Widespread formal entry-level training for police recruits
is a recent phenomenon. Until the late 1960s such training was found predominantly in the nation's larger municipal police departments and in state police agencies. In the mid
1950s four states—California, New York, Minnesota, and Montana—
pioneered in the move to encourage universal training for police
recruits by passing legislation mandating recruit training for local
agencies.

Since then an ever growing number of states have passed legislation
establishing a state-level council or agency authorized to set minimum training standards and certify police officers. In this chapter we
describe the variations in state legislation regarding entry-level police
training in effect in December 1974. Next we discuss individual
agency entry-level training requirements and how these requirements
have changed since 1967. Finally we discuss the types of entry-level
training producers and the variety of interorganizational arrangements for the production and consumption of entry-level training.

TRAINING LEGISLATION

By December 1974 all but three states had passed legislation requiring minimum entry-level training for newly appointed police officers
[1]. In some cases the state legislature itself determined the minimum training standards; in other states it delegated this power to a
council or agency. Only Hawaii, Missouri, and West Virginia had not
enacted legislation authorizing supervision of entry-level training

243

within the state, although Missouri did require all recruits from cities located in first-class counties to obtain 600 hours of training at a regional training academy.

Ten states had statutory requirements setting the minimum training hours for all full-time police officers. Twenty-one states prescribed minimum training standards for all full-time police officers through rules and regulations issued by a state agency or council. The requirements ranged from 114 hours in Georgia to 480 hours in Pennsylvania. The other 16 states had passed training requirements, but the legislation did not affect all police officers in those states. Mississippi, for example, had a statutory requirement covering only state police officers. Louisiana had regulations covering deputy sheriffs. Illinois had established a 240-hour minimum course for all full-time county and municipal police officers, but the course was not mandatory until January 1, 1976.

Training Required by Local Direct
Service Producers

Over 90 percent of all local direct service producers in the 80 SMSAs have training requirements for their police officer recruits. In many cases these requirements are the state minimums, but some local departments have set requirements that exceed those established by their state. The proportion of local direct service producers requiring training is smallest in the Plains states (Region 7) where only 70 percent of the local direct service producers located in Missouri and Iowa require entry-level training (Table 12–1). Many of those agencies not requiring entry-level training are in Missouri where only agencies located in first-class counties are required to give entry-level training to recruits. Almost all agencies in the South and West require some entry-level training.

Municipal police, county police, and sheriffs' departments are slightly more likely to require entry-level training than are campus and other local direct service producers (including local park police, housing police, and airport police). The latter agencies are less likely to be covered by state legislation or training council regulations. In some states (e.g., South Carolina) they are excluded from the state training programs provided for municipal and county officers. But more than four fifths of all types of agencies do require at least some training for their recruits.

Smaller departments are less likely to require entry-level training than are larger departments (Table 12–2). Of the 68 part-time departments for which we have data, half do not require their recruits to receive formal training. Some state training laws specifically exclude

Table 12–1.   Percent of Local Direct Producers Who Require Entry-Level Training: Region and Type of Producer

Types of Producers	Total	Northeast Regions			Midwest Regions		Southern Regions		Western Regions		
		1	2	3	5	7	4	6	8	9	10
Total	(1,108) 91	(62) 81	(153) 95	(119) 82	(198) 85	(30) 70	(252) 95	(131) 97	(29) 100	(110) 100	(24) 92
Municipal police	(866) 93	(54) 91	(133) 98	(107) 83	(160) 84	(24) 71	(188) 98	(88) 99	(20) 100	(73) 100	(19) 90
County sheriffs and police	(106) 92	(0) —	(9) 56	(2) 100	(24) 92	(4) 75	(28) 96	(19) 95	(4) 100	(11) 100	(5) 100
Campus police	(94) 82	(6) 0	(4) 100	(8) 75	(11) 91	(1) 0	(30) 83	(17) 88	(3) 100	(14) 100	(0) —
Other local direct service producers	(42) 86	(2) 50	(7) 100	(2) 50	(3) 33	(1) 100	(6) 67	(7) 100	(2) 100	(12) 100	(0) —

Note: Number in parentheses equals number reporting.

246 Patterns of Metropolitan Policing

Table 12-2. Percent of Local Direct Service Producers Who Require Entry-Level Training: Size and Type of Producer

Types of Producers		Number of Full-Time Sworn Officers Employed by Producer							
	Total	Part Time Only	1 – 4	5 – 10	11 – 20	21 – 50	51 – 150	More Than 150
Total	(1,108) 91	(68) 49	(249) 89	(277) 92	(165) 97	(176) 97	(109) 99	(64) 98
Municipal police	(866) 93	(63) 51	(218) 89	(219) 96	(124) 99	(119) 100	(77) 100	(46) 100
County sheriffs and police	(106) 92	(0) —	(4) 100	(8) 75	(17) 94	(31) 87	(28) 96	(18) 94
Campus police	(94) 82	(2) 50	(15) 73	(37) 81	(17) 82	(20) 90	(3) 100	(0) —
Other local direct service producers	(42) 86	(3) 0	(12) 100	(13) 77	(7) 100	(6) 100	(1) 100	(0) —

Note: Number in parentheses equals number reporting.

part-time officers. Almost all full-time departments do require some entry-level training. Eighty-nine percent of the smallest full-time producers (between one and four full-time sworn officers) have such a requirement. The percentage rises to over 90 for departments with between 5 and 10 full-time officers and to 97 percent and higher for departments with more than 10 full-time officers.

Number of Hours Required

Although most direct service producers require all officers to have some entry-level training, the number of hours required varies considerably. Fifteen percent of the local direct service producers require less than four weeks of training. Twenty-four percent require more than nine weeks.

Across the 80 SMSAs, 55 percent of local direct service producers who mandate some entry-level training require more than 240 hours (Table 12−3). Municipal police departments are more likely than county departments or campus police to require more than 240 hours. Larger producers are more apt than are the smaller departments to require more than 240 hours of entry-level training. Eight of 10 municipal departments with more than 20 full-time sworn officers require over 240 hours of entry-level training. Departments relying entirely on part-time officers are the least likely to require any training. When they do require it, they rarely require more than 240 hours.

There is considerable variation in number of hours required among regions (Table 12−4). Almost all agencies located in New England, New York and New Jersey, and the Rocky Mountain states (Regions 1, 2, and 8) require more than 240 hours of entry-level training. A very low proportion of the agencies located in Virginia and Pennsylvania, the Southwest, and the Plains states (Regions 3, 6, and 7) have such high requirements. A major factor in the number of hours required is, of course, the minimum number of hours required by state law. However, state laws do not exclusively determine the number of hours required by an individual agency.

As shown in Table 12−5, most municipalities located in New England, New York and New Jersey, and the Rocky Mountain states (Regions 1, 2, and 8)—the three regions in which the highest proportion of municipal agencies require more than 240 hours—require more than their state minimum. All agencies requiring training in the Plains states and Rocky Mountain states (Regions 7 and 8) require more than their state minimum.

Nationwide, 48 percent of all local direct police service producers whose officers receive entry-level training require more than the state

Table 12-3. Percent of Local Direct Producers[a] Who Require More Than 240 Hours of Entry-Level Training: Size and Type of Producer

Types of Producers	Total	Part-Time Only	Number of Full-Time Sworn Officers Employed by Producer					
			1 – 4	5 – 10	11 – 20	21 – 50	51 – 150	More Than 150
Total training requirement	(996) 55	(32) 6	(217) 33	(252) 52	(157) 64	(168) 68	(108) 74	(62) 74
Municipal police	(794) 59	(31) 6	(191) 32	(208) 58	(122) 72	(119) 81	(77) 80	(46) 78
County sheriffs and police	(92) 39	(0) –	(4) 25	(5) 0	(15) 13	(25) 32	(27) 56	(16) 62
Campus police	(76) 42	(1) 0	(11) 36	(29) 28	(14) 64	(18) 50	(3) 67	(0) –
Other local direct service producers	(34) 35	(0) –	(11) 55	(10) 30	(6) 17	(6) 17	(1) 100	(0) –

Note: Number in parentheses equals number reporting.
[a] Those that require some entry-level training.

Table 12-4. Percent of Local Direct Producers[a] Who Require More Than 240 Hours of Entry-Level Training: Region and Type of Producer

Types of Producers	Total	Northeast Regions			Midwest Regions		Southern Regions		Western Regions		
		1	2	3	5	7	4	6	8	9	10
Total	(996) 55	(49) 100	(144) 99	(98) 33	(165) 42	(20) 15	(240) 40	(127) 19	(26) 96	(105) 84	(22) 77
Municipal police	(794) 59	(49) 100	(129) 100	(89) 33	(133) 44	(16) 19	(184) 43	(87) 17	(18) 94	(72) 99	(17) 82
County sheriffs and police	(92) 39	(0) —	(5) 100	(2) 50	(22) 32	(3) 0	(27) 30	(18) 11	(3) 100	(7) 100	(5) 60
Campus police	(76) 42	(0) —	(4) 100	(6) 33	(9) 33	(0) —	(25) 20	(15) 47	(3) 100	(14) 57	(0) —
Other local direct service producers	(34) 35	(0) —	(6) 83	(1) 0	(1) 100	(1) 0	(4) 50	(7) 0	(2) 100	(12) 17	(0) —

Note: Number in parentheses equals number reporting.
[a]Those that require some entry-level training.

Table 12-5. Percent of Local Direct Service Producers[a] Mandating Training That Require More Hours of Entry-Level Training Than Mandated by State Minimum Standards: Region and Type of Producer

Location	Number Reporting	Percent Requiring More Than State Minimum			
		Municipal	County	Campus	Other
Total	(998)	(796) 49	(92) 48	(76) 41	(34) 32
Northeast					
Region 1	(49)	(49) 80	(0) —	(0) —	(0) —
Region 2	(144)	(129) 81	(5) 60	(4) 75	(6) 50
Region 3	(98)	(89) 1	(2) 50	(6) 0	(1) 0
Midwest					
Region 5	(167)	(135) 63	(22) 68	(9) 67	(1) 100
Region 7	(20)	(16) 100	(3) 100	(0) —	(1) 100
South					
Region 4	(240)	(184) 13	(27) 22	(25) 12	(4) 50
Region 6	(127)	(87) 49	(18) 39	(15) 53	(7) 0
West					
Region 8	(26)	(18) 100	(3) 100	(3) 100	(2) 100
Region 9	(105)	(72) 85	(7) 86	(14) 57	(12) 17
Region 10	(22)	(17) 12	(5) 0	(0) —	(0) —

Note: Number in parentheses equals number reporting.
[a] Those that require some entry-level training.

minimum number of training hours (Table 12—6). The larger the agency—particularly for municipal police departments—the more likely it will require more than the state-mandated minimum. Municipal and county agencies are more likely than campus and other local agencies to require more than the state minimum of entry-level training hours.

Table 12—6.   Percent of Local Direct Service Producers[a] Requiring More Hours of Entry-Level Training Than Mandated by State Minimum Standards: Type and Size of Producer

Type of Producer and Number of Full-Time Sworn Officers	Number Reporting	Percent Who Require More Than State Minimum
Total	998	48
Municipal police	796	49
No full-time officers	32	9
1 to 4 full-time officers	191	32
5 to 10 full-time officers	209	40
11 to 20 full-time officers	122	59
21 to 50 full-time officers	119	70
51 to 150 full-time officers	77	71
Over 150 full-time officers	46	80
County sheriffs and police	92	48
1 to 4 full-time officers	4	0
5 to 10 full-time officers	5	0
11 to 20 full-time officers	15	40
21 to 50 full-time officers	25	44
51 to 150 full-time officers	27	70
Over 150 full-time officers	16	50
Campus police	76	41
No full-time officers	1	0
1 to 4 full-time officers	11	18
5 to 10 full-time officers	29	38
11 to 20 full-time officers	14	50
21 to 50 full-time officers	18	44
51 to 150 full-time officers	3	100
Over 150 full-time officers	0	—
Other direct service producers	34	32
1 to 4 full-time officers	11	36
5 to 10 full-time officers	10	40
11 to 20 full-time officers	6	17
21 to 50 full-time officers	6	33
51 to 150 full-time officers	1	0

[a]Those that require some entry-level training.

Time for Completing Required Training

More than one third of the local direct service producers whose officers receive entry-level training require that entry-level training be completed during the first six months of employment (Table 12—7). In California all agencies must, by law, provide entry-level training for their recruits before street assignment. The other two western regions, the Rocky Mountain states and the Northwest (Regions 8 and 10), are at the opposite extreme: no agencies in the SMSAs we studied require training before street assignment. In Colorado and Montana (Region 8) state law requires entry-level training within the first two years of employment and few agencies require completion during the first six months.

Large agencies of all types are more likely than smaller agencies to require training during the first six months of employment (Table 12—8). Six of 10 municipal and county producers employing more than 150 full-time sworn officers require entry-level training of their recruits during the first six months of employment.

City Training Requirements: 1967 and 1975

In 1967 the International City Management Association studied recruit training practices in more than 1,200 city police departments across the country [2]. As shown in Table 12—9, the ICMA found that as one moved from larger to smaller cities, the proportion of departments requiring entry-level training declined. Only 75 percent of the police departments serving cities of 10,000 to 25,000 population required entry-level training in 1967. Now, however, 99 percent of the city police departments serving cities of that size have training requirements—a marked change [3]. Cities of less than 10,000 population were not included in the ICMA study, but 89 percent of these now require recruit training.

Change has occurred in all regions, but is most dramatic in the South. In 1967 only 65 percent of all municipal departments in the South serving more than 10,000 residents required entry-level training. One hundred percent now require it. Overall, ICMA found 82 percent of the departments serving cities of more than 10,000 population required entry-level training seven years ago. Today, however, nearly every city in this size range requires police recruits to complete a formal training program.

Hiring Previously Trained Officers

As the length of the required training period increases, some police chiefs have feared that departments will vie for officers trained by other departments. Two types of concern about "pirating" were

Table 12–7. Percent of Local Direct Producers[a] Who Require Entry-Level Training During First Six Months: Region and Type of Producer

Types of Producers	Total	Northeast Regions			Midwest Regions		Southern Regions		Western Regions		
		1	2	3	5	7	4	6	8	9	10
Total	(889) 34	(49) 2	(146) 23	(19) 16	(161) 19	(6) 83	(225) 47	(125) 14	(26) 0	(110) 100	(22) 0
Municipal police	(693) 32	(49) 2	(130) 19	(15) 20	(129) 19	(4) 100	(173) 48	(85) 12	(18) 0	(73) 100	(17) 0
County sheriffs and police	(94) 32	(0) —	(5) 60	(2) 0	(22) 14	(2) 50	(26) 36	(18) 11	(3) 0	(11) 100	(5) 0
Campus police	(69) 49	(0) —	(4) 50	(2) 0	(9) 33	(0) —	(22) 41	(15) 40	(3) 0	(14) 100	(0) —
Other local direct service producers	(33) 54	(0) —	(7) 43	(0) —	(1) 0	(0) —	(4) 75	(7) 0	(2) 0	(12) 100	(0) —

Note: Number in parentheses equals number reporting.
[a]Those that require some entry-level training.

Table 12–8.   Percent of Local Direct Producers[a] Who Require Entry-Level Training During First Six Months: Size and Type of Producer

Types of Producers	Total	Number of Full-Time Sworn Officers Employed by Producer						
		Part Time Only	1 – 4	5 – 10	11 – 20	21 – 50	51 – 150	More Than 150
Total	(885) 30	(17) 0	(163) 17	(229) 31	(149) 30	(160) 27	(105) 43	(62) 61
Municipal police	(693) 30	(17) 0	(142) 14	(187) 33	(115) 29	(113) 27	(74) 47	(45) 60
County sheriffs and police	(93) 29	(0) —	(4) 25	(6) 17	(14) 7	(25) 20	(27) 30	(17) 65
Campus police	(68) 40	(0) —	(7) 43	(28) 29	(13) 62	(17) 41	(3) 33	(0) —
Other local direct service producers	(31) 29	(0) —	(10) 30	(8) 25	(7) 43	(5) 0	(1) 100	(0) —

Note: Number in parentheses equals number reporting.
[a]Those that require some entry-level training.

expressed to us. First, smaller departments may pay the costs of training an officer only to find the officer lured away to a larger department offering broader career opportunities. This concern was evidenced in the Indiana Criminal Justice Planning Agency's description of increasing use of the state training program:

> Smaller departments are taking advantage of Law Enforcement Training Board basic training, especially as the Indiana Criminal Justice Planning Agency provides funds for replacement officers. A problem exists in that well qualified officers often accept positions with larger municipal departments after their training, due to the vast difference in salary and benefits offered by the larger departments [4].

The possibility of a large department hiring trained officers away from small departments was not the only concern voiced. The opposite pattern was also mentioned. Since small departments feel the cost of training officers somewhat more directly than large departments do (in terms of losing the services of an officer while in training), some chiefs worried that smaller departments would try to hire previously trained officers away from larger departments to save themselves the costs of training.

Across the country we find that more than 50 percent of the local direct service producers that require training for their officers report hiring at least a few officers who have received training before employment (Table 12–10); but only 9 percent of these producers hire only recruits who have prior training. Hiring practices are somewhat related to producer size. Larger municipal police departments are more likely to hire only untrained recruits and provide them with training after employment. Smaller departments are more likely to hire recruits with previous training. County agencies are more likely to hire previously trained officers. Campus and other local agencies are least likely to hire recruits who have already received their training.

In the Northeast states (Regions 1 and 2), and particularly in New England (Region 1), more agencies requiring training are likely to train all of their recruits after employment (Table 12–11). California and Arizona (Region 9) have among the highest training standards in the country, but their proportion of departments hiring officers after they had been trained by another department nearly matched the national average. (Most of the agencies we studied in Region 9 are in California, where the state pays most out-of-pocket training expenses.) Local direct service producers in the Northwest (Region 10) are more likely than those elsewhere to hire recruits who have already been trained.

Table 12–9. Recruit Training Requirement in City Police Departments, 1967 and 1975

Classification of City	ICMA Study 1967[a]		
	Percent With Formal Recruit Training		*Number Reporting*
Population group			
Over 500,000	100		22
250,000 to 500,000	100		25
100,000 to 250,000	99		85
50,000 to 100,000	95		178
25,000 to 50,000	81		298
10,000 to 25,000	75		606
Under 10,000	—		—
	Including Cities Under 10,000	*Excluding Cities Under 10,000*	*Including Cities Under 10,000*	*Excluding Cities Under 10,000*
Location				
Northeast	—	86	—	333
Midwest	—	88	—	406
South	—	65	—	221
West	—	89	—	254
Total cities	—	82	—	1,214

[a]Source: Robert Havlick, 1968.

THE PRODUCTION OF ENTRY-LEVEL TRAINING

All levels of government are involved in the production of entry-level training. When we examine the number of *producers*—including regional training academies, state academies, and federal academies counted for each SMSA they serve—local producers constitute about a fourth of the 382 producers (Table 12–12). However, when we examine the number of *agencies* producing entry-level training, local agencies constitute nearly half.

There are 31 regional training academies producing entry-level training for 1 or more of the 80 SMSAs. Most of these academies are organized through interjurisdictional arrangements. A number of local direct service producers in a metropolitan area organize an academy to serve most of the local direct service producers in the area. In some instances the regional academy is located at a college or university. A governing board composed of local police officials

Table 12–9. continued

Police Services Study 1975			
Percent With Formal Recruit Training		Number Reporting	
100		2	
100		9	
100		22	
100		58	
100		40	
99		139	
89		600	
Including Cities Under 10,000	Excluding Cities Under 10,000	Including Cities Under 10,000	Excluding Cities Under 10,000
90	100	291	103
83	97	184	60
98	100	281	66
98	100	114	41
92	100	870	270

may organize the curriculum and hire the instructors, while the college or university provides the space and administers the program. Some regional academies are located in separate facilities owned by the state, and a few have purchased their own facilities. Seventy-three state agencies produce entry-level training. Many of these train direct service police from several SMSAs, so there are 147 state producers of entry-level training. These include colleges and universities that organize police training programs.

The type of training academy used depends somewhat on the type and size of the police agency using this service. Only the very largest departments are likely to maintain their own academies (Table 12–13). Between 60 and 85 percent of all full-time municipal departments with fewer than 150 full-time sworn officers use regional or state academies. The use of different types of producers also varies considerably by region, as shown in Table 12–14 [5]. Use of regional academies is particularly pronounced in California and Arizona (Region 9), while the use of state agencies by local direct producers is high in the Plains states, the Rocky Mountain states, and the Northwest (Regions 7, 8, and 10).

Table 12–10.   Proportion of Recruits Hired With Previously Acquired Entry-Level Training: Type of Agency

Type of Local Direct Service Producer	Number Reporting	Percent of Local Direct Service Producers[a] Who				
		Hired No Recruits	Hired Only Untrained Recruits	Hired Some Recruits With Prior Training	Hired More Than Half With Prior Training	Hired All Recruits With Prior Training
Total	652	9	39	36	7	9
Municipal police	488	10	40	35	6	9
No full-time officers	29	28	14	34	7	17
1 to 4 full-time officers	119	24	26	29	3	18
5 to 10 full-time officers	128	3	40	38	11	9
11 to 20 full-time officers	61	5	41	39	8	7
21 to 50 full-time officers	56	4	64	32	0	0
51 to 150 full-time officers	59	2	42	48	5	3
Over 150 full-time officers	36	8	67	22	3	0
County police	76	3	22	51	15	9
Campus police	63	5	48	30	8	10
Other	25	12	52	20	4	12

Note: Rows may not total 100 percent due to rounding errors.
[a]Those that require some entry-level training.

Table 12–11. Proportion of Recruits Hired With Previously Acquired Entry-Level Training: Region

Location	Number Reporting	Percentage of Local Direct Service Producers[a] Who				
		Hired No Recruits	Hired Only Untrained Recruits	Hired Some Recruits With Prior Training	Hired More Than Half With Prior Training	Hired All Recruits With Prior Training
Total	652	9	39	36	7	9
Northeast						
Region 1	37	8	81	11	0	0
Region 2	70	4	60	27	1	7
Region 3	73	15	47	27	6	6
Midwest						
Region 5	105	12	48	31	4	6
Region 7	9	0	56	22	11	11
South						
Region 4	105	12	24	43	11	10
Region 6	119	7	14	56	11	12
West						
Region 8	25	8	40	44	0	8
Region 9	91	3	44	31	9	13
Region 10	18	6	17	33	17	28

Note: Rows may not total 100 percent due to rounding errors.
[a] Those that require some entry-level training.

Table 12–12.   Producers of Entry-Level Training: Type of Agency

Type of Agency	Number of Producers	Percent	Number of Agencies	Percent
Total	382	100	226	100
Local producers				
Municipal police	65	17	65	29
County sheriffs and police	16	4	16	7
Colleges and universities	15	4	15	7
Other local	5	1	4	2
Interjurisdictional regional training academies	38	10	31	14
State agencies				
State highway patrols	72	19	27	12
Law enforcement training academies	41	11	24	11
Colleges and universities	13	3	10	4
Other state training agency	21	5	12	5
Federal agencies				
Military agency	60	16	16	7
Civilian agency	36	9	6	3

Table 12–13. Types of Academies From Whom Local Direct Service Producers Who Require Training Receive Entry-Level Training: Type and Size of Producer

Type of Local Direct Service Producer	Number Reporting	Percent of Local Direct Service Producers[a] Receiving Training From					
		Own Academy	Another Department's Academy	Regional Academy	State Academy	Community College or University Academy	Other Type of Academy
Total	984	7	19	35	32	12	8
Municipal police	782	7	20	34	33	11	9
No full-time officers	29	3	31	10	3	3	52
1 to 4 full-time officers	182	1	14	23	40	8	18
5 to 10 full-time officers	208	1	26	33	31	15	5
11 to 20 full-time officers	123	1	26	43	34	13	2
21 to 50 full-time officers	118	1	19	48	36	9	2
51 to 150 full-time officers	76	13	15	49	32	13	1
Over 150 full-time officers	46	83	2	11	18	7	2
County sheriffs and police	93	9	17	38	36	14	1
1 to 4 full-time officers	4	0	0	25	75	0	0
5 to 10 full-time officers	5	0	0	40	40	20	0
11 to 20 full-time officers	15	7	7	60	40	0	0
21 to 50 full-time officers	26	0	19	32	54	12	4
51 to 150 full-time officers	27	19	26	26	22	19	0
Over 150 full-time officers	16	13	19	47	13	25	0
Campus	74	8	11	30	30	22	13
Other local producers	35	0	32	51	12	15	11

Note: Rows may total more than 100 percent since some agencies send recruits to more than one academy.
[a] Those that require some entry-level training.

Table 12–14. Types of Academies From Whom Local Direct Service Producers Who Require Training Receive Entry-Level Training: Region

Location	Number Reporting	Own Academy	Another Department's Academy	Regional Academy	State Academy	Community College or University Academy	Other Type of Academy
			Percent of Local Direct Service Producers[a] Receiving Training From				
Total	984	7	19	35	32	12	8
Northeast							
Region 1	50	6	52	10	42	0	0
Region 2	144	4	28	65	33	1	0
Region 3	98	3	9	0	26	6	60
Midwest							
Region 5	162	10	25	6	52	13	2
Region 7	19	16	17	6	78	0	0
South							
Region 4	234	9	18	31	18	31	2
Region 6	124	8	4	56	25	5	7
West							
Region 8	29	7	31	3	69	0	0
Region 9	102	4	14	83	7	12	5
Region 10	22	5	0	0	96	0	0

Note: Rows may total more than 100 percent since some agencies send recruits to more than one academy.
[a]Those that require some entry-level training.

ENTRY-LEVEL TRAINING
IN METROPOLITAN AREAS

The number of entry-level training producers in each SMSA is much lower than the number of direct service producers whose officers are trained (Table 12—15). There are four training producers in the median SMSA; the interquartile range is two through seven. The Provo-Orem/Utah SMSA is the only SMSA we studied that is served by a single training academy. The largest number of academies serving an SMSA is 13 (in the Salinas-Seaside-Monterey/California SMSA). The number of training producers per SMSA—multiplicity—is somewhat higher in the southern and western regions. Much of this difference is due to the large number of military bases in those regions, because the military and other federal agencies do not use state or local training facilities.

The number of agencies producing training increases with metropolitan area size. But, relative to consuming agencies, the number of producers decreases as SMSA size increases. The median number of training producers per consuming agency falls from 0.50 in SMSAs under 125,000 to about 0.29 in SMSAs of more than 500,000 population.

Paterson-Clifton-Passaic/New Jersey, with 92 consuming agencies and four producers of training, has the lowest ratio of academies to consuming agencies in the 80 SMSAs. The Meridan/Connecticut SMSA, on the other hand, with two academies and two consuming agencies, is the only 1 of the 80 SMSAs where the number of consuming agencies equals the number of producers. The number of training producers per 1,000 sworn officers also decreases as the size of the SMSA increases. In the smallest SMSAs the median number of training producers per 1,000 sworn officers is 14; it falls to 4 in the largest SMSAs.

Independence, Autonomy, and Dominance

Few direct service producers supply entry-level training for themselves. Independence—the percentage of direct service producers per SMSA that produce their own entry-level training—is low across the country (Table 12—16). Many of the agencies producing their own training are state or military. Agencies in metropolitan areas of more than 500,000 population are less likely to produce their own entry-level training than are agencies located in smaller SMSAs.

Autonomy—the percentage of direct service producers per SMSA relying entirely on their own agency's academy for entry level training—is similar to, but somewhat lower than, independence. In half

Table 12–15. Multiplicity in Entry-Level Training: Region and SMSA Population

Location	Number of SMSAs	Number of Training Producers in an SMSA		Number of Training Producers per Consuming Agency		Number of Training Producers per 1,000 Sworn Officers	
		Median	Range[a]	Median	Range	Median	Range
Total	80	4	2 – 7	.33	.21 – .50	9	6 – 14
Northeast							
Region 1	8	2	2 – 4	.33	.22 – .50	8	6 – 10
Region 2	4	2	2 – 4	.11	.04 – .15	2	1 – 3
Region 3	6	3	3 – 4	.11	.10 – .50	9	9 – 10
Midwest							
Region 5	16	3	2 – 5	.26	.20 – .45	11	8 – 14
Region 7	4	2	2 – 3	.22	.18 – .25	9	7 – 9
South							
Region 4	15	6	2 – 8	.33	.21 – .55	7	4 – 14
Region 6	14	5	3 – 7	.45	.38 – .58	9	7 – 18
West							
Region 8	4	6	1 – 7	.50	.07 – .75	8	5 – 19
Region 9	7	9	9 – 11	.44	.35 – .56	10	5 – 14
Region 10	2	—	2 – 2	—	.10 – .33	—	6 – 10

Metropolitan Population (1973 est.)						
50,000 to 124,999	20	2	2 – 4	.50	.29 – .67	14	11 – 19
125,000 to 249,999	26	3	2 – 5	.33	.21 – .50	10	7 – 15
250,000 to 499,999	21	7	4 – 8	.35	.20 – .50	8	6 – 10
500,000 and over	13	8	4 – 10	.29	.11 – .33	4	3 – 7

[a]Range is the interquartile range except for Region 10, where it is the full range of variation.

Table 12–16.   Independence, Autonomy, and Dominance in Entry-Level Training: Region and SMSA Population

Location	*Number of SMSAs*	Percent of Consuming Agencies per SMSA Who					
		Produce Their Own Training		*Use Only Their Own Academy*		*Are Served by Dominant Producer*	
		Median	*Range*[a]	*Median*	*Range*	*Median*	*Range*
Total	80	20	12 – 27	17	10 – 27	70	50 – 85
Northeast							
Region 1	8	17	11 – 25	17	11 – 25	77	60 – 83
Region 2	4	9	4 – 11	9	3 – 11	74	50 – 75
Region 3	6	7	4 – 21	7	4 – 21	83	64 – 94
Midwest							
Region 5	16	16	10 – 20	13	8 – 17	73	50 – 88
Region 7	4	20	12 – 22	20	12 – 22	80	75 – 88
South							
Region 4	15	23	14 – 33	17	6 – 29	64	52 – 89
Region 6	14	25	17 – 33	25	17 – 33	56	50 – 77
West							
Region 8	4	38	0 – 50	38	0 – 50	38	33 – 56
Region 9	7	26	24 – 38	26	16 – 38	55	40 – 70
Region 10	2	—	5 – 17	—	5 – 17	—	83 – 95

Metropolitan Population (1973 est.)							
50,000 to 124,999	20	25	14 – 33	25	13 – 33	67	50 – 83
125,000 to 249,999	26	17	12 – 27	16	9 – 25	83	60 – 89
250,000 to 499,999	21	25	16 – 36	21	11 – 33	70	46 – 80
500,000 and over	13	16	6 – 20	9	6 – 16	63	50 – 76

[a]Range is the interquartile range except for Region 10, where it is the full range of variation.

the SMSAs we studied, fewer than 17 percent of all agencies produce their own training exclusively. In half the metropolitan areas of more than 500,000 population fewer than 9 percent of the agencies produce their own training exclusively. No agency in three SMSAs— Gary-Hammond-East Chicago/Indiana, Lexington/Kentucky, and Provo-Orem/Utah—relies entirely on its own academy to produce entry-level training. Autonomy is highest in Pueblo, Colorado, where five of the nine direct service agencies rely entirely on their own academies.

While independence and autonomy are low for entry-level training, dominance—the percent of direct service agencies obtaining entry-level training from a single agency—is high. In half the SMSAs, 70 percent of the direct service police agencies obtain entry-level training from the dominant producer. The pattern of high dominance holds for most regions, although the Rocky Mountain states (Region 8) are an exception. In Montana and Colorado there are a larger number of entry-level training producers than in many regions and a higher tendency for local direct producers to produce their own training. Consequently, the dominant producer in these SMSAs serves a smaller percentage of all direct service producers.

Alternation and Duplication

Alternation and duplication are almost nonexistent for entry-level training, as shown in Table 12–17. The nationwide median for both measures is zero. Only in New York and New Jersey (Region 2) does any significant alternation occur. There, training academy scheduling has been so developed that direct producers can send their recruits to alternative training academies depending upon which one is scheduling training sessions next. Little duplication exists in any region, nor for any size of SMSA.

INTERORGANIZATIONAL RELATIONSHIPS AND AGENCY TRAINING REQUIREMENTS

The most stringent training requirements are found in metropolitan areas where there are comparatively high numbers of training producers relative to direct service producers requiring training and where many direct service producers provide their own training. Local direct service producers in metropolitan areas with more training producers per 10 consuming agencies are more likely to require more than 360 hours of entry-level training, to require training during the first six months of employment, and slightly more likely to require entry-level training than producers located in low multiplicity

Table 12–17. Alternation and Duplication in Entry-Level Training: Region and SMSA Population

| | | Percent of Consuming Agencies per SMSA Who | | | |
| | Number of SMSAs | Utilize Alternate Academies | | Use More Than One Academy Without Alternation | |
Location		Median	Range[a]	Median	Range
Total	80	0	0 – 0	0	0 – 11
Northeast					
Region 1	8	0	0 – 10	0	0 – 0
Region 2	4	26	23 – 35	0	0 – 1
Region 3	6	0	0 – 0	0	0 – 14
Midwest					
Region 5	16	0	0 – 17	0	0 – 0
Region 7	4	0	0 – 0	0	0 – 0
South					
Region 4	15	0	0 – 0	11	0 – 20
Region 6	14	0	0 – 0	0	0 – 6
West					
Region 8	4	0	0 – 0	0	0 – 0
Region 9	7	0	0 – 4	0	0 – 25
Region 10	2	—	0 – 0	—	0 – 0
Metropolitan Population (1973 est.)					
50,000 to 124,999	20	0	0 – 0	0	0 – 0
125,000 to 249,999	26	0	0 – 15	0	0 – 9
250,000 to 499,999	21	0	0 – 0	0	0 – 17
500,000 and over	13	0	0 – 6	11	6 – 17

[a]Range is the interquartile range except for Region 10, where it is the full range of variation.

metropolitan areas. A similar pattern exists for producers located in metropolitan areas where a high proportion of the agencies rely exclusively upon their own training academies (Table 12—18).

In metropolitan areas where most of the training is done by a single training producer, a smaller number of agencies require: (1) any form of entry-level training, (2) more than 360 hours of entry-level training, and (3) completion of training during the first six months of employment. In metropolitan areas where dominance of entry-level training is comparatively low, 46 percent of the agencies require that recruit training be completed in six months. In metropolitan areas where dominance is comparatively high, only 19 percent require an early completion of recruit training.

DIVERSITY IN DELIVERY
OF ENTRY-LEVEL TRAINING

In reviewing the patterns of entry-level training production in 80 SMSAs we find that 91 percent of all local direct service producers require some entry-level training of all recruits. More than half the departments that require entry-level training specify more than 240 hours, and about half these departments specify more than the minimum mandated by state law. However, less than one third of the departments requiring entry-level training require that it be completed during the first six months of employment. Larger local direct service producers are more likely than smaller producers to require entry-level training, to require more hours of training, and to require that it be completed during the first six months of employment.

Our findings also show that while local police departments constitute about 45 percent of the agencies producing entry-level training, regional, state, and federal training academies play an important role in the production of entry-level training in metropolitan areas. Very few smaller police departments attempt to conduct their own entry-level training. Most send their recruits to regional and state academies or to an academy operated by a large local department. Because of this, the number of training agencies serving each SMSA is considerably lower than the number of direct service producers.

While independence and autonomy of entry-level training are low compared to direct services, dominance is quite high. Alternation and duplication are almost nonexistent for entry-level training. More agencies are likely to have stringent entry-level training requirements in metropolitan areas with more training producers per 10 consuming agencies.

Table 12–18. Interorganizational Relationships in Metropolitan Areas and Agency Training Requirements

	Percent of Local Direct Service Producers That					
Training Interorganizational Relationships	*Require Entry-Level Training*		*Require More Than 360 Hours of Training*[a]		*Require Training Within Six Months of Employment*[a]	
	N	*Percent*	*N*	*Percent*	*N*	*Percent*
Total	1,108	91	998	24	887	30
Relative Multiplicity						
Low	526	89	524	20	423	21
Medium	340	95	315	23	308	38
High	177	92	159	38	156	39
Autonomy						
Low	559	90	501	16	414	26
Medium	336	92	304	23	280	38
High	213	94	193	40	193	31
Dominance						
Low	323	97	305	25	297	46
Medium	413	93	379	28	354	25
High	372	85	314	18	236	19

[a]Those that require some entry-level training.

✳ *Chapter 13*

Crime Laboratory Analysis

Stephen Mastrofski

Criminal laboratory services include a wide variety of activities necessary for collecting and scientifically analyzing evidence. This chapter focuses on the chemical analysis of substances for forensic purposes. Rather than examine the full spectrum of forensic scientific analyses that a crime laboratory might perform at one time or another, we have focused upon one type of commonly requested laboratory service requiring expert competence: chemical analysis. We included agencies in our study if they performed either narcotics analysis or other (non-narcotic) chemical analysis; for example, blood and hair. Although many police agencies have field testing equipment, we included only those agencies that could supply expert testimony for court proceedings.

In this chapter we first discuss the consumption and the production of crime laboratory analysis. Then we turn to a discussion of specialization and dominance in the structure of service delivery for laboratory analysis. In most of this chapter we do not distinguish between the two types of lab analysis included—narcotics analysis and other chemical analysis—as the patterns of delivery and use of both are identical in most cases.

USE OF CRIME LAB SERVICES

Nearly all direct service police agencies use crime lab analysis. Virtually all federal, state, county, and municipal direct police agencies use lab services. Nonusers are usually special investigative units that assist other local departments that make the requests for laboratory analysis. District attorney investigators in Alabama and Louisiana are typical nonusers.

What are crime lab consumers like? With the exception of certain nonusers noted above, the profile of lab users by type, size, and services produced is the same as the profile of direct service police agencies given in Chapter 4.

Duplication and Autonomy

Few consumers of crime lab analysis regularly use more than one laboratory (Table 13–1). California and Arizona (Region 9) have the

Table 13–1. Duplication in Crime Laboratory Analysis: Region and SMSA Population

Location	Number of SMSAs	Percent of Lab Consumers in SMSA Using More Than One Lab	
		Median	*Range*[a]
Total	80	0	0 – 9
Northeast			
Region 1	8	0	0 – 0
Region 2	4	0	0 – 0
Region 3	6	0	0 – 8
Midwest			
Region 5	16	0	0 – 14
Region 7	4	0	0 – 0
South			
Region 4	15	5	0 – 12
Region 6	14	0	0 – 0
West			
Region 8	4	0	0 – 0
Region 9	7	12	4 – 21
Region 10	2	—	0 – 0
Metropolitan Population (1973 est.)			
50,000 to 124,999	20	0	0 – 0
125,000 to 249,999	26	0	0 – 7
250,000 to 499,999	21	0	0 – 7
500,000 and over	13	4	0 – 13

[a]Range is the interquartile range except for Region 10, where it is the full range of variation.

highest multiple lab use, but even that region's multiple lab use is not very high. In addition, the most populated SMSAs tend to have the greatest multiple usage, although the relationship is not a strong one. The metropolitan area with the highest degree of multilab use is Gary-Hammond-East Chicago/Indiana. Here all 38 direct service producers report using the services of both the Northwest Indiana Criminal Toxiocology Laboratory (an interjurisdictional agency) and the Indiana State Police Crime Lab.

Whether law enforcement agencies use one or several labs for chemical analysis, most rely upon other agencies to provide them with this service. Many small agencies do not have the funds to invest in the equipment and expertise required for chemical analysis. Even large agencies often choose not to maintain their own labs. Fewer than one in five local police agencies with more than 150 sworn officers have their own labs. State and federal agencies conducting direct police services in metropolitan areas often have their own labs. They account for most of the autonomous consumers of lab service in the 80 SMSAs.

It is possible that a direct police agency might have its own lab and not be entirely autonomous for chemical analysis, but this is seldom the case in the SMSAs studied. Nearly every police agency that has its own crime lab does not routinely use other labs. The typical SMSA studied has a very low percentage of autonomous agencies; only 8 percent of the direct service producers in the median SMSA are autonomous for chemical analysis (Table 13−2). There is not much regional variation. The Southwest (Region 6) has the highest levels of autonomy. In New York and New Jersey, Virginia and Pennsylvania, the Midwest, and the Rocky Mountain states (Regions 2, 3, 5, 7, and 8) 25 percent or more of the SMSAs have no direct police agencies autonomous for chemical analysis.

An inverse relationship exists between SMSA size and chemical lab autonomy. SMSAs with the largest populations tend to have the lowest proportion of direct service producers who use their own chemical lab exclusively. This relationship is due to the constant number of autonomous state agencies among the 80 SMSAs. In most SMSAs there is at least one lab doing chemical analysis attached to a direct service police producer.

The SMSA with the greatest number of autonomous direct service agencies for lab analysis is Tampa-St. Petersburg/Florida. In this metropolitan area there are four law enforcement agencies providing lab analysis for themselves and other agencies: Pinellas County Sheriff, Florida Department of Criminal Law Enforcement, Federal Bureau of Investigation, and the U.S. Army Criminal Investigation Division.

Table 13-2. Autonomy in Crime Laboratory Analysis: Region and SMSA Population

Location	Number of SMSAs	Percent of Consuming Agencies per SMSA Who Use Only Their Own Lab		Percent of SMSAs Where No Direct Police Agency Is Autonomous
		Median	Range[a]	
Total	80	8	4 – 17	18
Northeast				
Region 1	8	11	3 – 25	13
Region 2	4	3	0 – 6	25
Region 3	6	2	0 – 8	33
Midwest				
Region 5	16	5	0 – 13	31
Region 7	4	6	0 – 9	25
South				
Region 4	15	7	4 – 13	13
Region 6	14	20	9 – 27	7
West				
Region 8	4	17	0 – 18	25
Region 9	7	8	6 – 8	0
Region 10	2	—	10 – 17	0
Metropolitan Population (1973 est.)				
50,000 to 124,999	20	17	5 – 25	20
125,000 to 249,999	26	9	6 – 17	15
250,000 to 499,999	21	7	5 – 11	10
500,000 and over	13	4	0 – 8	31

[a] Range is the interquartile range except for Region 10, where it is the full range of variation.

Although the number of direct service agencies relying exclusively upon their own organizations for chemical analysis is quite small, virtually every agency having its own lab routinely does chemical analyses for other police agencies. Many state lab producers are required by statute to supply lab service free of charge to other state and local agencies. Of the 39 local producers of lab service, only 2 reported charging fees for chemical analyses. The most common reason agencies offered for supplying the service to other agencies was responding to requests of agencies who want access to laboratory facilities.

PRODUCTION OF CRIME LAB SERVICES

Local producers of lab services who also produce direct police services are few. State and federal producers are more frequent and also more likely to produce direct services. Table 13–3 provides a breakdown by agency of the number of lab producers in all 80 SMSAs. It is useful here to recall the distinction we have made between "producers" and "agencies."

A lab producer is counted every time an agency, such as a state crime lab, provides services to a metropolitan area. Consequently, if a state lab serves three different SMSAs, there are three state "lab producers" in that state. Since each of these lab producers reflects the existence of only one organization for the provision of lab services, there is only one lab agency in the state. The term "producer" counts the number of different SMSAs served by the agency (SMSA incidence of production); the term "agency" refers to organizational entities regardless of the number of different metropolitan areas served.

Local Laboratories

Specific statutory authorization for local crime lab service exists in only two states: Oklahoma and Texas [1]. Nonetheless, local governments in many of the states have their own crime labs. The majority of local agencies producing crime lab analysis are located in the South, the Great Lakes states, and California and Arizona (Regions 4, 5, and 9). All multijurisdictional labs are in the Midwest and the West (Regions 5, 7, 8, 9, and 10). The South and West have all but one of the county labs.

Private labs are more common in the West. Three of the four private labs in that region are located in California. Three of the seven private labs in our study are located in medical laboratories and hospitals. No significant relationships appear when local lab agencies are

Table 13–3. Producers of Crime Laboratory Analysis: Type of Agency

Type of Agency	Number of Producers	Percent	Number of Agencies	Percent
Total	202	100	85	100
Local producers	39	20	38	45
Municipal police	16	8	16	19
County sheriffs and police	12	6	11	13
Multijurisdictional arrangements	4	2	4	5
Private laboratories	7	4	7	8
State police	92	45	38	45
Federal police	71	35	9	10
Military police	26	13	6	7
Civilian police	45	22	3	3

examined by population size of metropolitan areas, other than the tendency for these agencies to be located in the larger SMSAs.

State Laboratories

State agencies supply lab services to police agencies in all but 1 of the 80 SMSAs [2]. Seven states (California, Connecticut, Kentucky, Massachusetts, Oklahoma, Ohio, and South Carolina) have two different state agencies that supply lab services to direct service police agencies. State crime labs for chemical analysis have multiplied during the last decade. One report indicates that in 1966, 17 states had no crime labs at all [3]. Nine of these 17 states contain SMSAs included in our study sample, and each of these states now has a state laboratory.

Our legal research on the 50 states indicates that statutory authorization for state agencies to provide crime lab services now exists in 33 states (Table 13—4). Twenty-three of these states require agencies to maintain crime lab facilities. Ten states authorize agencies to operate labs, but do not require it. In the other states we studied, state agencies produce lab analysis without specific statutory authorization.

Federal Laboratories

Federal laboratories constitute an important resource for forensic analysis in metropolitan areas. Military law enforcement agencies from all armed services use the laboratory of the U.S. Army Criminal Investigation Division at Fort Gordon, Georgia. Three small crime laboratories are also operated by local military units in two of the SMSAs studied and are reported as separate crime lab analysis agencies in Table 13—3. Some military law enforcement agencies also use state and local civilian labs.

Nonmilitary federal agencies do not regularly perform laboratory analysis for the military. In addition to providing lab analysis for their own personnel, however, these agencies sometimes do provide lab services to state and local agencies. The FBI is by far the most extensive federal supplier of lab services to state and local agencies. During fiscal year 1974 the FBI performed more than one-half million laboratory examinations. Approximately one fifth of these were conducted for nonfederal law enforcement agencies in the United States [4]. These figures include forensic analyses of a much broader scope than those considered in our study. Most direct service agencies in the 80 SMSAs do not regularly use the FBI crime lab, although some agencies in various sections of the country do report regular use of this service.

Table 13–4.   Statutory Authorization of Crime Lab Services: State Agencies

State Name	Agency or Division Thereof Authorized for Crime Laboratory Analysis	Authority to Maintain a Crime Lab	Crime Lab Services				
		A	B	C	D	E	F
Alabama	State Toxicologist		•	•			
Alaska	Dept. of Public Safety		•	•	•	•	•
Arizona	Dept. of Public Safety		•	•	•	•	
California	Dept. of Justice	•		•	•		
Colorado	Bureau of Investigation	•					
Connecticut	State Police	•			•	•	
Connecticut	Commission of Medicolegal Invest.		•		•		
Delaware	Dept. of Public Safety	•	•	•			
Florida	Div. of Intelligence & Invest.		•	•	•	•	
Georgia	Crime Lab Division		•	•	•		
Illinois	Dept. of Public Safety		•	•	•		
Iowa	Dept. of Public Safety		•	•			
Louisiana	Dept. of Public Safety	•					
Maine	Dept. of Public Safety		•		•		
Massachusetts	Dept. of Public Safety	•		•	•		
Michigan	State Crime Detection Lab		•	•	•	•	
Mississippi	Dept. of Public Safety	•					
Nebraska	State Patrol		•	•	•	•	
Nevada	Dept. of Law Enforcement Assistance	•	•	•	•	•	
New Hampshire	Dept. of Safety	•					•
New Jersey	Dept. of Law and Public Safety		•	•	•	•	
New Mexico	State Police		•	•	•	•	

State	Agency	A	B	C	D	E	F
New York	State Police				•		
No. Carolina	Bureau of Investigation	•		•			
No. Dakota	Bureau of Criminal Investigation	•		•			
Oregon	State Police	•		•			
Tennessee	Dept. of Safety	•		•	•		•
Texas	Dept. of Public Safety	•		•	•	•	•
Utah	Dept. of Public Safety	•		•	•	•	
Vermont	State Health Laboratory				•		
Washington	State Patrol	•		•	•		
W. Virginia	Dept. of Public Safety	•		•	•	•	
W. Virginia	Office of Medical Examinations	•		•	•	•	
Wisconsin	Division of Law Enforcement Services	•		•	•		
Wyoming	Attorney General's Office				•	•	

Source: Thomas W. Kramer, Frank Anechiarico, and Larry Wagner (1976) "State Statutory Authorization of the Law Enforcement Functions of State, County, and Municipal Agencies" (Bloomington, Ind.: Workshop in Political Theory & Policy Analysis), Technical Report T-6.

Code for Table 13-4.

Authority to Maintain a Crime Lab

A — Permitted by state law to maintain a crime lab.
B — Required by state law to maintain a crime lab.

Crime Lab Services Authorized

C — Narcotics analysis.
D — Other chemical analysis.
E — Ballistics analysis.
F — Other analysis.

The Drug Enforcement Administration (DEA), which specializes in narcotics analysis, also supplies lab service to state and local agencies. Thirty-four percent of the approximately 43,000 examinations conducted by DEA in fiscal year 1975 were performed for state and local agencies [5]. Only a few of the state and local agencies located in the 80 metropolitan areas use the DEA lab regularly, however. The Bureau of Alcohol, Tobacco, and Firearms of the Department of the Treasury (ATF) also regularly analyzes evidence for agencies in a few of the metropolitan areas included in our study.

These statistics show a substantial laboratory service contribution by federal agencies to state and local agencies. Federal labs also often receive many difficult, nonroutine specimens from agencies regularly using state or local labs. Data collected in this study indicate, however, that by and large, civilian police in metropolitan areas do not regularly use federal agencies for chemical analysis of evidence. In half the 80 SMSAs no local direct service police agencies use federal labs on a regular basis. In the other 40 SMSAs only about 1 in 10 lab consumers is served regularly by a nonmilitary federal agency.

Multiplicity

The median number of labs serving an SMSA is two (Table 13–5). The SMSA served by the largest number of lab producing agencies is Vallejo-Fairfield-Napa/California. Seven different agencies process evidence for police agencies in that area (two private labs, one state lab, three military labs, and the FBI). Many SMSAs are served by only one lab producer. Waco, Texas is an example. Here all 12 direct police producers send their evidence for analysis to the Texas State Department of Public Safety.

The South and West (Regions 4, 6, 8, 9, and 10) have the highest median number of lab producers per SMSA; the Northeast (Regions 1, 2, and 3) has the lowest. This regional variation is due in large part to the heavy concentration of military agencies in metropolitan areas of the South and West. Ninety percent of the military direct service producers in the 80 SMSAs are in these two areas [6]. The median crime lab multiplicity for the 22 SMSAs with military law enforcement agencies is four; the median crime lab multiplicity for the 58 SMSAs with no military law enforcement agencies is two.

Median multiplicity for all 80 SMSAs when military units are excluded is also two. The regional variation is reduced significantly when nonmilitary agencies are considered alone (Table 13–6). This highlights the problem of inferring the availability of crime lab analysis in a metropolitan area from the total number of labs serving that

Table 13–5. Multiplicity in Crime Laboratory Production: Region and SMSA Population

Location	Number of SMSAs	Number of Laboratory Producers in an SMSA		Number of Laboratory Producers per 10 Consuming Agencies	
		Median	*Range[a]*	*Median*	*Range*
Total	80	2	1 – 3	1.5	.9 – 2.9
Northeast					
Region 1	8	2	2 – 2	2.5	1.3 – 3.3
Region 2	4	1	1 – 1	.5	.1 – .5
Region 3	6	2	2 – 3	1.4	.3 – 2.9
Midwest					
Region 5	16	2	1 – 2	1.1	.6 – 1.7
Region 7	4	1	1 – 2	.9	.6 – 1.0
South					
Region 4	15	3	2 – 4	1.4	1.0 – 2.7
Region 6	14	3	1 – 4	2.5	1.1 – 3.3
West					
Region 8	4	3	3 – 4	2.7	2.5 – 3.3
Region 9	7	4	3 – 6	2.0	1.2 – 2.5
Region 10	2	—	2 – 2	—	.9 – 3.3
Metropolitan Population (1973 est.)					
50,000 to 124,999	20	2	1 – 3	3.3	1.7 – 3.7
125,000 to 249,999	26	2	1 – 3	1.4	.9 – 2.7
250,000 to 499,999	21	4	2 – 4	1.7	1.0 – 2.5
500,000 and over	13	3	2 – 3	.9	.5 – 1.2

[a] Range is the interquartile range except for Region 10, where it is the full range of variation.

Table 13-6. Multiplicity in Nonmilitary Crime Laboratory Production: Region and SMSA Population

Location	Number of SMSAs	Number of Nonmilitary Laboratory Producers in an SMSA		Number of Nonmilitary Laboratory Producers per 10 Consuming Agencies	
		Median	Range[a]	Median	Range
Total	80	2	1 – 3	1.4	.9 – 2.7
Northeast					
Region 1	8	2	2 – 2	2.5	1.3 – 3.3
Region 2	4	1	1 – 1	.5	.1 – .5
Region 3	6	2	2 – 2	1.4	.3 – 2.2
Midwest					
Region 5	16	2	1 – 2	1.1	.6 – 1.7
Region 7	4	1	1 – 1	.9	.6 – 1.0
South					
Region 4	15	2	2 – 4	1.4	1.0 – 2.9
Region 6	14	2	1 – 3	2.2	1.1 – 3.3
West					
Region 8	4	2	2 – 3	2.7	2.7 – 2.9
Region 9	7	3	3 – 4	2.1	1.3 – 2.2
Region 10	2	—	2 – 2	—	.9 – 3.3
Metropolitan Population (1973 est.)					
50,000 to 124,999	20	2	1 – 2	2.5	1.7 – 3.3
125,000 to 249,999	26	2	1 – 2	1.3	.9 – 2.9
250,000 to 499,999	21	3	2 – 3	1.7	1.0 – 2.2
500,000 and over	13	3	2 – 3	.9	.5 – 1.3

[a]Range is the interquartile range except for Region 10, where it is the full range of variation.

area. Military labs provide forensic analysis only to military law enforcement agencies; their services are not generally available to civilian agencies in these metropolitan areas. Additionally, the number of labs serving an area may not be a reflection of their combined capacity to handle that area's volume of service requests, since the size of labs may vary considerably.

The ratio of lab producers to consumers of lab service is typically quite low. The median number of lab producers per 10 consumers in an SMSA is 1.5. New England, the Southwest, and the Rocky Mountain states (Regions 1, 6, and 8) have the highest ratios; New York and New Jersey (Region 2) have the lowest. The metropolitan area with the highest producer-consumer ratio is one of the smallest in the study—Owensboro/Kentucky, which has three consumers of lab service and four producers of the service (Kentucky State Police, Kentucky Department of Public Health, FBI, ATF). Paterson-Clifton-Passaic/New Jersey, the study's largest SMSA, has the lowest producer-consumer ratio: approximately 1 to 100.

When only nonmilitary producers are considered, the median ratio of lab producers to consumers drops to 1.4, but the only significant changes in median ratios are in the Southwest and California and Arizona (Regions 6 and 9). Most labs in New England, New York and New Jersey, and the Great Lakes states (Regions 1, 2 and 5) are state labs (Table 13−7). In the rest of the country, distribution among local, state, and federal lab producers is more nearly equal.

SPECIALIZATION IN CRIME LAB ANALYSIS

The type of chemicals analyzed varies somewhat by type of lab (Table 13−8). Seventy-one percent of the agencies doing crime lab analysis supply both narcotics and other chemical analyses to their consumers, while 18 percent supply narcotics analyses only, and 12 percent supply other chemical analyses only. Municipal and nonmilitary federal labs are more likely than other types of labs to supply narcotics analyses, but no other chemical analyses.

While the pattern of specialization for lab analysis is fairly clear-cut, specialization of crime lab agencies in terms of the other direct and auxiliary police services they may produce is less so. Local agencies usually fall into one of two categories. A local producer of crime lab analysis is either a highly specialized auxiliary agency (most often producing forensic analysis only) or an agency producing many police services including crime lab analysis (Table 13−9). The latter

Table 13-7. Distribution of Crime Lab Producers: Region and SMSA Population

Location	Number Reporting	Percent of Lab Producers in Each Region That Are		
		Local	State	Federal
Total	202	19	46	35
Northeast				
Region 1	17	0	94	6
Region 2	5	20	80	0
Region 3	14	14	43	43
Midwest				
Region 5	30	23	63	13
Region 7	6	33	33	33
South				
Region 4	44	21	39	41
Region 6	36	14	42	44
West				
Region 8	14	21	29	50
Region 9	32	25	22	53
Region 10	4	50	50	0
Metropolitan Population (1973 est.)				
50,000 to 124,999	42	12	57	31
125,000 to 249,999	52	15	60	25
250,000 to 499,999	71	18	32	49
500,000 and over	37	35	38	27

are all municipal and county agencies. Multijurisdictional and private agencies all specialize in chemical or forensic analysis.

In contrast to local lab agencies, state lab agencies show several patterns of crime lab service production. Seventeen of the 38 state lab agencies (45 percent) produce auxiliary services only; 15 of these 17 do lab analysis exclusively. Another 37 percent of the state agencies that produce crime lab analysis also produce a broad range of direct services; 18 percent fall into an intermediate class, producing

Table 13–8. Types of Crime Lab Services: Type of Agency

Type of Agency	Number Reporting	Percent of Labs Conducting		
		Narcotics Analysis	Chemical Analysis	Both Types of Analysis
Total	85	18	12	71
Local producers	38	18	11	71
Municipal police	16	31	6	63
County sheriffs and police	11	9	9	82
Multijurisdictional arrangements	4	0	0	100
Private laboratories	7	14	29	57
State laboratory	38	16	8	76
Federal laboratories	9	22	33	44
Military laboratories	6	17	33	50
Civilian laboratories	3	33	33	33

Table 13–9.   Range of Other Services Produced by Crime Laboratory Analysis Agencies: Type of Agency

Type of Agency	Number Reporting	Percent of Agencies Producing			Percent of Agencies Producing Other Auxiliary Services
		No Direct Services	1 to 2 Direct Services	3 to 5 Direct Services	
Total	85	51	9	40	52
Local agencies	38	44	5	51	54
Municipal	16	18	0	81	81
County	11	36	0	64	64
Multijurisdictional	4	100	0	0	0
Private	7	100	0	0	0
State agencies	38	45	18	37	58
Federal agencies	9	57	43	0	43
Civilian	3	100	0	0	0
Military	6	83	17	0	33

only one or two direct services. Fifty-eight percent of the state agencies producing crime lab analysis also produce other auxiliary police services.

In the 80 SMSAs, federal agencies that supply lab analysis tend to provide only a few of the direct services we examined, and most often only criminal investigation services. They often provide other auxiliary services, however, typically for themselves (training, for instance). None specializes exclusively in crime lab work, but several have extensive facilities primarily intended to support their own investigative forces.

DOMINANCE OF LABORATORY SERVICE PROVISION

Half the 80 SMSAs have a single laboratory producing chemical analysis for at least 96 percent of the direct police service agencies using lab analysis (Table 13–10). More than three fourths of the 80 metropolitan areas have dominant producers routinely serving at least 79 percent of the consumers. Although all regions report high median dominance measures, broader variation exists in the southern and western parts of the country. The much higher presence of the military in these regions and the greater number of consumers using several labs in the West contribute to this. There appears to be no strong relationship between the extent to which the dominant crime lab serves an SMSA and the size of that SMSA.

State agencies are the most dominant producers of criminal lab services in the 80 SMSAs. In 65 of the 80 SMSAs a state agency supplies chemical analysis to more direct police service agencies than any other type of lab. Only in the Plains states, the Rocky Mountain states, and California and Arizona (Regions 7, 8, and 9) are there substantial proportions of the metropolitan areas served by nonstate lab agencies. All but two of the dominant nonstate labs are associated with a local unit of government. More than 60 percent of the metropolitan areas in each population category are dominated by state agencies. In the largest SMSAs, local labs supply a significant portion of this service, however.

Table 13–11 compares the typical extent of the lab production for local, state, and federal producers. The median state chemical lab in these 80 metropolitan areas serves 85 percent of the SMSA police agencies on a regular basis. In 22 of the SMSAs, state agencies supply chemical analysis to *all* direct service producers using labs. In Paterson-Clifton-Passaic/New Jersey, the New Jersey State Police analyze evidence for all 91 of the direct police agencies. In spite of the fact

Table 13–10.   Dominance in Crime Laboratory Analysis: Region and SMSA Population

Location	Number of SMSAs	Percent of SMSA Consumers Served by Dominant Lab Producer		Percent of SMSAs Where Dominant Producer Is a		
		Median	Range[a]	Local Agency	State Agency	Federal Agency
Total[b]	80	96	79 – 100	19	81	4
Northeast						
Region 1	8	100	100 – 100	0	100	0
Region 2	4	100	88 – 100	25	75	0
Region 3	6	98	94 – 100	0	100	0
Midwest						
Region 5[c]	16	100	95 – 100	19	94	0
Region 7	4	95	80 – 100	50	50	0
South						
Region 4[d]	15	91	63 – 100	20	80	7
Region 6	14	73	64 – 100	21	79	0
West						
Region 8	4	67	55 – 67	0	50	50
Region 9	7	91	76 – 96	43	57	0
Region 10	2	—	83 – 95	0	100	0

Metropolitan Population (1973 est.)					
50,000 to 124,999[e]	20	100	67 – 100	15	80	10
125,000 to 249,999[e]	26	100	93 – 100	8	92	4
250,000 to 499,999	21	91	58 – 96	19	81	0
500,000 and over[e]	13	96	88 – 100	46	62	0

[a] Range is the interquartile range except for Region 10, where it is the full range of variation.
[b] Two dominant labs supply equal numbers of direct service producers in three SMSAs, so percent of SMSAs where dominant producer is a local, state, or federal agency is greater than 100 percent.
[c] State and local labs supply equal numbers of direct service producers in two SMSAs.
[d] Federal and state labs supply equal numbers of direct service producers in one SMSA.
[e] Two dominant labs supply equal numbers of direct service producers in one SMSA.

Table 13–11. Number of Crime Laboratory Analysis Consumers: Type of Producer

Type of Lab Producer	Number Reporting	Number of Lab Consumers per SMSA Served Regularly by This Type of Producer		Percent of Lab Consumers per SMSA Served Regularly by This Type of Producer		Number of SMSAs Where All Lab Consumers Are Served Routinely by This Type of Producer
		Median	Range[a]	Median	Range	
Local laboratory	34	4	1 – 14	20	6 – 80	2
State laboratory	73	9	6 – 18	85	55 – 100	22
Federal laboratory						
Military laboratory	25	2	2 – 3	20	17 – 22	0
Civilian laboratory	42	1	1 – 2	10	5 – 19	0

[a] Range is the interquartile range.

that this is the most fragmented of the 80 SMSAs, all its police agencies receive lab services exclusively from the State Police on a regular basis. For production of forensic chemical analysis, this SMSA is completely consolidated.

The various local agency laboratories rank a distant second in terms of the proportion of direct service producers served. They serve 20 percent of the direct service producers in the median SMSA. In two SMSAs (Gary-Hammond-East Chicago/Indiana and Springfield/Missouri) local labs serve all lab consumers. The metropolitan area where the dominant lab producer serves the smallest proportion of producers is Albuquerque/New Mexico. Four of the SMSA's 12 direct producers (25 percent) have chemical analyses conducted by the Albuquerque Police Department.

Federal agencies commonly serve the fewest direct service producers in these metropolitan areas. Federal civilian agencies regularly serve a median of 10 percent of an SMSA's direct service producers. Military labs provide for a median of 20 percent of an SMSA's direct producers, although in most cases this amounts to 100 percent of the area's military law enforcement agencies. In only one case does a federal lab come close to serving all direct service producers in a metropolitan area. This is in Provo-Orem/Utah, where the FBI crime lab produces chemical analysis for 14 of the 15 producers of direct police services.

PATTERNS OF CRIME LAB SERVICE

Crime lab analysis of evidence is a service available to virtually all metropolitan police agencies. Although this chapter has reviewed variations in the character of the crime lab industry from one type of metropolitan area to another, we should emphasize that the patterns of lab analysis production generally share more common features than differences. Few direct service police agencies conduct their own laboratory analysis. On the other hand, most labs are attached to or closely allied with law enforcement agencies.

Crime lab analysis in most areas is dominated by state laboratories. Much of the lab industry variation among SMSAs can be attributed to the heavy concentration of military agencies in the South and West, which inflates crime lab multiplicity and deflates the dominance of single lab producers in those regions.

Some significant variations among SMSAs, however, cannot be attributed to military presence. There is a considerably greater use of local agencies in the West than in other regions. The rapid and comparatively recent growth of western metropolitan regions in the

1960s may well account for the greater use of local producers there. Somewhat independent of this regional relationship is the tendency for larger metropolitan areas to have local lab producers. Areas with larger populations may have a volume of work large enough to realize economies of scale in operating their own crime laboratories.

The general implication of the data on these 80 metropolitan areas is that, in terms of crime lab analysis, many of the recommendations of study commissions have been implemented. Although the data do not permit evaluation of the adequacy of crime lab provision in these metropolitan areas, we find that crime lab service is commonly available to all police agencies and is typically provided to them through a state agency. Further research is needed to evaluate the adequacy of present patterns of crime lab producers' service delivery.

Chapter 14

An Overview of Auxiliary Service Delivery Patterns

The service delivery patterns for auxiliary services, except radio communications, are considerably different from those for direct services. A much smaller number of producers, some of whom are specialists in their particular field, produce these services. Most direct service producers, including many of the very largest, obtain entry-level training, detention, and laboratory analysis from other agencies.

Radio communications is the auxiliary service most commonly produced by direct service police agencies. Almost all county police and sheriffs' departments conduct their own radio communications regardless of agency size. For municipal police departments, campus police, and other agencies serving special districts, larger departments are more likely to conduct their own radio communications. It is important to note that many agencies—especially the smaller ones— have arrangements with other agencies to conduct radio communications for them during some parts of the day. In more than half the 80 metropolitan areas at least one patrol agency supplying its own radio communications also has an alternate supplier of this service. County sheriffs are the major alternate supplier of radio communications. Communications centers specializing in this service have been established in some SMSAs. Municipal police and other local agencies also supply radio communications for each other.

County sheriffs' departments are the most common local agencies supplying pretrial detention. In most states county sheriffs have the legal responsibility to maintain jails. Other arrangements are found, however. Connecticut has state jails; Kentucky and Pennsylvania have county jails that are independent of the sheriff; and in other metropolitan areas there are municipal or county jails not associated with direct police service agencies. A few municipal police departments also maintain their own jails, but they are the exception.

County sheriffs' departments produce pretrial detention in 62 of the 76 SMSAs where detention is conducted by local producers and contribute over 70 percent of the local detention capacity. Detention centers serve 24 of the 76 metropolitan areas and contribute about one fifth of the detention capacity. Municipal police departments produce pretrial detention in 17 SMSAs and contribute less than one tenth of the detention capacity. Detention is usually supplied on a county-by-county basis so that multicounty metropolitan areas have separate jails serving each of their counties. While county sheriffs' departments and detention centers typically supply detention services to all civilian police agencies operating in the county, most municipal police department jails are used exclusively by those departments themselves. The military maintains its own facilities for detaining military personnel.

Only the largest municipal police departments are likely to conduct their own entry-level training. Some of these departments also train police recruits for other police agencies in their areas. State and regional criminal justice training academies, colleges and universities, and technical institutes are other common producers of entry-level training. Entry-level training is required by more than 90 percent of the municipal police departments and county police and sheriffs' departments in the 80 SMSAs. Over 80 percent of all campus and other local police agencies also require entry-level training. The latter agencies are less likely to be subject to state requirements for recruit training. Federal and state agencies conduct their own training.

Few local direct service agencies conduct chemical analysis of evidence. Even the largest agencies use other agencies' laboratories rather than employing experts to identify narcotics, blood, and other substances. State agencies are the most common suppliers of this auxiliary service. In some states laboratory services are produced by the state police or state bureau of investigation. In others a separate state crime lab has been established. The two types of arrangements are equally common in the 80 metropolitan areas we studied. But there are also other arrangements. In the 20 metropolitan areas where they are found, municipal police department labs and sheriff's department labs are used by other local agencies. In a few metropolitan areas hospital laboratories are used as a common practice, and in four SMSAs regional crime labs have been organized. State agencies usually use state labs. Federal agencies usually use federal labs.

Most direct service producers use auxiliary services even if they do not produce them. The number of direct service producers in an SMSA who use each auxiliary service is shown as "fragmentation" in Table 14–1. For all four auxiliary services this is uniformly similar to the number of producers for the direct services studied.

Most direct police service producers obtain auxiliary services from other agencies. Thus, multiplicity scores are lower than scores for fragmentation. At least nine agencies produce radio communications in half the 80 SMSAs. The median number of producers for detention and chemical laboratory analysis is two. For entry-level training the median number is four. More than 20 SMSAs have as many producers as consumers of radio communications, and the median SMSA has 0.86 producers for every agency using this service. For entry-level training the median ratio of producers to consumers is 0.33. Detention and chemical analysis each have about seven agencies using the service for each producer of the service, or median ratios of 0.15 and 0.14, respectively.

While independence and autonomy are relatively high for radio communications, both measures are quite low for the other three auxiliary services. There is little coordination between producers of these services. Alternation in radio communications does occur among a few agencies in over half the 80 SMSAs. Duplication of production is not characteristic of any of the four auxiliary services.

Dominance, on the other hand, is much higher for auxiliary services than for direct services, particularly for detention and chemical laboratory analysis. In half the 80 SMSAs, at least 96 percent of the direct service producers using lab analysis are served by the dominant producer.

In many ways the patterns of auxiliary service delivery in the 80 SMSAs differ rather markedly from those expected. Major reports on police organization during the last decade have suggested that auxiliary services are not readily available to police. We have found a high utilization of auxiliary services. Economies of scale in the production of such auxiliary services as detention and chemical analysis may account for the low numbers of producers of those services. The "full-service" police department is certainly not a widely adopted model for metropolitan policing. Instead, even the largest local police agencies obtain auxiliary services from other agencies.

Table 14–1.   Structure of Service Delivery for Auxiliary Services in 80 Metropolitan Areas: Measures

	Radio Communications	Detention	Entry-Level Training	Chemical Laboratory Analysis
Fragmentation				
Median	13	14	13	12
Range[a]	8 – 21	9 – 22	8 – 20	8 – 22
Multiplicity				
Median	9	2	4	2
Range	6 – 17	1 – 3	2 – 7	1 – 3
Multiplicity per consuming agency				
Median	.86	.15	.33	.14
Range	.67 – 1.00	.09 – .25	.21 – .50	.09 – .27
Independence				
Median	83	10	20	8
Range	65 – 100	2 – 16	12 – 27	5 – 17
Autonomy				
Median	73	8	17	8
Range	50 – 92	0 – 13	10 – 27	4 – 17
Alternation				
Median	5	0	0	0
Range	0 – 17	0 – 12	0 – 0	0 – 0

Coordination				
Median	0	0	0	0
Range	0 – 0	0 – 0	0 – 0	0 – 0
Duplication[b]				
Median	0	0	0	0
Range	0 – 0	0 – 0	0 – 11	0 – 7
Dominance				
Median	25	88	70	96
Range	15 – 42	75 – 100	50 – 85	79 – 100

[a] Range is the interquartile range.
[b] Without alternation.

※ *Chapter 15*

Police Agency Cooperation: Patterns of Mutual Aid and Cross-Deputization

John P. McIver
Larry Wagner

Jurisdictional fragmentation has been cited as a major problem facing police. Critics charge that political boundaries can afford criminals "sanctuary" from police action. They insist, furthermore, that the traditional, usually informal provision of assistance between agencies is insufficient: cooperation must be achieved through formal means [1]. These conclusions, however, are based on the assumption that cooperation tends to be " . . . sporadic and informal, even for those agencies which are contiguous or overlapping" [2].

Many critics have theorized that increasing informal cooperation is not an effective means of improving the quality of police services. Informal arrangements are typically described as those in which one agency agrees to come to the assistance of another if needed. The clause "if needed" is usually applied to emergency situations only. Critics have asserted that these mutual aid agreements, while serving a valid purpose, do not " . . . materially add to the quality of services provided by a specific department nor do they improve the quality of personnel" [3].

These views are largely inaccurate. Undoubtedly, some jurisdictional boundaries lead to confusion and conflict among police agencies in metropolitan areas, but usually boundaries between agencies only limit the routine activities of departments. When extraordinary situations occur, such as a fleeing suspect or a police emergency, jurisdictional lines usually pose minimal restraint on police actions. We examined state legislation regarding powers of arrest and fresh pursuit across police jurisdiction boundaries. We also asked police officials about their arrangements for mutual assistance and whether their departments had given or received emergency assistance during the year preceding our survey. The results of both the legal and behavioral inquiries indicate that interagency cooperation is the rule.

FRESH PURSUIT

Police officers in most states have explicit authority to pursue suspects beyond the limits of their own jurisdictions [4]. However, that authority is subject to a variety of restrictions. Authority to pursue within the state is usually treated separately from authority to pursue across state lines.

Intrastate Fresh Pursuit

Thirty-nine states have intrastate fresh pursuit legislation—statutes authorizing county or municipal peace officers to pursue suspected criminals across municipal and county lines. These states are shown in Map 15-1.

Intrastate fresh pursuit is generally not a problem for officers employed by state-level law enforcement agencies. Most state law enforcement agencies have, by definition, statewide jurisdiction. State police may pursue suspected offenders anywhere within their state. County and local peace officers have more restricted jurisdictions.

Fresh pursuit legislation is not always uniformly applicable to county and local peace officers. In Maine, for example, county sheriffs may pursue a suspect anywhere in the state for any offense, but municipal peace officers are permitted by legislation to pursue only as far as the county lines. In South Carolina, sheriffs and their deputies may pursue into adjacent counties for any offense, but municipal peace officers may pursue only three miles beyond their own city limits.

Pursuit authority may also be limited by the type of offense. North Carolina county sheriffs are permitted to pursue suspected felons anywhere in the state, but are otherwise limited to their own counties. In Virginia all peace officers are given statewide authority to pursue suspected felons, but can pursue only into an adjacent jurisdiction for a misdemeanor committed in an officer's presence.

Of the 39 states having specific legislation on intrastate fresh pursuit, 22 authorize all county and municipal peace officers to engage in fresh pursuit throughout their state for any offense. An additional eight states authorize statewide pursuit under at least some circumstances. That 30 states authorize some form of statewide fresh pursuit contradicts any blanket assertion that police officers are unable

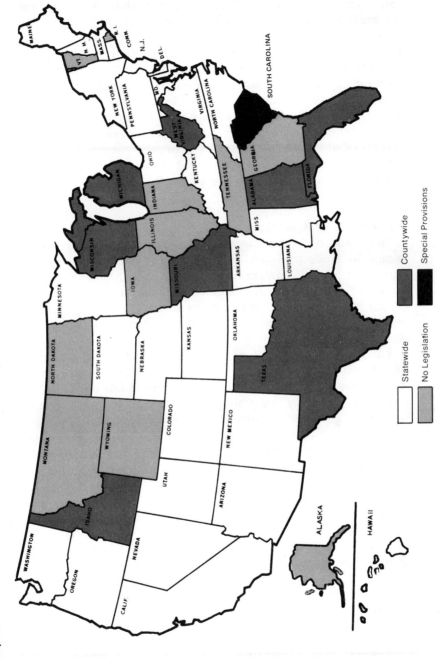

Map 15-1. Distribution of Intrastate Fresh Pursuit Legislation

to pursue beyond their own jurisdictions. Of the nine additional states having other forms of legislation regarding intrastate fresh pursuit, eight authorize countywide pursuit for any offense.

Eleven states have no legislation pertaining specifically to intrastate fresh pursuit. Lack of specific legislation does not, however, preclude intrastate fresh pursuit activity in these states. In states having no applicable statutes or case law, officers have the same right to arrest another person as do private persons under the common law. (Under common law a citizen may make an arrest only for an offense committed in his or her presence.) So, even in states with no legislation or case law specifically applicable to intrastate fresh pursuit, law enforcement officers are not helpless if a suspected criminal crosses jurisdictional lines: the citizen's arrest right extends statewide.

Standards of Knowledge

The standard of knowledge required of an officer before he can engage in fresh pursuit depends in many states upon the type of crime committed. For example, an officer in Alabama can make an arrest for a misdemeanor without a warrant only if the crime is committed in his presence. But to make an arrest for a felony the officer needs only to have reasonable cause to believe a felony has been committed.

For misdemeanors, 17 of the 39 states with fresh pursuit legislation grant officers authority to engage in fresh pursuit when they have reasonable cause to believe that a crime has been attempted or committed. Twenty-two states grant fresh pursuit authority for misdemeanors under the more limited condition that the crime was attempted or committed in the officer's presence. Practically all of the 39 states grant fresh pursuit authority with reasonable cause for felonies.

Interstate Fresh Pursuit

What authority does a pursuing officer have when a suspect flees across state lines? Here the legislation is more specific: a majority of states have extended broad authority to the police officer as exemplified by this statute:

> Any member of a duly organized state, county or municipal peace unit of another state of the United States who enters this state in fresh pursuit, and continues within this state in such fresh pursuit, of a person in order to arrest him on the ground that he is believed to have committed a felony in such other state, shall have the same authority to arrest and hold such

person in custody, as has any member of any duly organized state, county or municipal peace unit of this state, to arrest and hold in custody a person on the ground that he is believed to have committed a felony in this state [Kansas S.A. §62–632 (1937)].

A statute like this is designated a Uniform Act on Fresh Pursuit and has been enacted by 31 states. Ten more states have enacted variations of the Uniform Act. Of these 10, 2 have broadened the authority of the Uniform Act to include any offense. The other eight require reciprocity for their own Act to authorize interstate fresh pursuit. A police officer in any of these eight states can pursue across state lines into any other state that has passed a variant of the Uniform Act. By 1974 only nine states had not enacted any legislation on interstate fresh pursuit. Most of these states are located in the South (Map 15–2).

Police officers in most states have relatively broad powers to pursue fleeing suspects, particularly when a felony is suspected. Some states without specific intrastate authority have used their authority under the Uniform Act authorizing interstate fresh pursuit as authorization for fresh pursuit within their own state. So the actual practice concerning intrastate fresh pursuit may be somewhat understated.

PATTERNS OF INTERAGENCY ASSISTANCE

Eighty-six percent of local patrol agencies in the 80 SMSAs report that they assist other police departments outside their jurisdictions [5] (Table 15–1). Ninety-one percent report that they receive assistance from other agencies. Is this assistance "reciprocal"? In almost all cases the answer is yes. Only 3 percent of local patrol producers report assisting other agencies while not receiving assistance themselves. Seven percent report receiving assistance without themselves providing assistance. Together, both types of nonreciprocal assistance apply to only 10 percent of the patrol agencies. Ninety-three percent of all local patrol agencies in the 80 SMSAs report providing *or* receiving assistance.

Municipal police departments provide assistance outside their jurisdictions more often than other types of local patrol agencies. More than 90 percent of municipal patrol agencies indicate that their officers go beyond jurisdictional boundaries to assist other agencies. County sheriffs are slightly less likely to assist outside their jurisdictions. 77 percent provide aid outside their jurisdictions [6]. Special

Map 15–2. Distribution of Interstate Fresh Pursuit Legislation

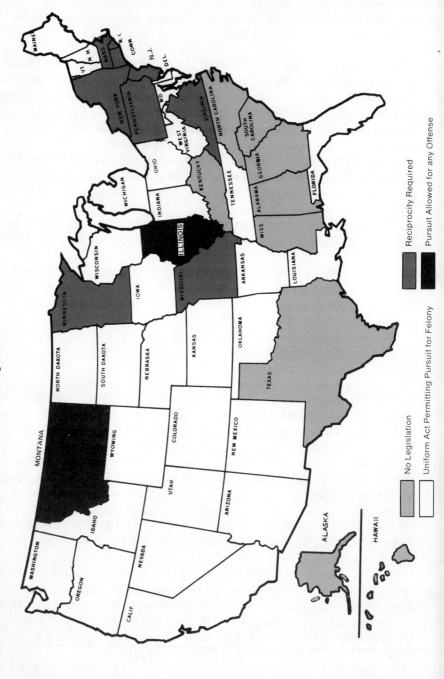

patrol producers and campus police agencies are much less likely to assist outside their jurisdictions. In some instances the legal powers of these officers are limited to the jurisdictions of their employing agency by state law: for example, to a college or university campus. These agencies are also less likely to share radio frequencies with other agencies, and so their officers are not as likely to be aware of another agency's need for emergency help.

More than 90 percent of municipal police agencies and about 80 percent of the county agencies report receiving assistance. Similar proportions of campus and other special district patrol producers report receiving assistance.

Mutual Aid Agreements

Although almost all local police agencies provide assistance to and receive assistance from other agencies, fewer local agencies enter into formal mutual aid agreements with other departments. About half the patrol agencies have some type of mutual aid agreement with at least one other agency. Municipal police departments are the most likely to organize such aid agreements. Fifty-one percent of the municipal police departments, but only about 30 percent of county agencies, campus police, and other specialized producers, belong to mutual aid pacts.

Significant regional differences exist in mutual aid pact membership. The Far West (Region 9) has the largest proportion of agencies who are parties to formal aid arrangements; the Rocky Mountain states (Region 8) have the smallest proportion. The large proportion of agencies in the Far West who have formal aid agreements is due principally to California law, which requires all police agencies to be members of formal mutual aid pacts.

Agency Size and Assistance

Agency size is related to interagency assistance among municipal police departments. The larger the municipal police department, the less likely it is to give or to receive assistance (see Table 15-1). Size makes little difference, however, in the percentage of agencies that belong to aid agreements. With the exception of the largest agencies (more than 150 sworn officers), approximately half of all municipal police departments are parties to formal mutual aid agreements. Only one quarter of the largest municipal departments participate in formal mutual aid pacts.

Department size is not so important for assistance to or from county police and sheriffs' departments. There is little relationship between the number of full-time sworn officers employed by a

Table 15—1. Assistance: Type and Size of Local Patrol Producer

Type of Patrol Producer	Number Reporting	Percent of Patrol Producers That		
		Provide Assistance to Other Police Agencies	Receive Assistance From Other Police Agencies	Belong to a Mutual Aid Agreement
Municipal police by number of full-time officers	841	92	92	51
Part-time only	62	95	98	53
1 to 4	213	92	95	46
5 to 10	206	95	95	50
11 to 20	119	93	96	58
21 to 50	119	93	94	64
51 to 150	76	87	79	57
Over 150	46	80	61	24
County sheriffs and police by number of full-time officers	91	77	79	30
1 to 4	2	50	50	0
5 to 10	4	75	100	0
11 to 20	16	69	75	31
21 to 50	27	85	85	22
51 to 150	26	69	65	31
Over 150	16	88	94	50

Campus police by number of full-time officers	93	56	87	32
Part-time only				
1 to 4	3	0	100	67
5 to 10	13	31	77	46
11 to 20	36	64	92	28
21 to 50	18	61	78	17
51 to 150	20	65	95	40
	3	33	67	33

Other local producers by number of full-time officers	38	53	97	32
Part-time only				
1 to 4	2	0	100	50
5 to 10	11	73	100	55
11 to 20	10	60	90	0
21 to 50	8	50	100	25
51 to 150	6	33	100	33
	1	0	100	100

Table 15–2. Percent of Local Patrol Producers That Are Parties to Formal Mutual Aid Agreements: Region and Type of Producer

Location	Type of Local Patrol Producer			
	Municipal Police	County Sheriffs and Police	Campus Police	Other Police Agencies
Total	51 (867)	29 (94)	32 (93)	32 (38)
Northeast				
Region 1	30 (57)	0 (0)	33 (6)	0 (1)
Region 2	70 (132)	40 (5)	25 (4)	17 (6)
Region 3	81 (108)	0 (2)	63 (8)	100 (2)
Midwest				
Region 5	50 (180)	26 (23)	42 (12)	0 (6)
Region 7	41 (22)	33 (3)	0 (1)	0 (0)
South				
Region 4	37 (169)	26 (27)	17 (29)	33 (3)
Region 6	9 (88)	6 (17)	24 (17)	29 (7)
West				
Region 8	0 (21)	0 (4)	0 (3)	0 (2)
Region 9	92 (71)	100 (8)	62 (13)	55 (11)
Region 10	58 (19)	40 (5)	0 (0)	0 (0)

Note: Number in parentheses equals number reporting.

county agency and its participation in interagency assistance. Larger county patrol agencies are, however, somewhat more likely to be members of formal mutual aid agreements.

Size of department is apparently not a factor in either interagency assistance or participation in formal mutual aid pacts for campus and other local patrol agencies. With few exceptions, agencies of these types report receiving assistance. Many of these agencies do not provide assistance, regardless of their size, and only one third belong to formal mutual assistance agreements.

Interagency assistance is more frequent than participation in formal mutual aid pacts for all types and sizes of departments. Most local patrol agencies are either providers and/or receivers of some on-the-street assistance from another patrol producer. In most cases patrol agencies both give and receive assistance whether or not they are parties to formal mutual assistance agreements.

Patterns of Deputization

"Deputization" means that police officers from one jurisdiction are given police powers in a jurisdiction or jurisdictions other than their own [7]. Almost two out of five local patrol agencies use some type of deputization arrangement. The most prevalent arrangement is a nonmutual one, where one agency's officers are deputized by a second agency, but the first agency does not deputize the second agency's officers.

The officers of over one third of the local patrol agencies we studied are deputized by other police agencies. Seventeen percent of the patrol producers deputize officers from other jurisdictions. Examination of deputization patterns for county and municipal police departments provides an explanation as to why a larger number of agencies have officers deputized by other agencies than deputize officers from other agencies.

Nearly 50 percent of the county agencies indicate that they deputize officers from other agencies, while only 16 percent of the municipal agencies and almost no campus agencies deputize officers from other agencies. In many instances county sheriffs deputize officers from the smaller municipal agencies operating within their jurisdictions. Deputization enables county sheriffs who may have many municipal departments within their overall jurisdictions to draw upon these departments for assistance within the county as a whole.

Fewer than 20 percent of the county patrol agencies have officers who have been deputized by other departments. Sheriff's department officers do not need to be deputized by municipalities to have

Table 15–3.   Percent of Local Patrol Producers Whose Officers Are Deputized by Other Police Agencies: Region and Type of Producer

Location	Type of Local Patrol Producer			
	Municipal Police	County Sheriffs and Police	Campus Police	Other Police Agencies
Total	35 (858)	16 (92)	45 (100)	38 (40)
Northeast				
Region 1	26 (55)	0 (0)	75 (8)	50 (2)
Region 2	8 (133)	0 (5)	25 (4)	14 (7)
Region 3	56 (109)	0 (2)	38 (8)	100 (2)
Midwest				
Region 5	34 (177)	4 (23)	29 (14)	50 (6)
Region 7	42 (24)	0 (3)	100 (1)	0 (1)
South				
Region 4	30 (158)	12 (26)	57 (30)	67 (3)
Region 6	25 (89)	17 (18)	24 (17)	0 (7)
West				
Region 8	33 (21)	0 (4)	100 (3)	100 (2)
Region 9	74 (73)	86 (7)	40 (15)	40 (10)
Region 10	63 (19)	50 (4)	0 (0)	0 (0)

Note: Number in parentheses equals number reporting.

Table 15–4. Percent of Local Patrol Producers That Deputize Officers From Other Departments: Region and Type of Producer

Location	Type of Local Patrol Producer			
	Municipal Police	County Sheriffs and Police	Campus Police	Other Police Agencies
Total	16 (862)	49 (94)	2 (96)	5 (41)
Northeast				
Region 1	15 (55)	0 (0)	0 (8)	0 (2)
Region 2	2 (133)	20 (5)	0 (4)	0 (7)
Region 3	51 (108)	0 (2)	0 (8)	50 (2)
Midwest				
Region 5	2 (179)	65 (23)	0 (14)	17 (6)
Region 7	9 (23)	0 (4)	0 (1)	0 (1)
South				
Region 4	7 (163)	58 (26)	3 (29)	0 (4)
Region 6	2 (89)	22 (18)	0 (16)	0 (7)
West				
Region 8	5 (21)	50 (4)	0 (3)	0 (2)
Region 9	69 (73)	86 (7)	8 (13)	0 (10)
Region 10	0 (18)	60 (5)	0 (0)	0 (0)

Note: Number in parentheses equals number reporting.

powers of arrest within the municipalities in their own county. This contrasts with municipal, campus, and other local police departments, which have more of their officers deputized by other agencies. Many of these are small departments. Across the country more than 50 percent of the departments with only part-time officers and more than 30 percent of the departments with 1 to 10 officers have their officers deputized by another agency.

Campus police departments are most likely to have their officers deputized by city, county, or state police. This deputization may give campus police their formal police powers, since in some states college and university security departments are not empowered to authorize their own officers. Campus police are not likely to deputize others. Most campuses lie within another police jurisdiction, and officers from other agencies with legal jurisdiction on a campus do not need their officers deputized.

Participation in Emergency Assistance

Only 50 percent of the patrol producers who both give and receive emergency assistance outside of their jurisdiction are members of mutual aid agreements (see Table 15−5). Clearly, assistance is available in many places without formal agreements. Twenty-six percent of the agencies that report neither giving nor receiving any external assistance belong to mutual aid agreements; so, belonging to a mutual aid pact is no guarantee that assistance has been provided. (Of course, there may have been no need for assistance in some of these cases.)

Almost 70 percent of the producers who report both giving and receiving emergency assistance are either members of mutual aid pacts or have some form of deputization agreement. Thus, most of the agencies reporting mutual assistance do have some formal arrangements between them, although the absence of formal arrangements does not preclude assistance.

One third of the agencies that report either "mutual" or "one-way" assistance also report their officers are deputized by another agency. Agencies are less likely to deputize other agencies' officers than to join mutual aid agreements. Fewer than one fifth of the patrol agencies that both provide and receive assistance deputize officers from other agencies. About 6 percent of the agencies that only give assistance deputize officers from other agencies. Deputization of the officers of other agencies in order to receive assistance is similarly infrequent. Fewer than 7 percent of the agencies receiving, but not giving, assistance deputize officers of other police agencies.

Table 15–5. Assistance Arrangements in Local Patrol Producers: Mutual Aid Agreements, Cross-Deputization, and Type of Assistance Relationship

	Type of Assistance Received or Given			
	Receive and Give Assistance	*Only Assist Others*	*Only Receive Assistance*	*None*
Is this agency a member of a mutual aid agreement?	(862) 51.2[a]	(32) 34.4	(75) 26.7	(65) 26.2
Are this agency's officers deputized by another police department?	35.8	34.4	40.0	13.8
Does this agency deputize officers from other police departments?	18.6	6.3	6.7	13.8

Note: Number in parentheses equals number reporting.
[a] Percent responding yes to question.

COOPERATION, NOT ISOLATION

We find much more cooperation among police agencies producing patrol services than expected from a reading of many descriptions of metropolitan policing that have appeared in national reports. Nationwide about 90 percent of all agencies give or receive emergency assistance outside their own jurisdictions. While the proportion of agencies that belong to formal mutual aid agreements is lower (nearly 50 percent of all patrol agencies), membership in such formal agreements is not necessary for emergency assistance to be given.

The existence of many separate jurisdictions does not limit fresh pursuit. Most states have legislation explicitly authorizing pursuit beyond local boundaries. As we saw earlier, patrol, traffic patrol, and traffic accident investigation are conducted in alternate times or places in most service areas that have more than one producer of the service. Coordination of criminal investigations is common. We conclude that cooperation among police agencies throughout the nation's metropolitan areas is extensive.

Chapter 16

Dividing the Work of Metropolitan Policing

The work of policing metropolitan areas in the United States is divided in various ways. One sort of division is geographic. Different officers are assigned responsibility for serving different parts of the SMSA. In some instances these officers are organized into separate departments. In other cases the geographic assignments are made to officers within the same police department.

Another way to divide the work of metropolitan policing is to assign officers to particular services and have them restrict their activities to those services. For example, some officers from a single department may be assigned to control traffic, others to patrol, and others to investigate reported crimes. Officers may even be assigned separately to traffic patrol and to traffic accident investigation. Similarly, there are service areas for which the department responsible for investigating residential burglary is different from the department investigating traffic accidents. Specialization is not practiced in all service areas, however. In some places general area patrol, traffic control, and criminal investigation are conducted by the same officer. Police generalists are found both in very small police agencies and in large departments using team policing.

PERSONNEL DEPLOYMENT IN DIRECT SERVICE AGENCIES

Small police departments are sometimes thought to make less efficient use of their employees than are large departments. Each department requires its own chief, and even very small departments often have assistant chiefs and others with titles that indicate management responsibilities. What observers often overlook, however, is the on-street presence of many police administrators, particularly in small departments. In departments with fewer than five full-time officers, the chief is a regular part of the patrol force. In somewhat larger departments the chief may not patrol, but still maintains supervisory contact with patrol operations. Rather than small departments removing officers from direct service activities and placing them in administrative assignments, the opposite appears to be the case.

Smaller municipal patrol agencies have a lower proportion of their officers assigned to administration and a higher proportion assigned to patrol (Figure 16−1). Campus and special district police make similar kinds of assignments. County sheriffs' departments do not fit this pattern because of the greater administrative burden most of them have, regardless of size, from court-related activities, such as maintaining jails, serving civil processes, doing bailiff duty, and keeping records related to these.

Municipal, campus, and special district departments with 10 or fewer officers assign, on the average, more than 90 percent of their officers to patrol. Municipal departments with more than 150 officers average less than 60 percent of their officers assigned to patrol. The percentage of officers assigned to patrol decreases as agency size increases. The reverse is true of assignments to administrative services. But the decreases in patrol assignment are not equaled by the increases in administrative assignment. Larger departments are more likely to assign personnel to other direct service or auxiliary service tasks.

Departments with more than 150 sworn officers assign, on the average, 15 percent of their sworn officers to criminal investigation, 8 percent to traffic control, and 3 percent to work with juveniles. These departments also average 13 percent of their officers assigned to administrative services, 2 percent to radio communications, and about 1 percent each to training, detention, and crime lab. The percentage figures show the proportionate difference in assignment, but they do not reveal the absolute differences. Fewer than 100 officers have full-time administrative assignments in the 467 full-time departments with 10 or fewer officers. The 48 departments with at least 150 officers together have more than 1,000 officers assigned to administrative services.

Administrative services are important. We do not intend to suggest that records, research, internal operations, legal assistance, and other staff services should be eliminated. But not all departments need to supply all these, and full-time sworn employees may not be needed

Figure 16−1. Average Percent of Sworn Officers Assigned to Patrol, Other Direct Services, Auxiliary Services, and Administration, by Size of Municipal Producer

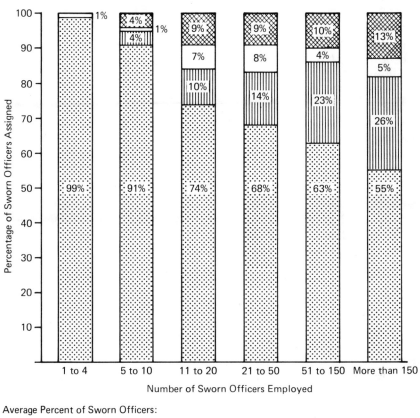

Average Percent of Sworn Officers:

Assigned to Patrol   Assigned to Auxiliary Services

Assigned to Other Direct Services   Assigned to Administration

to conduct such activities in smaller departments. Small departments usually put their emphasis on getting officers out on patrol.

AGENCY SPECIALIZATION IN DIRECT SERVICES

Large departments are more likely to conduct all the direct services we studied, but even large departments are sometimes specialized and produce only one or two of these direct services. Patrol is the only service not commonly regarded as potentially "specialized." Direct service agencies that are concerned only with traffic control are commonly viewed as specializing in traffic, and agencies whose primary activity is the investigation of reported crimes are seen as specializing in criminal investigation. In a similar way, there are some agencies that specialize in patrol, although they are commonly thought of as "limited service" rather than specialized agencies. These are mainly special district police, such as those of parks or hospitals, but some small municipal police departments also fit this classification.

Traffic control and criminal investigation are conducted in these patrol service areas by officers from other agencies with overlapping jurisdictions. Agencies specializing in patrol may be effective in meeting the distinct needs of some parts of a metropolitan area for some particular patrol activity. There may be no more reason for agencies specializing in patrol to supply other police services than there is for agencies specializing in traffic control to investigate homicide or agencies specializing in traffic accident investigation to patrol.

Most local police departments do not specialize in a single service, of course. Regardless of size, most local patrol agencies also supply their service areas with traffic control service—traffic patrol and accident investigation (Table 16-1). More than 90 percent of the municipal police departments with 11 or more officers supply all five of the direct services we examined. Smaller municipal police departments are less likely than larger agencies to conduct residential burglary investigation and even less likely to conduct homicide investigation. Sheriffs' or county police departments typically conduct criminal investigations in their service areas, regardless of their size.

As we saw in Chapter 7, small agencies that do investigate homicides are quite likely to receive the assistance of investigative specialists from other agencies. Thus, service areas patrolled by small local agencies are not without the services of investigative specialists. When serious crimes occur in these areas investigators from other agencies coordinate their investigation with officers of the small patrol agency, or they conduct the entire investigation and the local patrol agency does not participate.

Almost all county police and sheriffs' departments that patrol also investigate reported crime. Fewer of these departments conduct traffic control services, although a majority do so. Department size makes no difference in the services produced by county departments. Other local police agencies, including campus and other special district police, are less likely than either county or municipal police to conduct their own investigations of reported crime, but they are somewhat more likely than county agencies to be involved in traffic control. Larger campus and other special district agencies are somewhat more likely to conduct more direct police services, but the relationship of agency size to services produced is not as marked as it is for municipal police departments.

AUXILIARY SERVICE SPECIALIZATION

Auxiliary service production is similarly divided. There are a few police departments in which generalist police officers produce their own support services. The same officers are assigned to detention and to radio communications and may rotate to street duty that involves patrol, traffic control, and criminal investigation. But these arrangements are quite rare. Much more common is the department that obtains each auxiliary service from personnel who specialize in the production of that service. These personnel may be employees of the police agency using the auxiliary service, or they may be employed by another agency from which the police department obtains the support service.

Radio communications is usually produced within the department using the service. Pretrial detention, entry-level training, and chemical analysis of evidence are usually obtained from other agencies. In either case, however, the officers who use the auxiliary service in the conduct of patrol, traffic control, or criminal investigation do not also produce the support service. Others carry out the support service for the direct service officers to use as needed.

In many instances the producers of auxiliary services supply numerous police departments—thus, in many of the 80 metropolitan areas there is a single crime lab and often only one pretrial detention facility serving all police departments in the area. In metropolitan areas with military bases there are always at least two producers of these various services because of the separate provision for police services by the military services.

IS THERE A SYSTEM?

Whether it is preferable to have all police service production in a single department or to have departments organized along either geographic or service specific lines is an issue that requires further study. Some think that having all services within the same department facilitates communication and coordination of the separate services. On the other hand, in studying 80 SMSAs with extensive division of services among agencies, we find considerable interdepartmental communication and coordination of service.

Table 16–1. Production of Additional Services: Type and Size of Local Patrol Producer

Type of Local Patrol Producer and Number of Full-Time Sworn Officers	Number Reporting	Percent of Local Patrol Agencies Producing Direct Police Services			
		Traffic Patrol	Traffic Accident Investigation	Residential Burglary Investigation	Homicide Investigation
Total	1,159	93	90	83	69
Municipal police					
Part-time only	76	89	78	53	21
1 to 4	244	97	96	70	46
5 to 10	220	97	96	91	74
11 to 20	126	98	100	98	94
21 to 50	123	97	98	98	98
51 to 150	79	100	100	100	99
Over 150	48	100	100	100	100
County sheriffs and police					
1 to 4	3	100	100	100	100
5 to 10	5	60	80	100	100
11 to 20	16	69	50	87	87
21 to 50	28	68	61	100	100
51 to 150	27	67	63	100	96
Over 150	18	78	72	100	100
Other local patrol producers					
Part-time only	6	67	50	17	17
1 to 4	28	75	36	25	7
5 to 10	53	91	74	59	34
11 to 20	27	81	70	70	33
21 to 50	28	93	82	79	50
51 to 150	4	100	100	75	75

Table 16–1. continued

Type of Local Patrol Producer and Number of Full-Time Sworn Officers	Number Reporting	Percent of Local Patrol Agencies Producing Auxiliary Police Services			
		Radio Communications	*Entry-Level Training*	*Adult Pretrial Detention*	*Crime Lab Analysis*
Total	1,159	70	6	12	2
Municipal police					
Part-time only	76	25	0	0	0
1 to 4	244	38	0	0	0
5 to 10	220	67	0	6	0
11 to 20	126	90	0	6	0
21 to 50	123	96	1	9	0
51 to 150	79	95	15	17	6
Over 150	48	94	81	15	17
County sheriffs and police					
1 to 4	3	100	0	100	0
5 to 10	5	100	0	80	0
11 to 20	16	94	0	81	0
21 to 50	28	96	4	96	7
51 to 150	27	100	19	85	0
Over 150	18	89	11	89	28
Other local patrol producers					
Part-time only	6	50	33	0	0
1 to 4	28	54	7	0	0
5 to 10	53	72	0	0	0
11 to 20	27	89	7	0	0
21 to 50	28	86	4	0	0
51 to 150	4	100	0	0	0

Can coordination and cooperation of activities occur only under the direction of a single, overarching hierarchy? No; this assumption is clearly contradicted by the experience of many of the police agencies in the 80 metropolitan areas we studied. Many types of systematic relationships have been worked out among the agencies policing metropolitan areas. Agencies patrolling or controlling traffic for the same service area typically alternate their activities to avoid duplicating each other's work. Coordination of criminal investigations is a standard procedure for many police departments. Most direct service police agencies receive at least some auxiliary services from other agencies. Almost all local patrol agencies report giving and receiving emergency assistance.

Evaluation of these alternative ways of organizing the delivery of police services in metropolitan areas requires detailed study of the operations of police agencies. How do the service-related activities of generalist officers differ from those of specialist officers conducting the same service? How do communications among officers in different agencies differ from communications among officers in different divisions of the same agency? Do these differences in organization affect the kinds of service citizens receive from police?

The prescription that it is necessary to organize all service activities within a single, "full-service" police department is based more on abstract principles of bureaucratic organization than on examination of police experience. Police departments have worked out a variety of ways to cooperate. This is not to say that all divisions of labor among separate agencies are effective. There are occasional cases of confusion, noncooperation, and isolation between departments; but a department conducting a variety of police services may also have tense relationships among its specialized units.

Since each metropolitan area presents a different combination of agencies, personnel, and resources, an examination of the needs of each particular area is the best way to determine if changes are needed and the form any such changes ought to take.

Appendixes

✳ *Appendix A*

Glossary of Terms

AGENCY   An organization that, under a direct legal relationship to a governing authority, has its own budget and personnel. Agency refers to the entire organization, regardless of its regional divisions or the number of metropolitan areas it serves. An agency is not to be confused with a producer, that part of an agency serving a specified geographic region. The distinction is illustrated by the Federal Bureau of Investigation, a single *agency* producing one or more services in 41 of the 80 metropolitan areas we studied. The total number of FBI producers is, therefore, 41.

ALTERNATION   An organizational arrangement among two or more producers that serve the same service recipient, but systematically divide their production activities over space, over time, or among clientele. For example, alternation in space for traffic patrol occurs in a town where the state police patrol all state and federal highways within the municipal limits and the town police patrol all other public thoroughfares. Our measure of alternation in an SMSA is the fraction of all service areas receiving alternate service.

ALTERNATION, RELATIVE   The fraction of the SMSA population served by alternate producers. Relative alternation is an indicator of the proportion of an SMSA's population that receives a service under conditions where police agencies systematically divide their production activities over space, over time, or among clientele.

AUTONOMY   The extent to which service recipients rely exclusively on their own producers for any particular service. Autonomy of traffic patrol is the proportion of the service areas receiving traffic patrol exclusively from their own police agency.

AUTONOMY, RELATIVE   The proportion of the population of the metropolitan area living in service areas that regularly receive a given service only from their own police agency.

AUXILIARY PRODUCER Any agency or part of an agency that conducts activities designed to help police departments supply direct police services. Producers need not necessarily interact with citizens to produce auxiliary services (e.g., training, lab analysis).

AUXILIARY SERVICE An activity (such as radio communications, chemical analysis, training, detention) designed to help police departments supply direct police services (such as general patrol, traffic patrol, criminal investigation) to citizens.

COORDINATION An organizational arrangement among two or more departments serving the same service recipients. In a coordinated arrangement the participating departments interact to produce the service. An example of coordination in criminal investigation occurs when several departments' officers work on a case, sharing leads and maintaining a single case record. Our measure of coordination in an SMSA is the fraction of all service areas receiving a service from producers that coordinate.

COORDINATION, RELATIVE The proportion of the SMSA population receiving a given service from producers that coordinate.

CRIME LABORATORY ANALYSIS The processing of evidence by persons whose testimony is accepted as "expert" for presentation in court. Various kinds of laboratory analysis are required in criminal and accident investigation. In this study we limit our attention to the identification of narcotics and the chemical analysis of other substances like blood and hair.

CRIMINAL INVESTIGATION Activity undertaken to identify alleged criminals, to gather evidence for criminal proceedings, or to recover stolen goods. We focus our attention on two types of investigations: homicide investigation and residential burglary investigation. Homicide occurs less often, but is a more serious offense than residential burglary, which is an often encountered felony.

DIRECT PRODUCER Any agency or part of an agency that conducts activities designed to influence the safety of the citizens it serves and that does so through direct interaction with the citizens. In this study a direct producer is any agency or part of an agency that performs general area patrol, traffic patrol, traffic accident investigation, or criminal investigation.

DIRECT SERVICE An activity or set of related activities performed by officers having special powers of arrest and designed to influence the safety and satisfaction of the people in the service area. The service is produced by officers directly interacting with citizens (e.g., traffic patrol, criminal investigation) and is to be distinguished from auxiliary services, which do not necessarily require that officers interact with citizens.

DOMINANCE The extent to which a dominant producer produces a given service for the service recipients of a metropolitan area.

DOMINANCE, RELATIVE   The proportion of the SMSA population regularly served by the dominant producer.

DOMINANT PRODUCER   The producer serving the largest resident population on a regular basis for direct services, and the producer serving the largest *number* of direct service producers for auxiliary services.

DUPLICATION   A situation in which a police department or service area receives a service from two or more producers regularly, without coordination or alternation.

DUPLICATION, RELATIVE   The proportion of the SMSA population receiving a given service from two or more producers regularly, without coordination or alternation.

ENCLAVE   A territorially distinct area served by one police department, but also included in the jurisdiction of another police department (e.g., a college campus within a city).

ENTRY-LEVEL TRAINING   The department-required training of police recruits for an agency producing direct police services. By department-required we do not ignore or disregard state requirements; instead, we consider the number of training hours that a department specifies for its recruits. For many this requirement is the state minimum. For some the departmental requirement greatly exceeds the state minimum.

FRAGMENTATION   The division of the SMSA among service recipients. For direct services, fragmentation is the number of service areas for a given service within the metropolitan area. For auxiliary services it is the number of direct service producers in the metropolitan area receiving the service.

FRAGMENTATION, RELATIVE   The number of service areas per 100,000 residents in the SMSA.

GENERAL AREA PATROL   The organized surveillance of public places within a specified territory and response to reports of suspected criminal acts to prevent crime, apprehend offenders, or maintain public order.

GOVERNING AUTHORITY   A set of officials and procedures for determining provision of service. For example, a city council and the ordinances it enacts constitute the governing authority for a municipal police department.

INDEPENDENCE   The legal arrangement that exists between a producing agency and its own service recipient. Where the producing agency falls under the governing authority of the service recipients it serves, those service recipients are said to be independently served. The extent of service independence in an SMSA is the fraction of all service recipients receiving regular service from their own agency.

INDEPENDENCE, RELATIVE   The fraction of the SMSA population served by its own agencies.

INTERQUARTILE RANGE   A range of values (e.g., number of hours of training required) for a distribution of cases (e.g., police departments) starting at the lower end at the value of the case in the 25th percentile of the distribution and ending at the upper end at the value of the case in the 75th percentile of the distribution. Thus, the interquartile range shows the value limits of the middle 50 percent of the cases in a distribution.

IRREGULAR PRODUCER   An agency or part of an agency that produces a service only in unusual circumstances for a given service area (in the case of direct services) or a given direct producer (in the case of auxiliary services).

LOCAL DIRECT PRODUCER   A direct producer whose governing authority is located in the SMSA in which the producer is operating. This includes municipal police departments, county sheriffs, campus police divisions, special district police, and several multijurisdictional arrangements.

MEDIAN   A value in an ordered set of values below and above which there is an equal number of cases (e.g., the number of hours of training required by at least half the departments).

MULTIPLICITY   The number of producers supplying a service to a metropolitan area.

MULTIPLICITY, RELATIVE   The number of producers of a service to a metropolitan area relative to (1) SMSA population, or (2) the number of service recipients in the SMSA (clusters of residents in service areas for direct services, and producers of direct services for auxiliary services). Thus, in the first case relative multiplicity is the ratio of producers to each 100,000 residents of an SMSA. In the second case relative multiplicity is the ratio of producers to service areas for direct services and is the ratio of auxiliary producers of a service to direct producers for auxiliary services.

PATROL   (See GENERAL AREA PATROL.)

PRETRIAL DETENTION   The holding of an adult after arraignment, but before final court disposition of a case. Only agencies empowered to hold individuals in their facilities for more than 24 hours are included.

PRODUCER   An agency or that part of an agency that supplies a service to a recipient within an SMSA. For example, a state highway patrol may provide traffic patrol to service areas in all SMSAs in its state. When the state highway patrol is referred to as a producer to an SMSA, only that part of the agency and those personnel in that part of the agency serving the SMSA are included. When the state highway patrol is referred to as an agency, the entire organization and all its personnel are included. (See AGENCY.)

PRODUCTION   The performance of activities designed to alter events pursuant to police service goals, such as those that might be attached to traffic patrol— apprehension of offenders and prevention of accidents. An example of a production activity in traffic patrol is the use of speed monitoring devices, such as radar. A producer is an agency or part of an agency that performs such activity. Producers and service recipients interact in the production process, as contrasted with the provision process where producers and recipients interact separately with the governing authority.

PROVISION   The authorization, funding, procuring, and monitoring of service production. The governing authority serves as the focal point of activity between the service recipients and the service producer in the provision of a service. Examples of provision activities are taxation of citizens and authorization of agency budgets.

RADIO COMMUNICATIONS   The relaying of requests for police assistance to officers in the field, and the receipt of radioed requests for information or assistance from officers in the field.

REGULAR PRODUCER   An agency or part of an agency that supplies service on a regular basis to service areas (in the case of direct services) or other agencies (in the case of auxiliary services). There are four types of regular production:
1. Sole producer for service areas or direct police agencies
2. Coordination
3. Duplication
4. Alternation

SERVICE AREA   A portion of an SMSA having at least 100 residents, some way of making collective decisions about police services in the area, and a distinct legal arrangement with a producer of a direct police service. Thus, for each direct service the population of the metropolitan area is divided into mutually exclusive service areas, each served by one or more producers. The service areas for one direct service may differ from the service areas for another direct service since a community of people may have one arrangement for patrol and another for criminal investigations.

SERVICED POPULATION   For any given producer, the sum of the residents of all service areas in an SMSA receiving service from that producer.

SERVICE RECIPIENTS   For direct services—the residents of service areas. For auxiliary services—the producers of direct services in a metropolitan area.

SMSA   Standard Metropolitan Statistical Area. A designation specified by the U.S. Bureau of the Census to systematically identify metropolitan areas in the United States. An SMSA is defined (except in New England states) as a county, or group of contiguous counties, that contains at least one central city of 50,000 inhabitants or more or several cities with a combined population of at least 50,000. Contiguous counties are included in an SMSA if they meet criteria related to social and economic relationships to the central city. In the New England states SMSAs consist of clusters of contiguous cities and towns that meet similar criteria.

SWORN POLICE   Any individual given extraordinary power of arrest by virtue of statutory or other legally valid authorization.

TRAFFIC CONTROL   The monitoring of vehicular traffic and the investigation of traffic accidents. Because traffic patrol assignments may differ from traffic investigation assignments, we examine the delivery of each.

✳ *Appendix B*

Other Reports of the Police Services Study

Copies of the following technical reports are available at the indicated prices (postpaid) by writing to the Publications Secretary, Workshop in Political Theory and Policy Analysis, Indiana University, 814 East Third Street, Bloomington, Indiana 47401.

T-1   Larry Wagner. "Patterns of State Laws Relating to 'Fresh Pursuit.'"
[$1.00]

T-2   Larry Wagner and Thomas Kramer. "A Symposium of Recruitment Systems for Peace Officers."
[$1.00]

T-3   Thomas Kramer and Larry Wagner. "Statutory Provisions Regarding Entry-Level Training of Peace Officers."
[$1.00]

T-4   Elinor Ostrom. "A Historical Review of Entry-Level Training Legislation."
[$1.00]

T-6   Thomas Kramer, Frank Anechiarico, and Larry Wagner. "State Statutory Authorization of the Law Enforcement Functions of State, County, and Municipal Agencies."
[$5.50]

T-10   Eric Scott. "College and University Police Agencies."
[$1.75]

T-12   Roger B. Parks. "Police Patrol in Metropolitan Areas—
        Implications for Restructuring the Police."

                                                                [$1.50]

T-13   Roger B. Parks. "Victims' Satisfaction With Police: The
        Response Factor."

                                                                [$1.00]

T-14   Eric Scott. "Determinants of Municipal Police Expenditures:
        A Review Essay."

                                                                [$2.00]

T-15   John P. McIver. "Measures of Metropolitan Police Industry
        Structures—Service Structure Matrices for the Albany/
        Georgia SMSA."

                                                                [$1.00]

T-16   Elinor Ostrom. "Police Consolidation and Economies-of-Scale:
        Do They Go Together?"

                                                                [$1.00]

T-17   Gordon P. Whitaker. "Size and Effectiveness in the Delivery
        of Human Services."

                                                                [$1.00]

T-19   Elinor Ostrom, Roger B. Parks, and Gordon P. Whitaker. "A Public
        Service Industry Approach to the Study of Police in Metropolitan
        Areas."

                                                                [$1.75]

T-20   John P. McIver. "The Effects of State Laws on Municipal Police
        Departments: Mutual Assistance in Metropolitan Areas."

                                                                [$1.75]

T-25   Frances P. Bish. "The Limits of Organizational Reform."

                                                                [$1.75]

T-29   Gordon P. Whitaker and Stephen D. Mastrofski. "Equity in the
        Delivery of Police Services."

                                                                [$1.75]

T-31   Gordon P. Whitaker, Elinor Ostrom, and Roger B. Parks. "Using
        Citizen Surveys to Evaluate Policing."

                                                                [$1.00]

T–32   Elinor Ostrom, Roger B. Parks, Gordon P. Whitaker, and Stephen L. Percy. "Evaluating Police Organization."

[$1.75]

Fact sheets are available free of charge by writing to the Publications Secretary, Workshop in Political Theory and Policy Analysis, Indiana University, 814 East Third Street, Bloomington, Indiana 47401.

F–1   Elinor Ostrom. "The Topeka Major Case Squad."

F–2   Nancy M. Neubert. "The Major Investigative Team of Polk County."

F–3   Stephen D. Mastrofski. "The Tuscaloosa County Homicide Unit."

F–4   Nancy M. Neubert. "A Comparison of Major Case Squads in Four Metropolitan Areas."

F–5   Staff Research Unit, Kansas City/Missouri Police Department. "Kansas City Area Metro Squad."

F–6   Nancy M. Neubert. "The State Police of Crawford and Erie Counties."

F–7   Gary Miller. "The Universal City Joint Dispatching System."

F–8   Eric Scott. "The Intra-County Major Case Investigation Unit of Dane County."

F–9   John P. McIver. "The Worcester County Fraudulent Check Association: Community Cooperation in Law Enforcement."

Notes

Chapter 1

1. Early theoretical statements related to this approach include Vincent Ostrom, Charles M. Tiebout, and Robert Warren, "The Organization of Government in Metropolitan Areas: A Theoretical Inquiry," *American Political Science Review* 55 (December 1961): 831–842; and Vincent Ostrom and Elinor Ostrom, "A Behavioral Approach to the Study of Intergovernmental Relations," *The Annals of the American Academy of Political and Social Science* 359 (May 1965): 137–146. A related empirical study is that of Vincent Ostrom, *Institutional Arrangements for Water Resource Development—With Special Reference to the California Water Industry* (Springfield, Virginia: National Technical Information Service, April 1972).

Chapter 2

1. A Standard Metropolitan Statistical Area is a designation specified by the U.S. Bureau of the Census in order to systematically identify metropolitan areas in the United States. An SMSA is defined (except in the New England states) as a county, or a group of contiguous counties, that contains at least one central city of 50,000 inhabitants or more, or several cities with a combined population of at least 50,000. Contiguous counties are included in an SMSA if they meet the Census Bureau criteria related to social and economic relationships to the central city (e.g., suburban population commuting to work in the central city). In the New England states SMSAs consist of clusters of contiguous cities and towns that meet similar criteria.

2. This results in part from the definitions of SMSAs. In the New England portion of the Northeast region the Census Bureau includes a New England town in an SMSA only if its population density is greater than 100 persons per square mile. In other parts of the country entire counties are included in an SMSA if *any* part of the county is included. Sparsely populated Clark County, Nevada (which is the Las Vegas SMSA) has a population density of less than 35 persons per square mile, while its land area is 95 percent as big as Massachusetts.

3. These are Akron, Ohio; Austin, Texas; Birmingham, Alabama; El Paso, Texas; Nashville-Davidson County, Tennessee (treated by the Census as a consolidated city-county); Rochester, New York; San Jose, California; Tampa, Florida; and Tulsa, Oklahoma.

4. The data reported in Table 2−2 are at slight variance with data reported in our Summary Report, *Policing Metropolitan America*, due to 1973 population estimate errors in our data files for three SMSAs at the time that volume was published. These errors have been corrected, and the data presented here are correct.

5. We appreciate the cooperation we received from the FBI in making available to us a list of the NCIC Agency identifiers, as well as supplying us with additional data collected through the Uniform Crime Reports program.

Chapter 3

1. Those interested in the development of these concepts may want to read "Defining and Measuring Structural Variations in Interorganizational Arrangements," by Elinor Ostrom, Roger B. Parks, and Gordon P. Whitaker in *Publius* 4 (Fall 1974): 87−108, which presents our definitions of the concepts before intensive fieldwork. The changes made since that article appeared are primarily refinements that were necessary as we realized the variety of patterns was even greater than originally thought.

2. Data from this project are available from the Inter-University Consortium for Political and Social Research. Prospective users of these data should pay particular attention to this chapter.

3. See President's Commission on Law Enforcement and Administration of Justice, *The Challenge of Crime in a Free Society* (Washington, D.C.: Government Printing Office, 1967); Committee for Economic Development, *Reducing Crime and Assuring Justice* (New York: Committee for Economic Development, 1972); and Bernard L. Garmine, "The Police Role in an Urban Society," in Robert F. Steadman (ed.) *The Police and the Community* (New York: Committee for Economic Development, 1972).

Chapter 5

1. The National Commission on Productivity has focused a great deal of attention on police, particularly on the importance of getting a higher percentage of departmental personnel back out on the street patrolling. See their *Opportunities for Improving Productivity in Police Services* (Washington, D.C.: National Commission on Productivity, 1973).

2. Recall from Chapter 4 that municipal police departments include those of cities, towns, villages, boroughs, and townships. The Census Bureau distinguishes New England towns and townships in other regions from other types of municipalities. But where these units have their own police departments, we have found them to be quite similar to equivalent-sized municipalities in terms of internal organization and range of services supplied.

3. Note the shift here to a base of number of "producers" rather than number of "agencies." See the discussion of this distinction in Chapter 3.

4. The Meriden SMSA consists of the city of Meriden only and is patrolled exclusively by the Meriden Police Department. The Paterson-Clifton-Passaic SMSA consists of Bergen and Passaic Counties in New Jersey and is patrolled by 85 municipal and 2 county departments, as well as by a number of specialized local patrol agencies.

5. For a discussion focusing on these suppliers, see Eric J. Scott, "College and University Police Agencies," *Technical Report T-10*, Police Services Study (Bloomington, Ind.: Workshop in Political Theory and Policy Analysis, Indiana University).

6. Clarence M. Kelley, *Uniform Crime Reports for the United States—1973*, Washington, D.C.: U.S. Department of Justice.

7. Elinor Ostrom, et al., *Community Organization and the Provision of Police Services*, Beverly Hills, Calif.: SAGE Publications, 1973; Roger B. Parks, "Complementary Measures of Police Performance," in Kenneth M. Dolbeare (ed.) *Public Policy Evaluation*, Beverly Hills, Calif.: SAGE Publications, 1976.

8. The other type of arrangement for avoiding duplicate service delivery in service areas with two or more producers is coordination. Producers coordinate patrols when they work together in the deployment of their patrol personnel. Coordination of patrols occurs in few service areas. These are found in only about 15 percent of the 80 SMSAs.

9. In addition to data presented here, see Roger B. Parks, "Police Patrol in Metropolitan Areas—Implications for Restructuring the Police," in Elinor Ostrom (ed.) *The Delivery of Urban Services, Volume 10 Urban Affairs Annual Reviews*, Beverly Hills, Calif.: SAGE Publications, 1976.

Chapter 7

1. Peter W. Greenwood, Jan M. Chaiken, Joan Petersilla, and Linda Prusoff, *The Criminal Investigation Process, Volume III: Observations and Analysis* (Santa Monica, Calif.: The Rand Corporation, 1975). [R–1778–DOJ]

2. Stephen Mastrofski, "The Tuscaloosa County Homicide Unit" (Bloomington, Ind.: Workshop in Political Theory and Policy Analysis, Indiana University) discusses this agency in greater detail.

3. For a discussion of major case squads organized temporarily for specific investigations see Nancy Malacek Neubert, "Major Case Squads" and "The Major Investigative Team of Polk County"; Elinor Ostrom, "The Topeka Major Case Squad"; James C. McDavid, "The Major Case Squad of Greater St. Louis Metropolitan Area"; and the Staff Research Unit of the Kansas City, Missouri Police Department, "Kansas City Area Metro Squad." These reports are available from the Workshop in Political Theory and Policy Analysis, Indiana University, Bloomington, Indiana.

4. National Advisory Commission on Criminal Justice Standards and Goals, *Police* (Washington, D.C.: Government Printing Office, 1973).

5. Peter W. Greenwood and Joan Petersilla, *The Criminal Investigation Process, Volume I: Summary and Policy Implications* (Santa Monica, Calif.: The Rand Corporation, 1975). [R–1776–DOJ]

6. In addition to the volumes mentioned in Notes 1 and 5 above see Jan M. Chaiken, *The Criminal Investigation Process, Volume II: Survey of Municipal*

and County Police Departments (Santa Monica, Calif.: The Rand Corporation, 1975). [R-1777-DOJ]

7. See the reports in Note 3 above.

Chapter 8

1. Bruce Smith, *Police Systems in the United States*, 2nd revised edition (New York: Harper & Row, 1960), pp. 20-21.

Chapter 11

1. See, for example, American Bar Association Commission on Correctional Facilities and Services and Council of State Governments, *Compendium of Modern Correctional Legislation and Standards* (Chicago: American Bar Association, 1972); American Bar Association, Commission on Correctional Facilities and Services, Jail Standards Project, *Survey and Handbook on Jail Standards and Inspection Legislation* (Washington, D.C.: American Bar Association, 1974); National Advisory Commission on Criminal Justice Standards and Goals, Task Force Report on *Corrections* (Washington, D.C.: Government Printing Office, 1973); U.S. Advisory Commission on Intergovernmental Relations, *State-Local Relations in the Criminal Justice System* (Washington, D.C.: Government Printing Office, 1971).

2. National Advisory Commission on Criminal Justice Standards and Goals (1973), p. 294.

3. American Bar Association, Commission on Correctional Facilities and Services (1974), pp. 10-16.

4. Two agencies—the Midland County Sheriff and the Sonoma County Sheriff—produce detention, but no direct services, for SMSAs included in the study. These have not been counted as detention specialists because they do provide direct services elsewhere. A few of the detention centers do provide other auxiliary police services (e.g., dispatching). However, these services represent a small part of their regular work load.

5. In Virginia, counties provide services only to areas outside city boundaries. In county areas pretrial detention is produced by county sheriffs; in each of the 23 first-class cities there is also a city sheriff (a constitutional office with duties analogous to those of the county sheriffs).

6. In all Pennsylvania SMSAs, for example, pretrial detention is produced by county prison boards. In the San Antonio/Texas SMSA the Bexar County Detention facilities are the responsibility of an administrator appointed by the Commissioners Court; a similar arrangement is used for the Mercer County Jail in the Trenton/New Jersey SMSA. In Albuquerque/New Mexico city and county jail facilities were recently consolidated into a regional facility operated by the Bernalillo County Corrections and Detention Department.

7. National Advisory Commission on Criminal Justice Standards and Goals (1973), p. 300.

8. *Ibid.*, pp. 289-291.

Chapter 12

1. See Larry Wagner and Thomas Kramer, "Statutory Provisions Regarding Entry-Level Training of Peace Officers," *Technical Report T-3*, Police Services

Study (Bloomington, Ind.: Workshop in Political Theory and Policy Analysis, Indiana University, 1975).

2. Robert Havlick, "Police Recruit Training," *Municipal Yearbook, 1968* (Chicago: International City Managers' Association, 1968), pp. 340–341.

3. It should be pointed out that the samples for the ICMA study and our study are different. ICMA sent mail questionnaires to a sample of local units across the entire country, including rural areas. Our sample contains only agencies serving metropolitan areas. While many of the agencies included in our study are serving predominantly rural communities, we do not include any agencies that are located in counties that the Census Bureau would define as predominantly rural.

4. Indiana Criminal Justice Planning Agency, *1974 Indiana Comprehensive Plan for Law Enforcement and Criminal Justice*, 1 (Indianapolis, Ind.: Criminal Justice Planning Agency, 1973), p. 109.

5. The large proportion of agencies (60 percent) obtaining training from an "Other Type of Academy" in Virginia and Pennsylvania (Region 3) needs further explanation. At the time of our field interviews in Pennsylvania, considerable uncertainty about future training efforts existed. A bill had been signed establishing a Municipal Police Officers' Education and Training Commission to administer minimum training standards for all police officers in Pennsylvania. But considerable delay occurred in the appointment of the Commission, and local departments had little information about future standards and availability of programs. So, we coded recruit training information for Pennsylvania on the basis of that state's practice in 1974–75.

Agencies conducting recruit training varied considerably for local police agencies in Pennsylvania. The large departments sent their officers either to the State Police Academy in Hershey for a 400– to 480–hour course, to a Regional State Police Academy, or to one of the other three large academies in the state: the Allegheny County Police Academy (a federally funded regional academy), the Philadelphia Police Department Academy, or the Allentown Police Department Academy. Some of the larger departments, such as Reading, maintained their own training programs. The smaller departments required training for their recruits, but relied heavily on the 40–hour short courses offered at night at the local state police barracks. Short courses available at local barracks included: basic field instruction, traffic law procedure, and advanced field instruction. These local state police-run courses were counted in the "Other Type of Academy" classification.

Chapter 13

1. Thomas W. Kramer, Frank M. Anechiarico, and Larry Wagner, "State Statutory Authorization of the Law Enforcement Functions of State, County, and Municipal Agencies," *Technical Report T-6*, Police Services Study (Bloomington, Ind.: Workshop in Political Theory and Policy Analysis, Indiana University).

2. In Missouri the State Highway Patrol provides crime lab services, although direct producers in the Missouri SMSAs we studied do not report regular use of these facilities.

3. John Jay College National Survey of Crime Laboratories, Dr. Alexander Joseph, Director, "Study of Needs and the Development of Curricula in the Field of Forensic Science," in LEAA Project Report, *Crime Laboratories—Three Study Reports*, U.S. Department of Justice (Washington, D.C.: Government Printing Office, 1966), p. 5.

4. Clarence M. Kelley, *Crime in the United States, 1974*, U.S. Department of Justice (Washington, D.C.: Government Printing Office, 1975), pp. 18–20.

5. Richard S. Frank, Acting Chief of Forensic Sciences Division of the Office of Science and Technology, Drug Enforcement Administration, 1975: personal communication.

6. The percentage of direct service producers that are military in each region is as follows:

Northeast	%		*South*	%
Region 1	0		Region 4	6
Region 2	0		Region 6	11
Region 3	4			
			West	%
Midwest	%		Region 8	19
Region 5	1		Region 9	15
Region 7	2		Region 10	0

Chapter 15

1. David L. Norrgard, *Regional Law Enforcement: A Study of Intergovernmental Cooperation and Coordination* (Chicago: Public Administration Service, 1969).

2. *Ibid.*, p. 1.

3. President's Commission on Law Enforcement and the Administration of Justice, *Task Force Report: The Police* (Washington, D.C.: Government Printing Office, 1967b), p. 70.

4. The process of determining whether a state does or does not have legislation in this area involves a somewhat complex analysis. There may be a statute dealing with arrest powers, but jurisdictional limits are not mentioned. Or a statute dealing with the problem of intrastate fresh pursuit may have been repealed.

To illustrate, Iowa police officers are ordered to "pursue and arrest any person fleeing from justice." [Iowa Code Ann. §368A.17 and 18 (1973)] Although this duty is not limited by any reference to jurisdictional lines, a recent Iowa case has held that an officer seeking to make an arrest without a warrant outside his originating jurisdiction must be treated as a private person. [*State v. O'Kelly*, 211 N.W. 2nd 589 (1973)] Wyoming did have a statute permitting statewide pursuit: Wyo. Stat. §7–163 (1957), but Rule 56 of the Wyoming Rules of Criminal Procedure provided that this statute be superseded as of February 11, 1969. And in Illinois the intrastate fresh pursuit power was presumed by law enforcement officials to be defined by case law or by opinions of the Attorney General. Upon further investigation, however, citations verifying these authorities were not found.

The full citations to relevant statutes are contained in Larry Wagner, "Patterns of State Laws Relating to Fresh Pursuit," *Technical Report T-1*, Police Services Study (Bloomington, Ind.: Workshop in Political Theory and Policy Analysis, Indiana University, 1975).

5. The data on mutual assistance are based on three questions asked of police administrators in the 80 SMSAs:

- In situations other than civil disorders or natural disasters do your officers ever go outside the boundaries of (name of jurisdiction) to aid another department?
- Do officers from other departments ever come into (name of jurisdiction) to aid your force?
- Has your department entered into any mutual aid agreements with other departments in the area to handle requests for aid?

6. The responses to the survey questions on county police and sheriffs' mutual aid behavior are ambiguous. A positive response, for example, may indicate that the county agency cooperated with police departments in a neighboring county or that the county agency has assisted municipal police agencies that are not part of its normal service area. The assistance data for county agencies, therefore, should be interpreted with caution.

7. Data on deputization were based on two questions asked of police administrators:

- Are any of the officers working in this department deputized by any other police agency in the area?
- Has this department deputized police officers from any other police agency in the area?

About the Authors

Elinor Ostrom is Co-Director of the Workshop in Political Theory and Policy Analysis and Professor of Political Science at Indiana University in Bloomington, Indiana. She has had a long-standing interest in questions related to the effect of organizational arrangements on the output of urban public agencies and in the measurement of that output. She has written numerous articles on these questions, particularly as they relate to the area of law enforcement.

Roger B. Parks is a Research Associate with the Workshop in Political Theory and Policy Analysis and Co-Principal Investigator for the Police Services Study. He is the author of several recent articles dealing with questions of police organization, police relations with victims of crime, and police performance measurement. Work in progress includes an attempt to specify the way in which variations in police organizational arrangements are related to variations in police performance and to estimate the magnitudes of the specified relationships.

Gordon P. Whitaker is a political scientist interested in urban public services. His research includes efforts to measure the public consequences of public service activities and investigations of the ways political and administrative organization influence the services delivered. He taught at Brooklyn College of the City University of New York and is currently Assistant Professor of Political Science at the University of North Carolina at Chapel Hill.